D1087270

INTRODUCTION TO COMPUTERS AND DATA PROCESSING

Prentice-Hall
Series in Applied Mathematics

PRENTICE-HALL, INTERNATIONAL, INC., *London*
PRENTICE-HALL OF AUSTRALIA, PTY. LTD., *Sydney*
PRENTICE-HALL OF CANADA LTD., *Toronto*
PRENTICE-HALL OF INDIA PRIVATE LTD., *New Delhi*
PRENTICE-HALL OF JAPAN, INC., *Tokyo*

INTRODUCTION TO COMPUTERS AND DATA PROCESSING

DANIEL D. BENICE

Chairman, Computer Science
Montgomery College
Takoma Park, Maryland

Prentice-Hall, Inc.,   Englewood Cliffs, N. J.

© 1970 by
PRENTICE-HALL, INC.
Englewood Cliffs, New Jersey

All rights reserved. No part of this book
may be reproduced in any way, or by any
means, without permission in writing from
the publisher.

Current printing (last digit):

10 9 8 7 6 5 4 3 2 1

13-497543-1

Library of Congress Catalog Card Number: 70-126002
Printed in the United States of America

Thielman   15 Je '71   Math

30 July '12

TO SHARON

PREFACE

This text is intended for an introductory course in data processing and/or computer science. No previous knowledge of computers is assumed, and very little experience with algebra is required.

Many examples, illustrations, and exercises have been used in an attempt to make the book especially easy to read and understand. The author realizes that computer principles can be very confusing to someone who knows nothing about them.

The survey presented is broad enough to satisfy the reader planning to specialize and take additional computer courses, as well as the reader who may prefer only an introduction to the basic concepts. Those planning a career in programming should know what is expected; they should see flowcharting and programming languages in a first course. And students intending to take only an introductory course should not be shortchanged. Some familiarity with programming languages is part of a basic computer background.

The treatment of number systems is particularly simplified, and is novel in this context. I have found that the use of charts rather than algorithms makes the concepts easier to understand and easier to remember.

The explanation of EAM is intentionally brief. The chapter on RPG can be used to supplement it, if desired.

In many cases it will not be possible, or desirable, to study all five languages presented (System/360 Assembler, FORTRAN, COBOL, PL/1,

RPG). The independence of these chapters allows any of them to be omitted or included according to the needs of the reader.

Answers are given to enough problems to enable the reader to find and correct his errors in computational and programming problems. An annotated bibliography is supplied for those who seek additional references.

An instructor's manual is available, containing answers, suggestions, comments, and additional material — for example, an explanation of GET/PUT EDIT for PL/1 users whose compilers cannot work with GET/PUT DATA.

The author would appreciate receiving any comments or criticisms from the instructor or his students.

I am especially indebted to my brother, Ronald J. Benice, for his continual, searching criticism of several manuscript versions. I owe thanks to my friend and former colleague Paul J. Serafin for many invaluable suggestions which helped improve the text considerably.

I would like to acknowledge the assistance of Ken Cashman, College Production Editor for Prentice-Hall. His suggestions and overall diligence did much to lessen the burden of completing and editing the final manuscript. I wish to express my deep appreciation of my colleague Margaret G. Aldrich for her interest and encouragement.

Finally, special thanks are due my wife, Sharon, for her patience and typing assistance throughout this project.

DANIEL D. BENICE

Takoma Park, Maryland

CONTENTS

ix

INTRODUCTION TO COMPUTERS AND DATA PROCESSING

1

A BRIEF HISTORY
OF COMPUTING
AND COMPUTERS

INTRODUCTION

From the beginning the incentive for developing computing machines was a basic one: reduce the time wasted and errors produced when man did his own arithmetic; instead free him for creative work. By the 1940's there was an additional incentive: create computers which can carry out sequences of *logical* as well as arithmetic operations, and do them *so quickly* and so accurately that problems could be solved that were once considered impossible or too time consuming to even attempt.

ABACUS (Ancient)

The abacus was among the first devices used for computation, and has taken many forms over the years. The current forms are wooden or metal frames with columns of beads on thin rods. They are used as toys or novelties in our country, but merchants in China and other Asian countries use them for fast and accurate business calculations.

If you look at Fig. 1-1 you will see an abacus with several columns

1

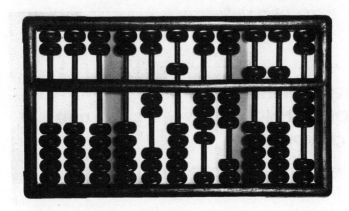

FIGURE 1-1. An Abacus. *Courtesy of General Electric Co.*

of beads, one for the units place of the number, one for tens, one for hundreds, and so on. Numbers are registered by moving the correct number of beads in each column.

Although the methods will not be explained here, it should be noted that the abacus can be used for addition, subtraction, multiplication (repeated addition), and division (repeated subtraction).

The abacus is an example of a *digital* computing device. In other words, it is a *counting* device rather than a *measuring* device; that is, each bead counts as "one" even if it is larger or smaller than another.

LOGARITHMS AND THE SLIDE RULE (1614, 1630)

The slide rule is the only *analog* computing device which will be mentioned in our history of computing. Numbers are represented by distances on a scale, and the distances are determined by the logarithms of the numbers.[1] As an example, multiplication of two numbers is carried out by adding their distances on the scale (see Fig. 1-2).

It should be emphasized that it is the *adding of distances,* rather than the counting of objects, that distinguishes this simple *analog* computer from digital computing devices.

[1] An understanding of *why* the slide rule works is dependent on an understanding of logarithms.

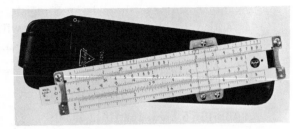

FIGURE 1-2. A Slide Rule. *Courtesy of Pickett Industries.*

MECHANICAL WHEEL CALCULATOR (1642)

Blaise Pascal developed the world's first mechanical adding machine in 1642. His calculator was essentially a set of interlocking geared wheels, one wheel for the units place of a number, one for the tens, and so on (see Fig. 1-3). The number 15, for example, would be entered by moving the units wheel 5 and the tens wheel 1. To add 23 to this number we move the units wheel 3 more and the tens wheel 2 more. The result is that the units wheel has moved 8 and the tens wheel 3. The resulting sum then is 38.

Additionally, the gears are set up so that if a "carry" is necessary, it will be handled as required to produce the correct result. As an

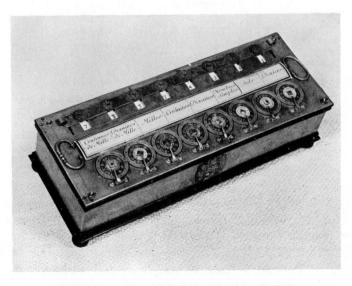

FIGURE 1-3. Pascal's Calculator. *Courtesy of IBM Corp.*

example, suppose there is an 8 registered on a particular wheel and 5 is added to that wheel. The result will appear as a 3 on the wheel, and 1 will be carried to the next wheel.

BABBAGE'S ENGINES (1812-1834)

It was in 1812 that Charles Babbage, a mathematician, became particularly annoyed by the inaccuracies he found in the tables of calculations he was using. At that time mathematical tables were prepared by hand computation. This, of course, was a time-consuming and error-producing process.

Babbage soon began work on an automatic calculating machine which would be able to generate many kinds of tables. The machine was called a *Difference Engine,* because tables would be constructed by the machine using a method known as *differences* (see Fig. 1-4).

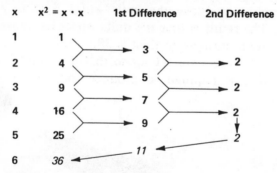

The chart shows how tables can be computed using the method of differences. Values for x from 1 to 5 are supplied along with the squares of the numbers (in the next column). You can see how the square of the next number, 6, is determined using differences. Just follow the arrows. Similarly, we can quickly get $7^2 = 49$, and so on.

FIGURE 1-4. Computation Using Differences.

Unfortunately, Babbage never completed his Difference Engine. While working towards its completion, he envisioned a more elaborate, general-purpose *Analytical Engine.* Meanwhile the British government, which was funding the development of the Difference Engine, noted Babbage's "lack of progress" and withdrew the funds. As a result, he was unable to complete either machine (see Fig. 1-5).

FIGURE 1-5. Babbage's Difference Engine. *Courtesy of IBM Corp.*

BOOLEAN ALGEBRA (1854)

George Boole, a mathematician, developed a system for representing logical statements in terms of mathematical symbols. Using the symbols and some rules one could determine whether a statement was logically true or false.

His methods were not widely accepted, and it was not until the next century that his ideas were applied.

PUNCHED CARD (1880-1890)

Herman Hollerith developed the modern machine-readable punched card and the associated mechanical card-processing equipment. Hired by the Bureau of the Census, he developed and used his inventions on the huge volume of data collected in the 1890 census.

SWITCHING LOGIC (1938)

Claude Shannon applied Boolean algebra to systematic representation of complex switching networks. Shannon's result simplified teaching and research in the design of circuits like those to be found in future electronic computers.

MARK I   (1937-1944)

In 1937, Howard Aiken of Harvard University designed a huge mechanical calculator capable of performing a long *sequence* of arithmetic and logical operations. His proposed calculator received instructions in code from punched paper tape, produced the results, and had storage, control, and arithmetic units. But the Mark I was relatively slow because the speed of its calculations depended on the speed of many electromechanical components.

IBM agreed to construct Aiken's calculator, and the completed machine was presented to Harvard University in 1944 (see Fig. 1-6).

FIGURE 1-6. Mark I. *Courtesy of IBM Corp.*

ENIAC (1943-1945)

The Electronic Numerical Integrator And Calculator (ENIAC) was designed by J. P. Eckert and J. W. Mauchly of the University of Pennsylvania. It was the first *electronic* computer (it used 18,000 vacuum tubes!), and was much faster than Mark I. However, the machine had no internal storage. It had to receive its instructions externally via switches and plugs, a very serious limitation.

It should be noted that ENIAC was a special purpose computer, designed to handle mathematics problems in ballistics and aeronautics.

EDVAC (1945-1952)

The Electronic Discrete Variable Automatic Computer (EDVAC) was also developed by the Eckert and Mauchly team. It was larger than ENIAC, used binary (base 2) numbers for arithmetic operations, and stored its instructions internally.

UNIVAC I (1951)

The first electronic computer which was available commercially was the UNIVAC I (Universal Automatic Computer). Unlike its predecessors, it was used for non-scientific data processing.

UNIVAC was built by Remington Rand (now Sperry Rand), a company originated by Eckert and Mauchly.[2] It used magnetic tape for input and output. Previously, computers had used the considerably slower punched cards and paper tape. Also, UNIVAC was the first computer to accept and process *alphabetic data,* as well as numeric data.

---

[2]It is also interesting to note that it was Herman Hollerith who established one of the companies which merged to eventually become International Business Machines, Incorporated–IBM.

SECOND GENERATION COMPUTERS (1959)

It was not long before UNIVAC (division of Sperry Rand) was joined by IBM and others in tremendous competition to develop a new series of computers. The original problem, that of building a working computer, had been solved. But this first generation of computers was not a refined one. The computers used vacuum tubes as basic components of internal circuits. As a result the machines were bulky (huge!), needed considerable power to run, and produced so much heat that strict air-conditioning requirements were needed to protect the computer parts and keep the computer working. The first generation computers were not as reliable as many had hoped. They were fast, but not fast enough. They had internal storage capacity, but not enough.

Research soon led to the development of computers which used transistors instead of vacuum tubes. These *second generation* computers, as they were called, were much smaller, required less power, and produced considerably less heat. The use of transistors also increased reliability and processing speed (shorter circuits!). These computers also had much greater storage capacity.

THIRD GENERATION COMPUTERS (1964)

In 1964, *third generation* computer systems appeared on the market. They have many advantages over their predecessors, including features lacking in the second generation machines.

One new design uses solid state logic microcircuits for which conductors, resistors, diodes, and transistors have been miniaturized and combined on half-inch ceramic squares (see Fig. 1-7). Another design uses (smaller) wafers on which the circuit and its components are etched. Each wafer is called a monolithic integrated circuit (see Fig. 1-8). The smaller circuits allow faster execution of instructions. Faster computers make otherwise impractical or impossible jobs quite feasible. The new components are more reliable, so maintenance is reduced. Larger capacity storage devices are available and at lower cost per bit of storage.

Many manufacturers of third generation computers have produced

FIGURE 1-7. Transistors for Third Generation Solid-State Microcircuit vs. Transistor Used in Second Generation Computers. *Courtesy of IBM Corp.*

series of similar and compatible computers.[3] What this means is that programs which run on one computer of a given series will also run on most larger models of that series.[4] In other words, they accept and execute the same instructions and handle the same forms of data. This is a first for third generation computers.

There are several advantages which result from this compatability. The user (a bank, airline, research center, etc.) can rent a small

FIGURE 1-8. Third Generation Monolithic Integrated Circuit. *Courtesy of RCA, Information Systems Division.*

[3]International Business Machines calls theirs the System/360, Xerox Data Systems makes the Sigma family, and National Cash Register manufactures the Century Series of computers, etc.

[4]A *program* is a list of instructions (directions) for the computer to execute (follow).

computer at the beginning and replace it with a larger one when needed; and he does not have to rewrite all his programs or change the form of his data. There are employer-employee advantages. It is now much easier for persons skilled in operating or programming one computer to adjust to "different" computers. Similarly the employer has an easier time finding job applicants with experience using the equipment he has.

Most third generation systems are designed to handle both scientific and commercial data processing with equal ease. This is particularly valuable for installations which do both kinds of data processing. Previously, such installations either had *two* computers (one scientific, one commercial) or settled for inferior processing of one type of data.

Along with third generation computers, newer and faster equipment has been introduced for handling input and output. This will be discussed in detail in Chapter 6 (see Fig. 1-9).

Incidentally, along with the third generation computers has come the more popular use of the word nanosecond. A *nanosecond* is one

FIGURE 1-9. A Third Generation Computer System. *Courtesy of IBM Corp.*

billionth (10^{-9} or 1/1,000,000,000) of a second. Some processing speeds (for example, switching time and cycle time) should be measured in nanoseconds to be meaningful. For other (slower) speeds the term microsecond is sufficient. A *microsecond* is one millionth (10^{-6} or 1/1,000,000) of a second, and is used as a unit of time in second and third generation computers. The word *millisecond* means one thousandth (10^{-3} or 1/1000) of a second, and is still another unit used to indicate processing times for computers.[5]

CURRENT MANUFACTURERS

At present there are dozens of manufacturers of high speed computers. A partial list includes:

Burroughs Corporation (B)[6]
Control Data Corporation (CDC)
Digital Equipment Corporation (PDP)
General Electric Company (GE)
Honeywell (H)
International Business Machines Corporation (IBM)
National Cash Register Company (NCR)
RCA Corporation (RCA)
Xerox Data Systems (formerly Scientific Data Systems) (XDS)
UNIVAC division of Sperry Rand (UNIVAC)

SCALE OF COMPUTERS

Computers are usually placed in one of three scales: small, medium, or large. The scale is determined by size, speed, and capability. The greater these specifications, the larger the scale of the computer. Also, the greater the scale of the computer the higher the price of rental or purchase.

---

[5] A *picosecond* is one trillionth (10^{-12}) of a second, and is used occasionally as a unit of time.
[6] Included in parentheses are the letters which generally precede the model numbers of the manufacturer's computers.

Photo of XDS Sigma 7. *Courtesy of Xerox Data Systems.*

Computer rentals run from less than $2000 to more than $200,000 per month, depending on the scale and the type of computer within that scale.[7] Similarly, purchase prices range from less than $100,000 to several million dollars.

Photo of PDP-10. *Courtesy of Digital Equipment Corp.*

[7]The rental "month" is usually defined as a certain number of computer hours of use in a thirty-day period.

EXERCISES 1.1

1. What is an important difference between an analog computer and a digital computer? Give an example of each, but do not use the slide rule or abacus.

2. What do we mean by "creative" work?

3. Compare first, second, and third generation computers. List their differences and similarities.

4. The second generation computers were basically excellent machines. Why then did the computer companies spend fortunes in the research and development of a new, third generation of computers?

5. What are the essential differences between a desk calculator and an electronic computer?

6. In the chapter example which demonstrated the use of differences (see Fig. 1-4), we found that the *second* differences were constant. This was because the formula in x involved x^2, or 2 as the highest power of x. Other functions such as $3x^2 + 7$, $x^2 + 2x - 1$, etc. would also have constant second differences. Similarly, functions like x^3, $2x^3 + 7x^2 - x + 6$, etc. have constant *third* differences (since x^3 is highest), and so on for higher powers of x.

   With this in mind, use differences to complete the two charts below—even though the form of the function is not supplied.

   (a)

x	function
1	3
2	12
3	33
4	72
5	135
6	___
7	___

   *(b)

x	function	first diff.	second diff.	third diff.
1	3			
		6		
2	___		4	
		___		0
3	___		___	
		___		
4	___			

   *Answers to starred exercises are given at the end of the book.

*7. (a) How many microseconds are there in two seconds?
   (b) How many microseconds are there in 500 nanoseconds?
   (c) How many nanoseconds are there in 3 milliseconds?
   (d) Which is the greatest period of time: 5 milliseconds, 800 microseconds, or 10,000 nanoseconds?
   (e) Which is the shortest period of time: 300 nanoseconds, .2 microsecond, or .1 millisecond?

8. UNIVAC I was the first computer to accept and process alphabetic data. Why was this an important development?

"I don't have the heart to tell him that figure's for monthly rental, not purchase."

© DATAMATION

2

THE PUNCHED CARD
AND EAM EQUIPMENT

THE PUNCHED CARD

The *punched card* was introduced to standardize the recording of data and to provide a simple means of communicating with the machines that process data. This standard size, permanent record is also called a *data processing card*.

The standard card has 80 numbered columns and 10 printed rows–a row of 0's, a row of 1's, 2's, 3's, etc. (see Fig. 2-1). Data is recorded by punching small rectangular holes in the columns. Specifically, one can record any digit from 0 through 9 by punching

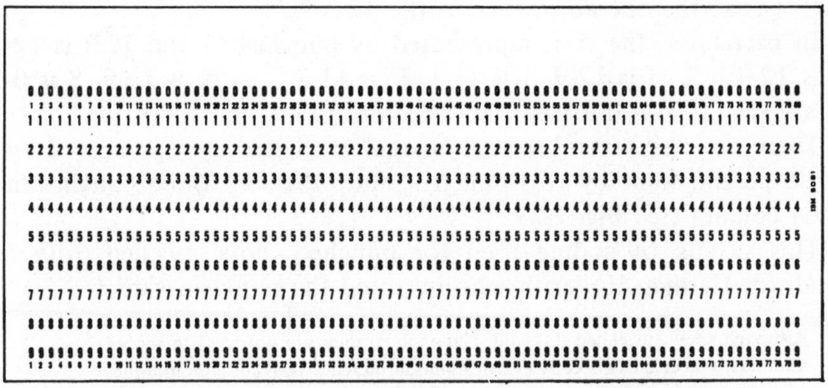

FIGURE 2-1. A Data Processing Card (actual size is 7 3/8 inches by 3 1/4 inches). *Courtesy of IBM Corp.*

a hole through that digit, in any desired column. Such holes or punches are referred to as *numeric punches,* since the punch has recorded a particular *number* in the card. If you wish to record the three-digit number 438, use three consecutive card columns. For example, punch the 4 in column 35, the 3 in column 36, and the 8 in column 37 (see Fig. 2-2).

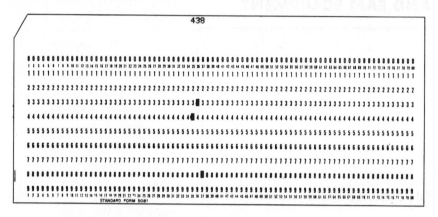

FIGURE 2-2. The Number 438 Recorded on a Punched Card.

To represent letters on punched cards we need two punches in the column where the letter is desired. One of these is a nonzero numeric punch (1, 2, 3, . . . , 9) and the other is a *zone punch.* There are three different zone punches. The 0-punch is used as a numeric punch when alone; however, it is a zone punch when an additional numeric punch occurs in the same column. The others are the 11-punch and the 12-punch. The *unlabeled* row above the 0-row is the 11-row; the one above that is the 12-row.[1]

In particular, the A is represented by punches 12 and 1, B is 12-2, C is 12-3, . . . , I is 12-9, J is 11-1, K is 11-2, . . . , R is 11-9, S is 0-2, T is 0-3, . . . , Z is 0-9 (see Fig. 2-3).

There are also several special characters. Some are represented by a single punch, some by two punches, and others by three punches in a given column (see Fig. 2-3).

This system of coding used for punched cards is called *Hollerith code,* for Herman Hollerith who invented the punched card.[2]

[1] Although they are called 11- and 12-punches, they are *not* used to record numbers; you need two consecutive numeric punches to record the number 11 or the number 12.

[2] In 1969, IBM introduced a 96-column card. See Chapter 7 for a picture and discussion.

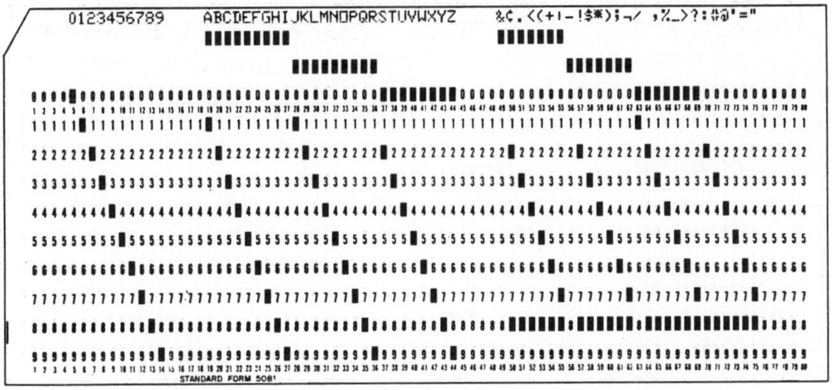

FIGURE 2-3. A Punched Card Showing the Character Set.

USES

Listed here are some common uses for punched cards, most of which you have probably seen already.

pay checks
bills
drivers' licenses
college registration forms
savings bonds
invoices
purchase orders

ADDITIONAL TERMINOLOGY

A punched card might contain the social security number, name, course, section number, and instructor of a student enrolled in a college course. A specific number of consecutive columns would be reserved for the student's social security number, for his name, etc. These groups of consecutive card columns which are reserved for specific units of information are called *fields*. In our example there is a social security number field, a student name field, and so on. We often use punched cards which are printed with field headings in order to improve readability (see Fig. 2-4).

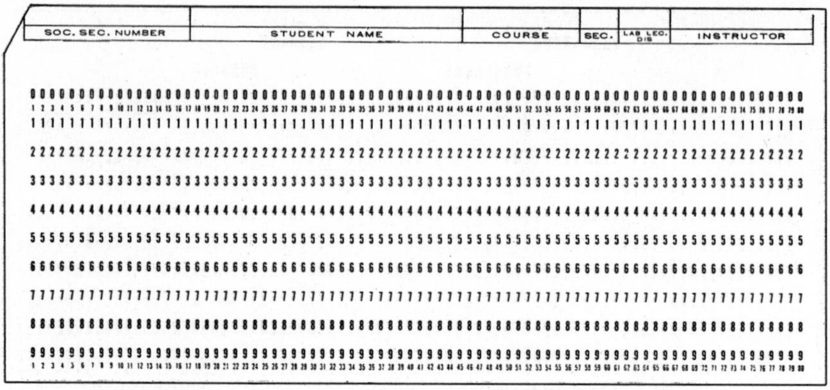

FIGURE 2-4. A Card with Printed Field Headings.

For efficient processing and record keeping it is desirable to record all information about one transaction or put all portions of an individual record on one data processing card. This is the *unit record principle,* and the (EAM) equipment used for card processing is often called *unit record equipment.*[3]

Often codes and various abbreviations are needed in order to fit all the information on one 80-column card. For example, a date like November 12, 1970 is often written as 11-12-70, and might appear in six consecutive card columns as 111270.

There are numerous techniques used to help distinguish and separate cards containing different types of data. These techniques include the use of (1) different colored cards (2) cards with different colored stripes across the top (3) cards with corner cuts at the top. Corner cuts, one per card, are also used to help determine when a card is upside down or backwards in a deck.

INTRODUCTION TO EAM

Punched cards can be processed by *Electric Accounting Machines,* or "EAM." Such punched card equipment includes sorters, collators, and tabulators.

Before beginning a discussion of the various machines used to process data, an introduction is in order.

---

[3]Note that records are made up of fields, and fields are made up of characters.

The words *hopper* and *stacker* are sometimes used interchangeably, but we will use hopper to mean a device which holds cards to be fed for processing; stacker will mean a device which accepts and holds cards after they have been processed.

A *file* is a collection of records. If the records are on cards, then we say that a deck of cards is a file of records.

A duplicate of a data processing card is sometimes called a *detail* card. The original is then called a *master*. Such terminology is especially appropriate when discussing the reproducer.

Data processing machines use wire brushes to "read" the holes in punched cards; punched holes are produced by metal punch dies.

Since most machines perform more than one function, and since many of these functions are complicated, wired panels are used to direct and control operations. Changes in wiring cause changes in operation (see Fig. 2-5).

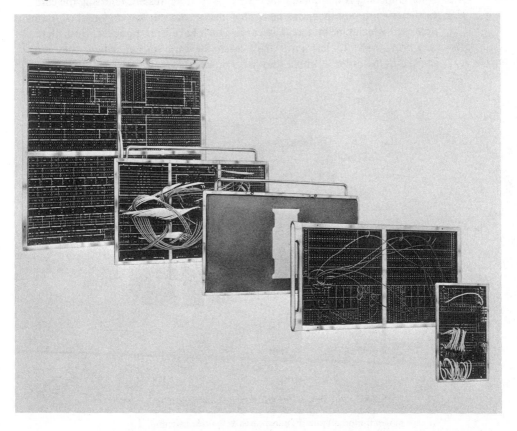

FIGURE 2-5. Wired Control Panels. *Courtesy of IBM Corp.*

THE CARD PUNCH MACHINE

Keypunching is the process by which we record (punch) information on (into) data processing cards. It is done using a *card punch* machine (see Fig. 2-6).[4]

The process:

1. Blank cards are placed in the card hopper (see Fig. 2-6).
2. The "FEED" key is depressed (see Fig. 2-7). This sends a blank card to the card bed for punching.
3. The "REG" key is depressed. This registers the card, thus allowing punching to begin (see Fig. 2-7).
4. Information is punched into the card by depressing keys (just like typing!). The result will contain both holes and printed interpretation. The holes are punched at the punching station (see Fig. 2-6).
5. When punching is completed the "REL" key is depressed, releasing the card to the left into another card bed. This makes room in the original bed for a new card which can be fed. The cards which have been punched work their way from right to left until they reach the card stacker, where they are stacked in the order in which they were punched (see Fig. 2-6).

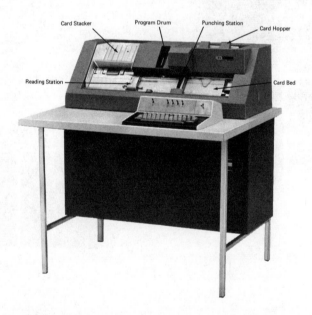

FIGURE 2-6. IBM 029 Card Punch. *Courtesy of IBM Corp.*

[4]The card punch is more popularly known as a *keypunch* machine.

FIGURE 2-7. Keyboard of 029 Card Punch. *Courtesy of IBM Corp.*

It is often desirable to duplicate a punched card. This can be done as follows:

1. Feed and register the card you want to duplicate.
2. Release it to the middle card bed.
3. Feed and register a blank card into the first card bed.
4. Depress the "DUP" key. This will cause both the original and the blank to move from right to left at the same rate. As the original moves it passes the reading station, where its holes are sensed. This information is relayed to the punching station and punched into the card in the punch bed.

After a deck of cards has been punched, it can be checked for keypunching errors by using a *verifier* (see Fig. 2-8). The verifier operator places the punched deck in the card hopper and proceeds to "punch" the same original data into the already punched cards. However, no actual punching occurs. Instead the following check is made: if the verifier operator has depressed the same key as the keypunch operator originally had (that is, if the "holes" match) the card moves to the next column and the procedure continues. If no discrepancy occurs for the entire card, then a notch is entered on the right side of the card, indicating that the card is correctly punched. However, if there is an inconsistency in any column the card remains

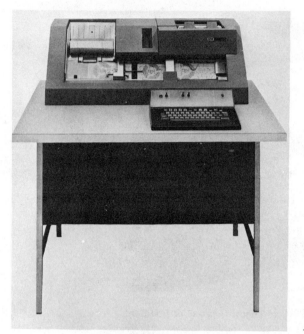

FIGURE 2-8. A Verifier. *Courtesy of IBM Corp.*

stationed at that column and an error light is turned on. The discrepancy has occurred because either the original punch is incorrect, or else the verifier operator has made a "punching" error. The operator has three tries to get the punches to agree (if the attempts fail, then the error is clearly on the punched card). A notch is then automatically entered above the column where the error is.

PROGRAM CARD

A *program card* (or *drum card*) can be used to give basic instructions to the keypunch machine. Instructions are punched in a card and it is wrapped around the drum of the machine (see Fig. 2-9). Drum cards are used to simplify the keypunching process, especially when the same information or similar information is to be punched in the same fields on each card. Automatic skipping of columns and automatic duplication of columns, for example, will increase efficiency and reduce errors.

The first punched column of each field of a drum card contains an

FIGURE 2-9. Program Card on Drum.
Courtesy of IBM Corp.

instruction in the form of a 0, 1, 11, or blank. All other columns contain 12-punches. The *12*-punches define the field, indicating which columns should be punched according to the preceding instruction.

A *0*-punch will cause automatic duplication (when the AUTO SKIP DUP switch is on).

An *11*-punch will cause automatic skipping.

A *blank* instruction permits manual punching.

When drum cards are used, the keyboard is ordinarily numeric. A *1* instruction punch shifts the keyboard from numeric to alphabetic. However, the 1-punch must appear in *every* column in which alphabetic punching is desired, not just the first.[5]

EXAMPLE 2-1.   The drum card in Fig. 2-10 will cause the following:

1. Duplication of data from columns 1-10 of the previously punched card into columns 1-10 of the card being punched.
2. Manual punching permitted in columns 11-17.
3. Skipping of columns 18-35.
4. Alphabetic punching in columns 36-40.

[5]When a drum card is *not* used the keyboard is set for alphabetic punching and the NUMERIC key must be depressed each time a digit is being punched.

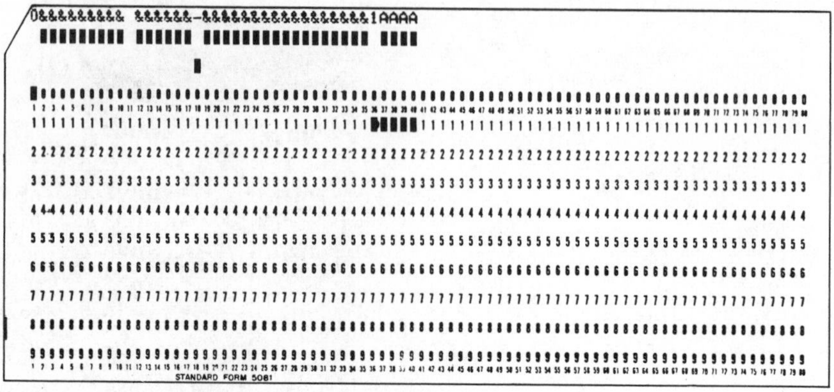

FIGURE 2-10. Drum Card for Example 2-1.

You can see from Fig. 2-10 that a 12-punch can be recorded by depressing the ampersand (&) and an 11-punch by a hyphen (-). In columns 37-40, where both 12- and 1-punches are needed, we simply punch an A (code 12-1).

THE REPRODUCER

Although the keypunch machine can be used to duplicate punched cards, it is not efficient for duplicating a large number of cards or making many copies of a set of punched cards. The *reducer* is used for efficient duplication of punch cards (see Fig. 2-11).

Reproducing

Reproducing is the card for card duplication of a file. The cards to be duplicated are placed in the read hopper and blank cards are placed in the punch hopper. One at a time the original cards pass by 80 sensing brushes which sense all the holes, one row at a time. A control panel receives the signal and directs the punching of corresponding holes in the blank cards (see Fig. 2-12).

After each card is punched it is verified. Both the original and the duplicate pass by comparing brushes to check that the duplicate is in fact the same hole-for-hole as the original. If there is a disagreement anywhere, the reproducer automatically stops.

FIGURE 2-11. The Reproducer. *Courtesy of IBM Corp.*

Gangpunching

Gangpunching is a process by which many blank cards are punched with the data from a single master card. There are two types.

Straight Gangpunching

In *straight gangpunching* the information on one master card is punched into many blank cards. The master is placed in front of a deck of blank cards. The new deck (master plus blanks) is placed in the punch hopper. The master passes by the punch brushes; its holes are sensed and punched into the blank behind it. Next the newly punched duplicate (called a *detail card*) passes the brushes and the blank behind it is punched according to the holes in this detail card. This process continues until all blank cards have been punched. The result is an entire file of detail cards, each identical to the master (see Fig. 2-13).

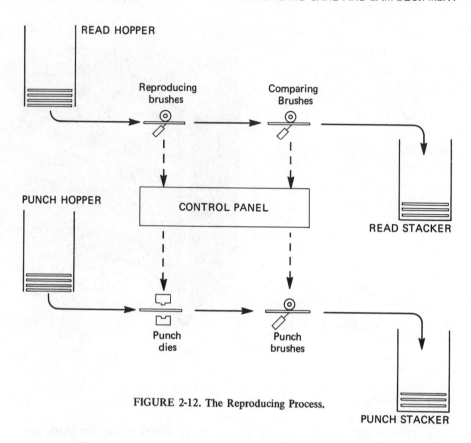

FIGURE 2-12. The Reproducing Process.

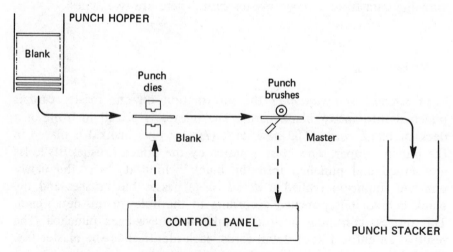

FIGURE 2-13. Gangpunching.

Interspersed Gangpunching

Suppose you would like 50 copies of one master card, 100 copies of a second master, and 75 copies of a third. *Interspersed gangpunching* is a process which will produce the desired results. The procedure is basically an extension of straight gangpunching. Place 50 blanks behind the first master; follow that with the second master and 100 blanks, and the third master and 75 blanks. We have one operation with one large deck (if straight gangpunching were used, we would have to use three separate decks and have three operations).

Consider the problem which arises when the last duplicated card of the first group is being sensed. As it is sensed, the master of the second group is passing the punch dies. What happens? Does this second master get ruined by being punched with the unwanted information being sensed? The answer, of course, is no! The master cards have been punched (before this whole operation began) with an X (or 11) punch. This is sensed by special brushes and the card is allowed to pass by the punch dies without being punched.[6]

Mark Sensing

In *mark sensing* special pencil marks on data processing cards are sensed, and corresponding holes are punched in these same cards. An electrographic pencil is used to make the marks, and special mark sensing brushes are used to sense them and transmit impulses to the punch dies (see Fig. 2-14).

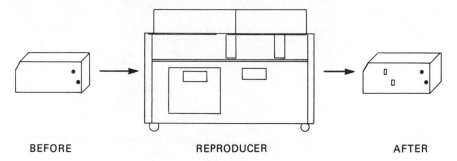

BEFORE   REPRODUCER   AFTER

FIGURE 2-14. Punching Mark-Sensed Cards.

[6]When used for control purposes, the 11 zone is sometimes called X and the 12 zone Y.

THE INTERPRETER

The *interpreter* is a machine designed to read the holes that have been punched into cards and print on the cards the characters which the holes represent. This is often very helpful, since the reproducer produces punched holes but no printed interpretation (see Fig. 2-15).

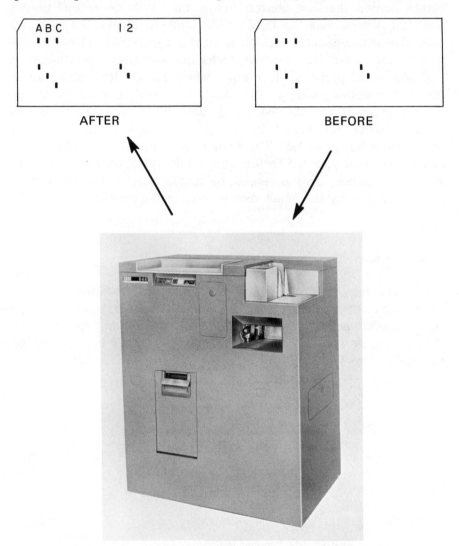

FIGURE 2-15. Interpretation of Cards by Interpreter. *Courtesy of IBM Corp.*

THE SORTER

The *sorter* is used to arrange decks of cards. They can be sorted into either alphabetic or numeric order. In this section we shall explain the numeric sort in some detail and only mention how the alphabetic sort is done.

The cards to be sorted are placed in the hopper and read one at a time. The sorter reads one column of a card and sends it to the pocket corresponding to the punch that was sensed. A sense brush and contact roller combination is used to sense the punch, open the corresponding chute, and send the card to the proper pocket via the determined chute. The sorter has a pocket for each punch 9, 8, 7, 6, 5, 4, 3, 2, 1, 0, 11, 12, and a reject pocket for blanks (see Fig. 2-16).

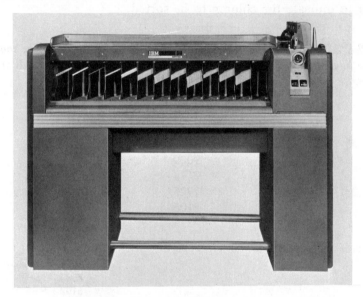

FIGURE 2-16. A Sorter. *Courtesy of IBM Corp.*

Numeric Sorting

To simplify our discussion of numeric sorting, let us assume that all card columns to be sorted contain only the digits 0 through 9, and only one per column. We shall not use or concern ourselves with the 11, 12, or reject pockets.

Our problem in numeric sorting is to arrange cards in order according to the numbers which are punched in them. For example, we might arrange a deck numerically according to the four-digit numbers in columns 21-24 of each card. But wait a minute! How can we sort four-digit numbers if our sorter can only sense one digit, not four? Since our sorter can only sort one column, we simply "sort" the cards four times. Each column sort is called a *pass*. We require four passes.

The procedure used to sort our four-digit numbers might appear strange at first. It is the *reverse digit method*–so called because the first pass sorts according to the *last* (right most) digit. The second pass sorts according to the second last digit, and so on, until the last pass sorts according to the first digit.[7] The operator uses a manual selector to indicate the column to be sorted.

EXAMPLE 2-2. Use the sorter and the reverse digit method to arrange the cards below in numerical order (we show only the numbers from the cards and not the entire card).

$$1009$$
$$4583$$
$$5102$$
$$2141$$
$$9000$$
$$0178$$
$$1925$$
$$8106$$
$$3333$$

The cards are placed in the sorter hopper.

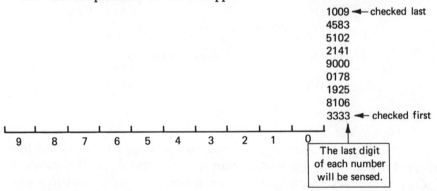

[7]See Exercise 9.

The first pass produces the results indicated below.

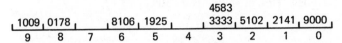

The cards are gathered (by the operator) from left to right and stacked for the next pass. Those from the 9 pocket appear at the top of the stack. Those from the 0 pocket are on the bottom. The cards are now in order with respect to the last digit of each.

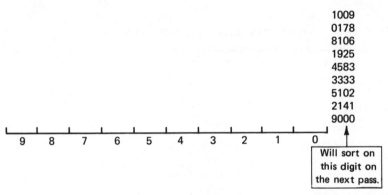

The second pass sorts on the second last digit. This produces the results below.

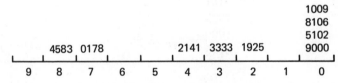

The cards are stacked (below, right) and are in order according to the last two digits (83, 78, 41, 33, 25, 09, 06, 02, 00). A third pass is used to sort according to the third last digit.

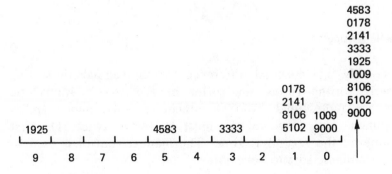

The cards are stacked (below, right) and a fourth pass is used to sort the cards according to the first digit. This, of course, is the final pass.

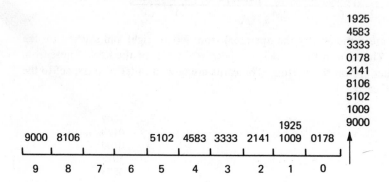

The final result is:

9000
8106
5102
4583
3333
2141
1925
1009
0178

Alphabetic Sorting

There is only one essential difference between alphabetic sorting and numeric sorting (using the sorter of Fig. 2-16). Alphabetic characters are represented by *two* punches--a zone punch and a numeric punch. Thus *each* column must be sorted twice. The first sort is numeric; the second is zone. The manual control is used to switch from numeric sort to zone sort.

THE COLLATOR

In this section we will study five basic *collator* operations:

merging
matching
match-merging
selecting
sequence-checking

Except in the case of sequence-checking it is assumed that all decks used are in correct order according to numbers which appear in the same field on each. It should be obvious, during the study of each process, that the process will usually fail if we do not use ordered decks.

In our discussions we will specify pockets (stackers), but this is only an attempt to make the explanations clearer. The choices are arbitrary and are determined by the control panel wiring.

As in the case of the reproducer, sensing is by brushes.

The collator which we describe here has five pockets (see Fig. 2-17). Some collators have four.

FIGURE 2-17. A Collator. *Courtesy of IBM Corp.*

Merging

Merging is the combining of two ordered decks of cards into one ordered deck.

One of the decks is placed in the primary hopper, the other in the secondary hopper. They are placed so that the smallest numbered cards of each deck will be sensed first. Then the first cards in each hopper are compared. The smaller numbered one is ejected into pocket 3; the larger remains in its hopper and is compared with the next card in the other hopper. Again the smaller numbered card is dropped into pocket 3. The process continues until all cards from both hoppers have been dropped into pocket 3. The result is an ordered deck in pocket 3 (see Fig. 2-18).

If two cards being compared have the same number, then both are dropped, primary first, into pocket 3.

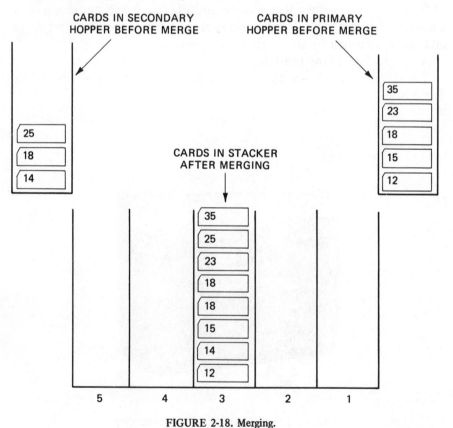

FIGURE 2-18. Merging.

Matching

In the *matching* process two ordered decks are separated into four decks, as follows: (1) cards from the primary hopper which have a matching numbered card in the secondary hopper are sent to pocket 2. The matching card from the secondary is sent to pocket 4. (2) Unmatched primary cards go to pocket 1. Unmatched secondary cards go to pocket 5.

Although the control and final results of matching differ considerably from those of merging, the mechanics of the comparing step are the same. That is, two cards (one from each hopper) are compared. If they are the same, both are ejected. If they differ, the smaller (only) is ejected. But control is different. If both are ejected they are sent to separate pockets, as indicated above. If only one is ejected it is sent to the proper pocket, as indicated above (see Fig. 2-19).

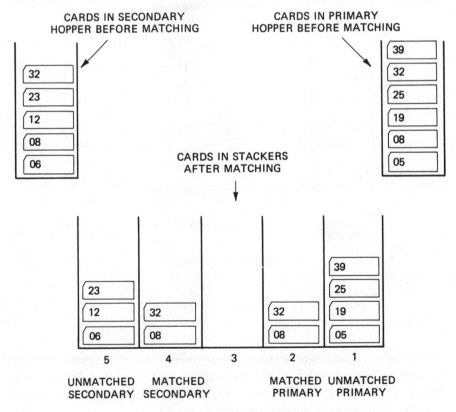

FIGURE 2-19. Matching.

Match-Merging

The *match-merge* is similar to the matching process. The *only* difference is that the cards which match are merged together into stacker 3, rather than separated as in matching (see Fig. 2-20).

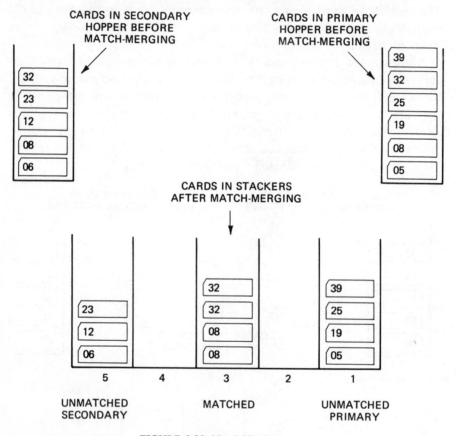

FIGURE 2-20. Match-Merging.

Selecting

A file of cards can be searched for all cards which have a special punch, a certain number, or any number in an interval. When found, these cards are removed from the file and dropped into a separate pocket. This process is called *selecting*.

Sequence-Checking

Sequence-checking is used to check that all cards in a deck are in order.

Let us assume that the cards are supposed to be in ascending order; that is, lowest first, highest last. The cards are placed in the primary hopper and a comparing procedure follows.

The second is compared with the first. If the second is larger than the first, then these two are in order. However, if the second is smaller than the first, then the order is incorrect. In this latter case the collator stops and an error light is turned on. The operator must remove the cards which are out of order, correct the order, and restart the collator.

Once the first two have been compared and found to be in order (or corrected after an error indication), the first is dropped into pocket 1. Next, the procedure is repeated with the third being compared with the second. The entire process is repeated until all cards are in the pocket.

THE CALCULATOR

The purpose of the *calculator* is to perform the simple, routine arithmetic calculations of addition, subtraction, multiplication, and division (see Fig. 2-21).

FIGURE 2-21. A Calculator. *Courtesy of IBM Corp.*

The calculator operates under directions from a wired control panel. Numbers are read from a card, or possibly several cards, and a series of calculations is performed using the numbers. The result is punched into the original card or into the card which follows, as instructed by the control wiring.

It should be noted that the same prewired set of operations will be applied to the data of all cards placed in the hopper and not just to the first card.

As an example, control could be wired to multiply the number in columns 10-12 by the number in columns 27-28, subtract from this product the number in column 30, and punch the result into columns 50-54. This same procedure would be followed for all cards placed in the hopper.

THE ACCOUNTING MACHINE

The *accounting machine*, or tabulator, is used to summarize data from punched card input and produce printed reports as output (see Fig. 2-22).

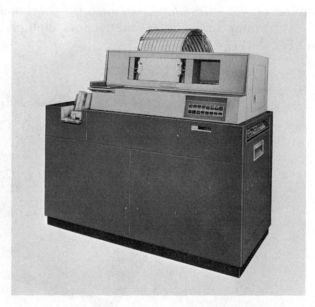

FIGURE 2-22. An Accounting Machine. *Courtesy of IBM Corp.*

Counters are used to accumulate totals and thus compress data into a presentable form. The accumulated data is printed on a report form in a format specified by the control wiring.

The functions of the calculator and accounting machine are merely sketched here to complete our discussion of EAM. Such processing can also be handled by a *computer*, using the Report Program Generator (RPG) language. RPG is discussed in detail in Chapter 15.

EXERCISES 2.1

1. Why do you think exactly two punches are used to represent letters?

2. What do you think would happen if you did not depress the "REL" before feeding a new blank card to be punched?

3. List the steps in punching a card and then duplicating it.

4. In alphabetic sorting we sort by numeric punch first. Why can't the first sort be by zone punch, or can it?

5. How can we determine whether or not a card has been verified?

6. It often happens during merging that one hopper becomes empty while the other still has cards. What would you expect to happen at this point?

7. Sort the numbers below step by step using the reverse digit method:

$$7301$$
$$9420$$
$$7302$$
$$4600$$
$$1111$$
$$5050$$
$$8000$$

8. Why would anyone use a sorter to sort a deck of cards if he could use the sequence-checking operation of the collator? Is there a situation where you would prefer sequence-checking to sorting?

9. Try the *forward* digit method of sorting for Example 2-2. Does this method produce a properly sorted deck?

10. Given the cards in the hoppers below, show what each of the five pockets of a collator contains after (a) matching (b) merging (c) match-merging.

	18
	07
	07
16	06
15	05
07	04
04	03
03	02
02	01

secondary	primary
hopper	hopper

11. Decode and write the interpretation for the following data processing card.

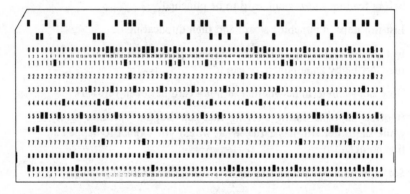

12. Darken the areas where punches should be to enter the message
COMPUTER SCIENCE & DATA PROCESSING beginning in
column 10.

3

NUMBER SYSTEMS

INTRODUCTION

This chapter presents a study of number systems. Specifically, we shall study the decimal, binary, octal, and hexadecimal number systems. In future chapters we will see how these ideas are applied to coding and programming for digital computers. We will also see applications to computer design and data representation.

PRELIMINARY MATHEMATICS

The ideas of *base* and *exponent* are important for an understanding of number systems.

10^3 is the same as $10 \times 10 \times 10$.
5^4 is the same as $5 \times 5 \times 5 \times 5$.
2^6 is the same as $2 \times 2 \times 2 \times 2 \times 2 \times 2$.

In these examples 10, 5, and 2 are *bases*, whereas 3, 4, and 6 are *exponents*. The base is multiplied by itself; the number of times it appears as a factor is determined by the exponent. Thus $10^4 = 10 \times 10 \times 10 \times 10$. The base *10* appears *four* times, since 4 is the exponent.

THE DECIMAL NUMBER SYSTEM (BASE 10)[1]

We can make some observations about the number system we are most familiar with.

1. All numbers are made up of digits selected from 0, 1, 2, 3, 4, 5, 6, 7, 8, 9.
2. The contribution of a digit to the total value of a number depends not only on what it is (i.e., 1, 2, 3, etc.) but also on *where* it is.

Let us examine the number 372, which can be written as

$$3 \times 100 + 7 \times 10 + 2 \times 1$$

The 2 contributes 2 to the total value of the number.
The 7 contributes 70 to the total value of the number.
The 3 contributes 300.

Consider the place values of another whole number, 25,164.

. . .	10,000	1000	100	10	1
. . .	2	5	1	6	4

$$\begin{cases} 2 \times 10,000 \\ + 5 \times 1000 \\ + 1 \times 100 \\ + 6 \times 10 \\ + 4 \times 1 \end{cases}$$

This can also be written as

. . .	10^4	10^3	10^2	10^1	10^0
. . .	2	5	1	6	4

Now we list some properties of *base 10* numbers.

1. *Ten* digits are used. They are 0, 1, 2, 3, 4, 5, 6, 7, 8, 9.
2. Column (place) values begin at 1 and increase by factors of *10* as we go from right to left.
3. The total value of a number is "computed" by multiplying the digits in the columns by their column values and adding all of the products.

[1]The expressions "base 10" and "decimal" will be used interchangeably.

THE BINARY NUMBER SYSTEM (BASE 2)

We establish the *binary* number system by using *2* as the base instead of 10, and by using *two* digits instead of ten. We list the properties of this different number system.

1. *Two* digits are used. They are 0, 1.
2. Column (place) values begin at 1 and increase by factors of 2 as we go from right to left.

We have charts as indicated below.

. . .	16	8	4	2	1

or

. . .	2^4	2^3	2^2	2^1	2^0

The binary number 1101, which we will write as $(1101)_2$ to indicate that it is a base two number, can be placed in a chart as

8	4	2	1
1	1	0	1

and considered as

$$1101 = 1 \times 8 + 1 \times 4 + 0 \times 2 + 1 \times 1$$
$$= \quad 8 \quad + \quad 4 \quad + \quad 0 \quad + \quad 1$$
$$= \quad 13.$$

In other words, $(1101)_2$ is the same as the base ten number 13, or

$$(1101)_2 = (13)_{10}.$$

EXAMPLE 3-1. Write $(1001010)_2$ as a decimal number. The chart

64	32	16	8	4	2	1
1	0	0	1	0	1	0

yields

$$1 \times 64 + 0 \times 32 + 0 \times 16 + 1 \times 8 + 0 \times 4 + 1 \times 2 + 0 \times 1.$$

When computed, we find $(1001010)_2 = (74)_{10}$.

EXAMPLE 3-2. Convert $(11101)_2$ *to base 10.* The chart

16	8	4	2	1
1	1	1	0	1

yields

$1 \times 16 + 1 \times 8 + 1 \times 4 + 0 \times 2 + 1 \times 1$. This is $(29)_{10}$.

It should be clear that the reverse process will convert a decimal number to binary. The problem is that of fitting the number to a binary chart.

EXAMPLE 3-3. Change $(52)_{10}$ *to binary.* We need only go as far as the 32's column in the binary chart, since 64 is greater than the number, 52, which we are converting.

~~64~~	32	16	8	4	2	1

← 52

√

We now indicate, by a 1 in the proper column, that one 32 is contained in 52. Removing this 32 leaves a remainder of 20 to be placed in the other columns.

32	16	8	4	2	1
1					

$52 - 32 = \textbf{20}$ left.

√

There is a 16 contained in the 20 which remains. Placing a 1 in the 16's column leaves a remainder of 4.

32	16	8	4	2	1
1	1				

$20 - 16 = \textbf{4}$ left.

√

There are no 8's in 4, so we have zero 8's in our number.

32	16	8	4	2	1
1	1	0			

$4 - 0 = \textbf{4}$ left.

√

There is a 4 in the 4 which remains. Marking this in the proper column leaves us with no remainder.

32	16	8	4	2	1
1	1	0	1		

$4 - 4 = \textbf{0}$ left.

√

Since there is 0 left, we have no 2's and no 1's; but 0's must be put in these columns to serve as place holders.

32	16	8	4	2	1
1	1	0	1	0	0

$$\checkmark \checkmark$$

Thus $(52)_{10} = (110100)_2$.

EXAMPLE 3-4. Change $(67)_{10}$ to binary. There is a 64 in 67. When removed and charted we have *3* left $(67 - 64 = 3)$. The 3, of course, is a 2 and a 1. Thus we have a 64, a 2, a 1, and the rest zeros.

64	32	16	8	4	2	1
1	0	0	0	0	1	1

$$(67)_{10} = (1000011)_2.$$

THE OCTAL NUMBER SYSTEM (BASE 8)

If we use *8* as the base, and use *eight* digits, we have the foundation of the *octal* number system.

1. The *eight* digits, 0, 1, 2, 3, 4, 5, 6, 7, are used.
2. Column (place) values begin at 1 and increase by factors of *8* as we go from right to left.

We have charts as indicated below.

...	512	64	8	1

or

...	8^3	8^2	8^1	8^0

Accordingly, the octal number $(327)_8$ can be placed in a chart as

64	8	1
3	2	7

and considered as

$$327 = 3 \times 64 + 2 \times 8 + 7 \times 1 = 215.$$

In other words,

$$(327)_8 = (215)_{10}$$

and we have a convenient method for changing octal numbers to their decimal equivalents.

Consider the reverse process, that of converting a base ten number to base eight. The mechanics are the same as for the conversion from base ten to base two, except we fit the decimal number to an *octal* chart.

EXAMPLE 3-5. Change $(59)_{10}$ to octal. We use the chart

8	1

and note that it is unnecessary to extend the chart to include the 64's column, since 64 is larger than the number, 59, which we are fitting to the chart.

There are seven 8's in 59. Thus we have a 7 in the 8's column, and a remainder of 3.

8	1
7	

$\sqrt{}$ $59 - 56 = 3$ left.

Clearly the 3 that remains is three 1's. We place a *3* in the 1's column, leaving a remainder of zero.

8	1
7	3

$\sqrt{}$ $3 - 3 = 0$ left. Thus, $(59)_{10} = (73)_8$.

EXAMPLE 3-6. Convert $(135)_{10}$ to octal. There are two 64's in 135. The remainder is 7.

64	8	1
2		

$\sqrt{}$ $135 - 128 = 7$ left.

There are no 8's in 7. The remainder is 7.

64	8	1
2	0	

$\sqrt{}$ 7 is left.

There are seven 1's in 7. The remainder is 0.

64	8	1
2	0	7

$\sqrt{}$ Thus $(135)_{10} = (207)_8$.

THE HEXADECIMAL NUMBER SYSTEM (BASE 16)

There are *sixteen* digits in the *hexadecimal* number system, and *16* is used as the base.

1. The *sixteen* digits, 0, 1, 2, 3, 4, 5, 6, 7, 8, 9, A, B, C, D, E, F, are used. We use A to represent 10, B for 11, C for 12, D for 13, E for 14, and F for 15. This convention is used because the numbers 10, 11, 12, 13, 14, 15 are not digits, but rather combinations of two digits each. Their use as "digits" would be confusing, as is shown in Example 3-7 below.
2. Column (place) values begin at 1 and increase by factors of *16* as we go from right to left.

We have the following charts:

. . .	256	16	1

or

. . .	16^2	16^1	16^0

So the hexadecimal number $(2A4)_{16}$ can be charted as

256	16	1
2	A	4

and converted.

$$2 \times 256 + 10 \times 16 + 4 \times 1 = 676$$

Thus, $(2A4)_{16} = (676)_{10}$, and we have a way of converting a hexadecimal number to decimal.

EXAMPLE 3-7. Justification of the use of symbols A, B, C, D, E, F. Suppose that $(2A4)_{16}$ were written $(2104)_{16}$; that is, without the use of the symbol A. The reader might understand this to mean

$$2 \times 16^3 + 1 \times 16^2 + 0 \times 16^1 + 4 \times 16^0$$

rather than

$$2 \times 16^2 + 10 \times 16^1 + 4 \times 16^0,$$

which is intended.

EXAMPLE 3-8. Change $(523)_{10}$ to hexadecimal. Using a hexadecimal chart, we begin by recording the two 256's which are in 523. The remainder is 11.

256	16	1
2		

$523 - 512 = 11$ left.

√

There are no 16's in 11. The remainder is 11.

256	16	1
2	0	

11 is left.

√

There are eleven 1's in 11. We use "B" for 11.

256	16	1
2	0	B

Thus $(523)_{10} = (20B)_{16}$.

√

EXERCISES 3.1

In 1-23 change each to a number in the indicated base.

    1. $(1100)_2$ to base 10

* 2. $(10011)_2$ to base 10

* 3. $(11010)_2$ to base 10

    4. $(15)_{10}$ to base 2

* 5. $(33)_{10}$ to base 2

* 6. $(87)_{10}$ to base 2

    7. $(17)_8$ to base 10

    8. $(54)_8$ to base 10

* 9. $(77)_8$ to base 10

  10. $(29)_{10}$ to base 8

*11. $(50)_{10}$ to base 8

  12. $(99)_{10}$ to base 8

  13. $(AB)_{16}$ to base 10

*14. $(F9)_{16}$ to base 10

*15. $(13C)_{16}$ to base 10

16. $(38)_{10}$ to base 16

17. $(96)_{10}$ to base 16

*18. $(208)_{10}$ to base 16

*19. $(139)_{10}$ to base 2

20. $(139)_{10}$ to base 8

21. $(101110)_2$ to base 10

*22. $(347)_8$ to base 10

*23. $(5DE)_{16}$ to base 10

24. The first twelve counting numbers in base 10 are 1, 2, 3, 4, 5, 6, 7, 8, 9, 10, 11, 12. What are the first twelve counting numbers in base 3? In base 4? In base 5?

25. In what bases is the number 12305 unacceptable?

ADDITION IN DIFFERENT NUMBER SYSTEMS

A further understanding of number systems can be gained by studying addition of numbers in different bases.

EXAMPLE 3-9. Addition in base 10. This example might seem trivial, but if you can *understand* the procedure (not just the mechanics), then addition in other number bases will be nearly as simple.

$$\begin{array}{r} \text{Add:} \quad 29 \\ 48 \\ 15 \\ \underline{13} \end{array}$$

If the addition is performed correctly, the result obtained will be 105. But what can we learn about number systems from this? Again, if you *understand* how to add you realize that upon adding the digits in the first column you get $9 + 8 + 5 + 3 = 25$. But 25 is not *one* digit, so 25 cannot appear in *one* column. So you do something like "put down 5 and carry 2." What this means is that $25 = 2 \times 10 + 5$; there are two tens in 25, with 5 left over. The 5 left over is five *ones*, so this is placed in the first (one's) column. The "two tens" indicates that a 2 should be added to the second (ten's) column. Thus the phrase "carry 2."

Perhaps we have already learned enough to apply these ideas to addition in base 2.

EXAMPLE 3-10. Add in binary

$$
\begin{array}{r}
10 \\
11 \\
\hline
\end{array}
$$

In the first column we have $0 + 1 = 1$. So our result at this point is

$$
\begin{array}{r}
10 \\
11 \\
\hline
1
\end{array}
$$

In the second column we have $1 + 1$. This is "2." But we don't have a digit called 2 in base 2 (only 0 and 1). In fact, since the base is 2, we find that $2 = 1 \times 2 + 0$, one two and no ones, or "put down 0 and carry 1." Our result at this stage is

$$
\begin{array}{r}
^{1}10 \\
11 \\
\hline
01
\end{array}
$$ (the small boldface "1" is the 1 being carried)

Moving left to the next column, and adding, we get our final result

$$
\begin{array}{r}
^{1}10 \\
11 \\
\hline
101
\end{array} \quad \checkmark
$$

EXAMPLE 3-11. Addition in base 2.

	1	11	111	111	
111	111	111	111	111	
101	101	101	101	101	
	0	**00**	**100**	**1100**	The result is 1100.

EXAMPLE 3-12. Addition in base 2.

	1	11	1011	1011	
101	101	101	101	101	
111	111	111	111	111	
101	101	101	101	101	
	1	**01**	**001**	**10001**	$\checkmark$

EXAMPLE 3-13. Addition in base 8.

	1	
37	37	
24	24	7 + 4 is "11" in base *10*, but this is $1 \times 8 + 3$ since we
	3	are adding in base *8*.

$$\begin{array}{r} 1 \\ 37 \\ 24 \\ \hline 63 \end{array} \checkmark$$

EXAMPLE 3-14. Addition in base 8.

$$\begin{array}{r} 2 \\ 746 \\ 157 \\ 567 \\ \hline 4 \end{array}$$ 6 + 7 + 7 = "20" = 2 × 8 + 4

$$\begin{array}{r} 22 \\ 746 \\ 157 \\ 567 \\ \hline 14 \end{array}$$ 2 + 4 + 5 + 6 = "17" = 2 × 8 + 1

$$\begin{array}{r} 122 \\ 746 \\ 157 \\ 567 \\ \hline 714 \end{array}$$ 2 + 7 + 1 + 5 = "15" = 1 × 8 + 7

$$\begin{array}{r} 122 \\ 746 \\ 157 \\ 567 \\ \hline 1714 \end{array}$$ \checkmark

EXAMPLE 3-15. Addition in base 16.

$$\begin{array}{cc} & 1 \\ A9 & A9 \\ 89 & 89 \\ \hline & 2 \end{array}$$ 9 + 9 = "18" = 1 × 16 + 2

$$\begin{array}{r} 11 \\ A9 \\ 89 \\ \hline 32 \end{array}$$ 1 + A + 8 = "19" = 1 × 16 + 3

$$\begin{array}{r} \tiny{1\ 1} \\ A9 \\ \underline{89} \\ 132 \quad \surd \end{array}$$

EXAMPLE 3-16. Addition in base 16.

$$\begin{array}{cc} & \tiny{1} \\ B3E & B3E \\ 127 & 127 \\ \underline{1F3} & \underline{1F3} \\ & 8 \end{array}$$ E + 7 + 3 = "24" = 1 × 16 + 8

$$\begin{array}{c} \tiny{1\ 1} \\ B3E \\ 127 \\ \underline{1F3} \\ 58 \end{array}$$ 1 + 3 + 2 + F = "21" = 1 × 16 + 5

$$\begin{array}{c} \tiny{1\ 1} \\ B3E \\ 127 \\ \underline{1F3} \\ E58 \quad \surd \end{array}$$

EXERCISES 3.2

Perform the additions in the bases indicated.

*1. Base 2.   (a) $\begin{array}{r} 101 \\ \underline{111} \end{array}$ (b) $\begin{array}{r} 1000 \\ \underline{1111} \end{array}$ (c) $\begin{array}{r} 1011 \\ \underline{111} \end{array}$

(d) $\begin{array}{r} 10011 \\ 1100 \\ \underline{10001} \end{array}$ (e) $\begin{array}{r} 101 \\ 110 \\ \underline{100} \end{array}$ (f) $\begin{array}{r} 1100 \\ 1011 \\ \underline{11} \end{array}$

*2. Base 8.   (a) $\begin{array}{r} 73 \\ \underline{6} \end{array}$ (b) $\begin{array}{r} 347 \\ \underline{450} \end{array}$ (c) $\begin{array}{r} 54 \\ 36 \\ \underline{21} \end{array}$

(d) $\begin{array}{r} 103 \\ 235 \\ 777 \\ \underline{111} \end{array}$ (e) $\begin{array}{r} 64 \\ 37 \\ \underline{12} \end{array}$

*3. Base 16. (a)   89 (b)   AB (c)   1DF
                25   CD   AB8
                                        E14

            (d) 5CE (e) A34
                 F72   17E
                 123   101

4. Base 4. (a)   31 (b) 222   (c)   333
                20   101   111
                       231   230

SUBTRACTION IN DIFFERENT NUMBER SYSTEMS

We can subtract in different number bases in essentially the same way that we subtract in base 10.

EXAMPLE 3-17. *Subtraction in base 10.*

   947
   263

We first subtract 3 from 7, and get 4.

   947
   263
      4

Next we *try* to subtract 6 from 4. However, 6 is larger than 4, so we "borrow 1" from the 9. Since the 9 is one column to the left of 4, the borrowed 1 is actually a borrowed *10*. Also, the 9 is reduced to an 8.

  10
  847
  263
    4

We subtract 6 from $(10 + 4)$.

  1 0
  847
  263
   84

Finally, we subtract 2 from 8.

```
 10
847
263
───
684  √
```

We can check the answer, 684, by adding 684 and 263 to get 947.

EXAMPLE 3-18. Subtraction in base 8.

```
63
47
──
```

We cannot subtract 7 from 3, so we "borrow 1" from the 6. The borrowed 1 is worth *8* when placed in the column containing the 3, since we are computing in *base 8*. Also, the 6 is reduced to 5.

```
 8
53
47
──
```

After subtracting we get

```
 8
53
47
──
 4
```

Next we subtract 4 from 5

```
 8
53
47
──
14
```

Thus

```
63
47
──
14  √
```

To check our result we add 47 and 14. This produces 63.

```
 1
47
14
──
 3        (7 + 4 = "11" = 1 × 8 + 3)
```

1
47
14
──
63

Subtraction in other bases is similar. In base 2 each borrowed 1 is worth 2. In base 16 each borrowed 1 is worth 16.

EXERCISES 3.3

Perform the subtractions in the bases indicated.

*1. Base 8.   (a) 52   (b) 35   (c) 126   (d) 540
                    33   27   53   307

*2. Base 16.   (a) 87   (b) 5C   (c) A6   (d) FB
                    39   38   69   ED

*3. Base 2.   (a) 11   (b) 101   (c) 1111   (d) 10111
                     1   10   101   1010

MULTIPLICATION IN DIFFERENT NUMBER SYSTEMS[2]

Multiplication of numbers in different number bases is similar to multiplication in base 10.

EXAMPLE 3-19. Multiplication in base 10.

            425
            381
            ───
            425
           3400
           1275
          ──────
         161925

---

[2]No continuity is lost if this section is omitted.

Multiplication in base 10 can be done efficiently because we know the multiplication table for all digits 0 through 9.

×	0	1	2	3	4	5	6	7	8	9
0	0	0	0	0	0	0	0	0	0	0
1	0	1	2	3	4	5	6	7	8	9
2	0	2	4	6	8	10	12	14	16	18
3	0	3	6	9	12	15	18	21	24	27
4	0	4	8	12	16	20	24	28	32	36
5	0	5	10	15	20	25	30	35	40	45
6	0	6	12	18	24	30	36	42	48	54
7	0	7	14	21	28	35	42	49	56	63
8	0	8	16	24	32	40	48	56	64	72
9	0	9	18	27	36	45	54	63	72	81

Note that the italic digits above indicate the carry (if any).

In base 2 the multiplication table is

×	0	1
0	0	0
1	0	1

(no carries)

EXAMPLE 3-20. Multiplication in base 2.

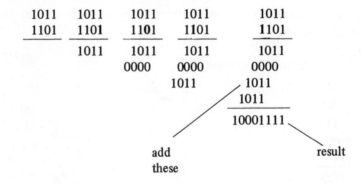

The table below indicates the results of multiplying digits in base 8. Again the italic digit indicates any carry.

X	0	1	2	3	4	5	6	7
0	0	0	0	0	0	0	0	0
1	0	1	2	3	4	5	6	7
2	0	2	4	6	*10*	*12*	*14*	*16*
3	0	3	6	*11*	*14*	*17*	*22*	*25*
4	0	4	*10*	*14*	*20*	*24*	*30*	*34*
5	0	5	*12*	*17*	*24*	*31*	*36*	*43*
6	0	6	*14*	*22*	*30*	*36*	*44*	*52*
7	0	7	*16*	*25*	*34*	*43*	*52*	*61*

In an attempt to make the table clearer we justify that $5 \times 7 = 43$.

Since $5 \times 7 = 35$ in base 10, and $(35)_{10} = (43)_8$, then $5 \times 7 = (43)_8$.

EXAMPLE 3-21. Multiplication in base 8 using the table above.

$$\begin{array}{r} 45 \\ 73 \\ \hline \end{array}$$

$$\begin{array}{r} 45 \\ 73 \\ \hline {}^1 7 \end{array} \qquad 3 \times 5 = 17$$

$$\begin{array}{r} 45 \\ 73 \\ \hline 1 \\ 147 \end{array} \qquad 3 \times 4 = 14$$

or

$$\begin{array}{r} 45 \\ 73 \\ \hline 157 \end{array} \qquad \text{so far.}$$

$$\begin{array}{r} 45 \\ 73 \\ \hline 157 \\ {}^4 3 \end{array} \qquad 7 \times 5 = 43$$

$$\begin{array}{r} 45 \\ 73 \\ \hline 157 \\ 4 \\ 343 \end{array} \qquad 7 \times 4 = 34$$

$$\begin{array}{r} 45 \\ 73 \\ \hline 157 \\ 403 \\ \hline 4207 \; \checkmark \end{array}$$

or

The table below shows the results of multiplying digits in base 16. Again, the italic digit indicates any carry.

X	0	1	2	3	4	5	6	7	8	9	A	B	C	D	E	F
0	0	0	0	0	0	0	0	0	0	0	0	0	0	0	0	0
1	0	1	2	3	4	5	6	7	8	9	A	B	C	D	E	F
2	0	2	4	6	8	A	C	E	*10*	*12*	*14*	*16*	*18*	*1A*	*1C*	*1E*
3	0	3	6	9	C	F	*12*	*15*	*18*	*1B*	*1E*	*21*	*24*	*27*	*2A*	*2D*
4	0	4	8	C	*10*	*14*	*18*	*1C*	*20*	*24*	*28*	*2C*	*30*	*34*	*38*	*3C*
5	0	5	A	F	*14*	*19*	*1E*	*23*	*28*	*2D*	*32*	*37*	*3C*	*41*	*46*	*4B*
6	0	6	C	*12*	*18*	*1E*	*24*	*2A*	*30*	*36*	*3C*	*42*	*48*	*4E*	*54*	*5A*
7	0	7	E	*15*	*1C*	*23*	*2A*	*31*	*38*	*3F*	*46*	*4D*	*54*	*5B*	*62*	*69*
8	0	8	*10*	*18*	*20*	*28*	*30*	*38*	*40*	*48*	*50*	*58*	*60*	*68*	*70*	*78*
9	0	9	*12*	*1B*	*24*	*2D*	*36*	*3F*	*48*	*51*	*5A*	*63*	*6C*	*75*	*7E*	*87*
A	0	A	*14*	*1E*	*28*	*32*	*3C*	*46*	*50*	*5A*	*64*	*6E*	*78*	*82*	*8C*	*96*
B	0	B	*16*	*21*	*2C*	*37*	*42*	*4D*	*58*	*63*	*6E*	*79*	*84*	*8F*	*9A*	*A5*
C	0	C	*18*	*24*	*30*	*3C*	*48*	*54*	*60*	*6C*	*78*	*84*	*90*	*9C*	*A8*	*B4*
D	0	D	*1A*	*27*	*34*	*41*	*4E*	*5B*	*68*	*75*	*82*	*8F*	*9C*	*A9*	*B6*	*C3*
E	0	E	*1C*	*2A*	*38*	*46*	*54*	*62*	*70*	*7E*	*8C*	*9A*	*A8*	*B6*	*C4*	*D2*
F	0	F	*1E*	*2D*	*3C*	*4B*	*5A*	*69*	*78*	*87*	*96*	*A5*	*B4*	*C3*	*D2*	*E1*

EXAMPLE 3-22. Multiplication in base 16.

$$\begin{array}{r} A3 \\ 94 \\ \hline \end{array}$$

$$\begin{array}{r} A3 \\ 94 \\ \hline C \end{array} \quad (4 \times 3 = C)$$

$$\begin{array}{r} A3 \\ 94 \\ \hline 28C \end{array} \quad (4 \times A = 28)$$

$$\begin{array}{r} A3 \\ 94 \\ \hline 28C \\ {}^1B \end{array} \quad (9 \times 3 = 1B)$$

$$
\begin{array}{r}
A3 \\
94 \\
\hline
28C \\
1 \\
5AB
\end{array}
\qquad (9 \times A = 5A)
$$

$$
\begin{array}{r}
A3 \\
94 \\
\hline
28C \\
5BB \\
\hline
\end{array}
$$

$$
\begin{array}{r}
A3 \\
94 \\
\hline
28C \\
5BB \\
\hline
5E3C \;\checkmark
\end{array}
$$

EXERCISES 3.4

Perform the multiplications in the bases indicated.

*1. Base 2. (a) 101 (b) 1110 (c) 1111 (d) 1011
                 101   1001   1010   1000

*2. Base 8. (a) 16   (b) 73   (c) 145 (d) 235
                 24   37   65   437

*3. Base 16. (a) 45   (b) A7   (c) CB   (d) 18F
                 21   D8   3E   69A

ADDITIONAL CONVERSIONS

Binary and Octal

It is a simple matter to convert binary numbers to octal, and octal numbers to binary. First let's see how to convert binary numbers to octal.

You *could* change the binary number to decimal, and the decimal number to octal.

$$(\quad)_2 \longrightarrow (\quad)_{10} \longrightarrow (\quad)_8$$

But this is two conversions, and a longer process than is necessary. Observe the table below.

Binary	Octal
000	0
001	1
010	2
011	3
100	4
101	5
110	6
111	7

What you should notice is that if we take binary digits three at a time (3 columns) they correspond to (and convert to) octal digits. In fact, all of the possible binary triplets (000 through 111) convert to all of the possible octal digits (0 through 7).

EXAMPLE 3-23. Change $(111011100001)_2$ to octal.
Group the binary digits in threes, beginning at the *right*.

$$111 \quad 011 \quad 100 \quad 001$$

Convert each group of three binary digits to one octal digit.

$$7 \quad\quad 3 \quad\quad 4 \quad\quad 1$$

Thus

$$(111011100001)_2 = (7341)_8.$$

Although it does not seem to matter in the example above, if you begin grouping from the *left* in the next example you will get an incorrect result; whereas grouping from the *right* leads to a different and correct result.

EXAMPLE 3-24. Change $(1101011111010)_2$ to octal.

$$1101011111010 = 1 \quad 101 \quad 011 \quad 111 \quad 010$$
$$= 1 \quad 5 \quad 3 \quad 7 \quad 2$$
$$= (15372)_8.$$

We can readily change numbers from octal to binary by replacing each octal digit with its three-digit binary equivalent.

EXAMPLE 3-25. Change $(7306)_8$ to binary.

$$\left.\begin{array}{l} 7 = 111 \\ 3 = 011 \\ 0 = 000 \\ 6 = 110 \end{array}\right\} \qquad \text{so} \qquad (7306)_8 = (111\ 011\ 000\ 110)_2 .$$

It should be clear that all of the zeros in the above result are needed as place holders. Removal of any zeros will make the answer wrong. (This statement might seem more convincing if you try the following: remove one or more zeros and convert the number back to octal. You will fail to get 7306.)

Binary and Hexadecimal

Just as every octal digit can be represented by 3 binary digits, so can each hexadecimal digit be represented by *4* binary digits.

Binary	Hexadecimal
0000	0
0001	1
0010	2
0011	3
0100	4
0101	5
0110	6
0111	7
1000	8
1001	9
1010	(10) A
1011	(11) B
1100	(12) C
1101	(13) D
1110	(14) E
1111	(15) F

EXAMPLE 3-26. Change $(10110101001)_2$ to hexadecimal. Grouping from the *right*, in fours, we get

$$101 \qquad 1010 \qquad 1001 = (5A9)_{16} .$$

EXAMPLE 3-27. Change $(F7CD)_{16}$ *to binary.*

$$F = 1111$$
$$7 = 0111$$
$$C = 1100 \quad \text{so} \quad (F7CD)_{16} = (1111 \ 0111 \ 1100 \ 1101)_2 .$$
$$D = 1101$$

Octal and Hexadecimal

We know enough already to use a shortcut for converting numbers from octal to hexadecimal, and vice versa.

Again, we *could* change from octal to hexadecimal by changing to base 10 first, and then to hexadecimal.

$$(\quad)_8 \longrightarrow (\quad)_{10} \longrightarrow (\quad)_{16}$$

But this involves two somewhat complicated computations.

How about using base 2 as an "intermediate" base?

$$(\quad)_8 \longrightarrow (\quad)_2 \longrightarrow (\quad)_{16}$$

EXAMPLE 3-28. Change $(74351)_8$ *to base 16.*

$$\begin{aligned}
(74351)_8 &= (111 \ 100 \ 011 \ 101 \ 001)_2 \\
&= (111 \ 1000 \ 1110 \ 1001)_2 \\
&= (78E9)_{16} .
\end{aligned}$$

Similarly, we can convert numbers from base 16 to base 8.

$$(\quad)_{16} \longrightarrow (\quad)_2 \longrightarrow (\quad)_8$$

EXAMPLE 3-29. Change $(A57)_{16}$ *to octal.*

$$\begin{aligned}
(A57)_{16} &= (1010 \ 0101 \ 0111)_2 \\
&= (101 \ 001 \ 010 \ 111)_2 \\
&= (5127)_8
\end{aligned}$$

FRACTIONS AND DECIMALS

We know that .94 in base 10 means any of the following:

$$9 \times \frac{1}{10} + 4 \times \frac{1}{100}$$

or   9 X .1   + 4 X .01

or   9 X 10^{-1} + 4 X 10^{-2}.

But what does $(.11)_2$ mean? We find that $(.11)_2$ can be expressed in the following ways which parallel the representations above:

$$1 \times 2^{-1} + 1 \times 2^{-2}$$

or $1 \times \frac{1}{2}$ $+ 1 \times \frac{1}{4}$

or $1 \times .5$ $+ 1 \times .25$.

These forms simplify to ¾ or .75.

That is,

$$(.11)_2 = (.75)_{10}.$$

EXAMPLE 3-30. Change $(.1011)_2$ to decimal.

$$(.1011)_2 = 1 \times \frac{1}{2} + 0 \times \frac{1}{4} + 1 \times \frac{1}{8} + 1 \times \frac{1}{16}$$

$$= .5 + 0 + .125 + .0625$$

$$= (.6875)_{10}.$$

EXAMPLE 3-31. Change $(.375)_{10}$ to binary. This conversion is made by fitting the number to a binary chart; that is, fit .375 to

$\frac{1}{2}$	$\frac{1}{4}$	$\frac{1}{8}$	$\frac{1}{16}$	. . .

or to

.5	.25	.125	.0625	. . .

Beginning at the left, we find that there are *no* .5's in .375. Thus

.5	.25	.125	. . .
0			

There is a .25 in .375. Thus

.5	.25	.125	. . .
0	1		

, and .375 − .25 = .125 is left.

The .125 remaining gives

.5	.25	.125
0	1	1

And the result is exact, since removing .125 from .125 leaves a remainder of zero. Thus $(.375)_{10} = (.011)_2$.

EXAMPLE 3-32. Change $(.56)_8$ to base 10.

$$(.56)_8 \text{ means } 5 \times 8^{-1} + 6 \times 8^{-2}$$

or

$$5 \times \frac{1}{8} + 6 \times \frac{1}{64}$$

or $5 \times (.125) + 6 \times 6 \times (.015625)$.

These simplify to $\frac{46}{64}$ or .718750. Thus, $(.56)_8 = (.718750)_{10}$.

EXAMPLE 3-33. Change $(.3)_{16}$ to base 10.

$$(.3)_{16} = 3 \times \frac{1}{16} \text{ or } .1875$$

Thus,
$$(.3)_{16} = (.1875)_{10}.$$

Conversion of fractions and decimals from base 10 to base 8 and from base 10 to base 16 are left as exercises.

EXERCISES 3.5

Change each to a number in the indicated base.

* 1. $(111000)_2$ to base 8
  2. $(101111)_2$ to base 8
* 3. $(10111)_2$ to base 8
  4. $(35)_8$ to base 2
  5. $(46)_8$ to base 2
* 6. $(217)_8$ to base 2

7. $(1011)_2$ to base 16

* 8. $(10001101)_2$ to base 16

* 9. $(1010101)_2$ to base 16

10. $(E7)_{16}$ to base 2

11. $(9F)_{16}$ to base 2

*12. $(1AC)_{16}$ to base 2

*13. $(777)_8$ to base 16

*14. $(1574)_8$ to base 16

*15. $(ABC)_{16}$ to base 8

*16. $(DEF)_{16}$ to base 8

*17. $(1.001)_2$ to base 10

*18. $(1.11)_2$ to base 10

*19. $(110.1)_2$ to base 10

*20. $(9.375)_{10}$ to base 2

*21. $(7.4)_8$ to base 10

*22. $(C.4)_{16}$ to base 10

*23. $(76.625)_{10}$ to base 8

*24. $(29.75)_{10}$ to base 16

25. $(11.011)_2$ to base 10

26. $(.1111)_2$ to base 10

27. $(3.7)_8$ to base 10

28. $(29.25)_{10}$ to base 2

29. $(3.12)_4$ to base 10

30. $(3.4)_5$ to base 10

4

COMPUTER LOGIC AND BOOLEAN ALGEBRA

BOOLE AND SHANNON

In 1854, an English mathematician named George Boole published a book which explained how logical statements could be transformed into mathematical symbols. Additionally, he explained how you could calculate the truth or falsity of related statements by using rules designed for just that purpose. This "mathematics" which Boole developed is known as *Boolean algebra* or symbolic logic.

Our interest here is in Claude Shannon's application of Boolean algebra. In his Master's thesis (M.I.T., 1938), Shannon showed how Boolean algebra could be applied to the design and simplification of complex circuits involved in electronic computers.

We shall study this "switching logic," as it may be called, but limit our discussion to simple switching circuits and gates. Our interest will be in the logic of the circuit, not in the electronics. However, you should realize that the ideas contained below apply equally well for thin films, magnetic cores, transistors, and other components of computer circuits.

NOTATION

To facilitate the discussion of switching circuits we use the following notation:

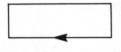
A circuit, with the arrow indicating the direction of current flow.

An *open* switch, or switch in *off* position.

A *closed* switch, or switch in *on* position

EXAMPLE 4-1.[1]

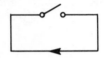
The switch is open (off). No current will flow through it

EXAMPLE 4-2.

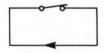
The switch is closed (on). Current will flow through it.

SERIES AND PARALLEL CIRCUITS

Series Circuits

All switches must be closed for current to flow through a *series* circuit.

---

[1] Actual sources of current will not be supplied. For convenience and ease in discussion, assume the current source to be at the left and the direction of flow clockwise.

EXAMPLE 4-3.

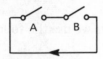

Both A and B must be closed for current to flow through the circuit.

EXAMPLE 4-4.

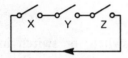

All three switches X, Y, and Z must be closed in order to have current flow.

Parallel Circuits

Current will flow through a *parallel* circuit if any (one or more) of the switches is closed.

EXAMPLE 4-5.

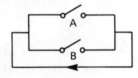

Current will flow through the circuit if either A or B is closed, or if both are closed.

EXAMPLE 4-6.

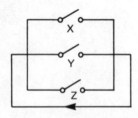

Current will flow through the circuit if any (one or more) of the switches is closed.

The Use of Charts

The results of Example 4-3 (series) can be presented simply and clearly with the introduction of charts.

A	B	CURRENT
open	open	no flow
open	closed	no flow
closed	open	no flow
closed	closed	flow

We introduce the following notation:

> 0 means open switch or no flow of current
> 1 means closed switch or flow of current
> means the logical "AND" operation; for example, $A \cdot B$ is read as "A AND B."

If we apply this new notation to the chart above, we get

A	B	$A \cdot B$
0	0	0
0	1	0
1	0	0
1	1	1

This chart provides us with an arithmetic table.

$$0 \cdot 0 = 0$$

$$0 \cdot 1 = 0$$

$$1 \cdot 0 = 0$$

$$1 \cdot 1 = 1$$

Thus

$A \cdot B = 1$ only when $A = 1$ and $B = 1$.
$A \cdot B = 0$ otherwise.

Recall that this is a series circuit, where current flows only when both switches are closed. No current flows otherwise.

Now let us return to the example with two switches in parallel. This can be charted as

A	B	CURRENT
open	open	no flow
open	closed	flow
closed	open	flow
closed	closed	flow

or as

A	B	A + B
0	0	0
0	1	1
1	0	1
1	1	1

Using "+" as the logical "OR" operation, $A + B$ is read A **OR** B, and we have the following arithmetic table:

$$0 + 0 = 0$$
$$0 + 1 = 1$$
$$1 + 0 = 1$$
$$1 + 1 = 1$$

We have

$A + B = 1$ if either A is 1, or B is 1, or both are 1.
$A + B = 0$ only if both A and B are 0.

Although the result $1 + 1 = 1$ seems strange, remember that this is not addition, but rather the *logical OR* operation. With this in mind, the result is quite reasonable.

LABELING AND DRAWING CIRCUITS

We can now label and draw simple switching circuits.

EXAMPLE 4-7. Label the circuit at the right to indicate under what conditions current will flow. Current will flow if *A and B* are closed. Thus the label is *A · B.*

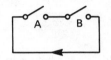

EXAMPLE 4-8. Label the circuit at the right.[2] The label should be *C + F,* since current will flow if either *C or F* is closed.

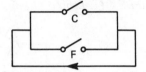

EXAMPLE 4-9. Label the circuit at the right. The label is *A · B + C,* since current will flow if *A* and *B* are both closed *or* if *C* is closed. Thus

$$(A \cdot B) \, or \, (C),$$

which is written

$$A \cdot B + C,$$

is the label.

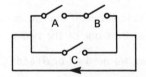

EXAMPLE 4-10. Label the circuit at the right. Observe that *P* must be closed or no current will flow. Also, either *Q* or *R* must be closed. Then current will flow through the circuit. Thus,

$$P \, and \, (Q \, or \, R),$$

or

$$P \cdot (Q + R) \text{ is the label.}$$

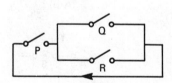

Note that the parentheses above are needed because the hierarchy of operations is the same as in arithmetic: multiplication before addition (AND before OR).

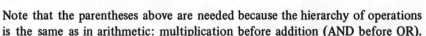

[2]When we ask for the "label" we shall always mean the label which indicates under what conditions current flows.

Without parentheses we have $P \cdot Q + R$, which is

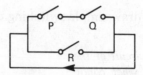

and this is not what we had originally.

EXAMPLE 4-11. Label

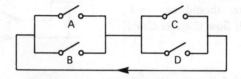

Following the path of current we see that for current to flow two conditions are necessary:

1. at least one of the two switches A, B must be closed.
2. at least one of the two switches C, D must be closed.

Thus, we need $(A$ or $B)$ and $(C$ or $D)$; that is, $(A + B) \cdot (C + D)$ is the label.

EXAMPLE 4-12. Draw a circuit which represents the Boolean expression
$$(A \cdot B) \cdot (C + D).$$

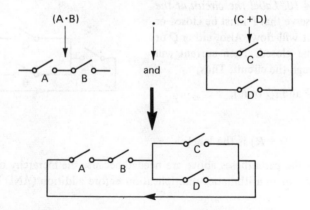

The original label could have been written as $A \cdot B \cdot (C + D)$.

EXAMPLE 4-13. Draw $(A + B + C) + X \cdot Y$.

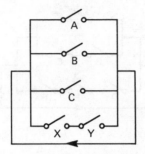

The original label could have been written as $A + B + C + X \cdot Y$.

EXERCISES 4.1

1. Show the binary chart for three switches in series.

2. Show the binary chart for three switches in parallel.

3. Shown below is a very simple computer. It answers the question: "Are both of the switches closed?" If the answer is yes, the light is turned on as an indication. If the answer is no, the light is not turned on. Draw a computer of this type which will answer the question: "Is at least one of the three switches closed?" Indicate how the answer will be given.

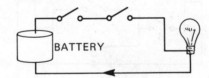

*4. Label

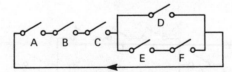

5. Draw $(A + B) + (C \cdot D)$.

* 6. Label

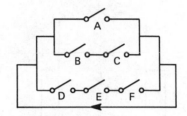

* 7. Label

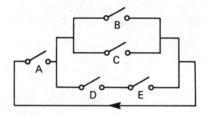

8. Draw $(A + B + C) \cdot (D + E \cdot F) + G$.

9. Draw $A \cdot (B \cdot D + E + C \cdot F)$.

10. Draw $X + Y + W \cdot Q + R$.

*11. Label

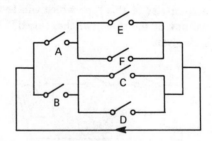

12. Draw $[(A + B + C) \cdot (D \cdot E + F)] \cdot H + I$.

*13. Label

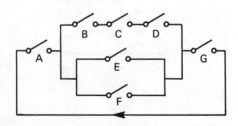

*14. Compute the value of each Boolean expression.
     (a) $1 + 0 + 0 \cdot 1$ (b) $1 \cdot 1 \cdot 1$
     (c) $1 + (1 \cdot 0 \cdot 1)$ (d) $0 \cdot (1 + 1)$
     (e) $1 \cdot (0 + 1 \cdot 0 + 0)$

GATES

Many of the basic functions of the arithmetic and control units of the computer are carried out using circuitry consisting of combinations of *gates*.[3] These functions include

1. adding binary numbers[4]
2. decimal to binary encoding
3. binary to decimal decoding
4. comparing two numbers
5. timing
6. counting
7. retaining arithmetic results

Each gate is a circuit. It accepts input(s) in the form of pulse (1) or no-pulse (0) and produces an output of pulse or no-pulse (1 or 0).

AND Gate

An *AND gate* is like a series circuit. Its output is a pulse (1) if all of its inputs are pulses. The standard AND gate for two inputs is illustrated below.

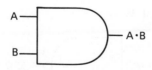

[3] A *gate* is a basic logic circuit.
[4] See Exercise 8 for this application.

OR Gate

An *OR gate* is like a parallel circuit. Its output is a pulse if any of its inputs is a pulse. The standard OR gate for two inputs is illustrated below.

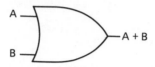

Inverter

The *inverter* changes an input to its opposite state. If the input is a pulse, the output will be a no-pulse. If the input is a no-pulse, the output will be a pulse. Symbolically we say that an input A has an output $\overline{A}$ (read as A-bar). $\overline{A}$ represents *not-A,* the complement of *A.* The inverter is illustrated below.

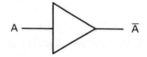

NAND Gate

An AND gate followed by an inverter is called a *NAND gate*. It can be illustrated as

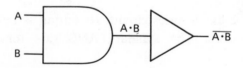

but is usually abbreviated as

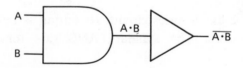

It can be charted in binary as

		AND ↓	NAND ↓
A	B	$A \cdot B$	$\overline{A \cdot B}$
0	0	0	1
0	1	0	1
1	0	0	1
1	1	1	0

NOR Gate

An OR gate followed by an inverter is called a *NOR gate.* It can be illustrated as

but is usually abbreviated as

It can be charted in binary as

		OR ↓	NOR ↓
A	B	$A + B$	$\overline{A + B}$
0	0	0	1
0	1	1	0
1	0	1	0
1	1	1	0

XOR Gate[5]

For two inputs A and B, the *XOR gate* is represented by the Boolean expression $A \cdot \overline{B} + \overline{A} \cdot B$. It is illustrated as

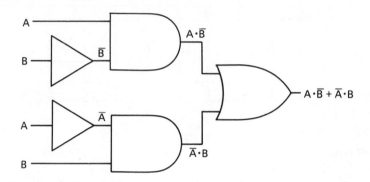

or in the abbreviated form

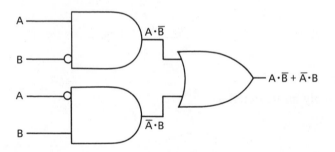

It can be charted as

						XOR
A	B	$\overline{A}$	$\overline{B}$	$A \cdot \overline{B}$	$\overline{A} \cdot B$	$A \cdot \overline{B} + \overline{A} \cdot B$
0	0	1	1	0	0	0
0	1	1	0	0	1	1
1	0	0	1	1	0	1
1	1	0	0	0	0	0

[5]XOR stands for *exclusive OR*.

In words, if either *A* or *B* (*but not both*) is a pulse, then the result is a pulse. Otherwise the result is no-pulse.

"Shouldn't that be an Exclusive—Or?"

EXERCISES 4.2

1. Draw an AND gate for three inputs. Also, draw a simple series circuit having three switches.

2. Draw an OR gate for three inputs. Also, construct the corresponding binary table.

3. Make a binary table which describes the effect of the inverter on pulse and no-pulse.

4. Draw and chart in binary a NAND gate having three inputs.

5. Draw and chart in binary a NOR gate having three inputs.

6. Draw and make a binary chart for two inverted inputs to an OR gate; that is, let the inputs pass through inverters before they reach the OR gate.

7. Draw and make a binary chart for two inverted inputs to an AND gate.

8. Verify that the following circuit will produce the arithmetic sum of two binary inputs. The result is shown for 0 + 1. Show that it also works for 1 + 0, 0 + 0, and 1 + 1. When the circuit forks in two directions, the pulse (or no-pulse) goes in *each* direction.

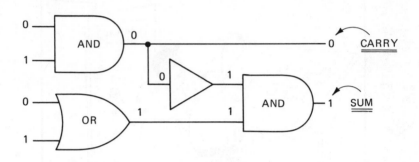

* 9. Label

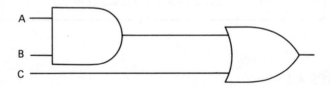

10. Draw $(A + B) \cdot (C + D)$.

*11. Label

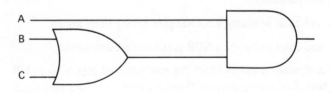

12. Draw $(A + B) \cdot C.$

*13. Label

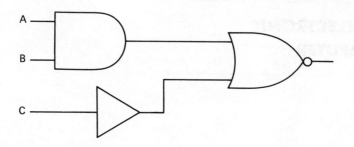

14. Draw $A \cdot B + C \cdot D.$

5

THE ELECTRONIC
COMPUTER

Since nearly all of the remaining chapters deal with computers, it is appropriate at this point to define "computer" and introduce important concepts that will be studied in detail later.

DEFINITION

By an *electronic computer* we shall mean a high speed machine which can accept and store data and instructions, process the data according to the instructions, and produce the results in some usable form, all virtually automatically.

We shall discuss the definition by indicating the directions in which its key words lead us.

High speed. The speeds (time) associated with processing are measured in milliseconds, microseconds, and nanoseconds (see Chapter 1).

Accept data and instructions. Data and instructions that are accepted by a computer are called *input*. Input is discussed in detail in the next chapter.

Store data and instructions. The computer processes data according to instructions. Both the data and the instructions must be in the computer's *storage* during such processing. Storage is treated in detail in the next chapter.

Instructions. Data is processed according to instructions supplied to the computer. A list of instructions to the computer is called a *program.* The person who writes the instructions is called a *programmer.*

The instructions can be arithmetic (for example, add, subtract, multiply, divide), logical (for example, compare, transfer), and input/output (for example, read, write, print, punch).

Produce results. The results produced by a computer are called *output.* Different kinds of output are discussed in the next chapter.

Automatic. The computer will process data according to the program after the operator initiates computer operation. After initialization all instructions of the program can usually be carried out, as programmed, with no additional help from the operator. Manual operation, including initialization, is handled using controls at the *console* of the computer (see Fig. 5-1).

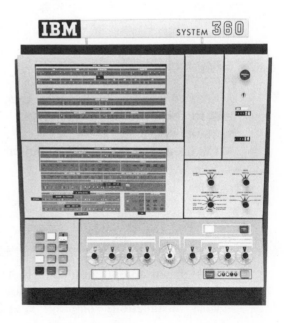

FIGURE 5-1. A Computer Console.
Courtesy of IBM Corp.

COMPUTER PROGRAMMING

We have said that a program is a list of instructions, and that a programmer writes such programs. However, there is more to programming than just writing instructions. We list (in order) the steps in the complete computer programming process:

1. Analysis
2. Flowcharting
3. Coding
4. Debugging
5. Documentation
6. Production

We now explain each of these steps.

Analysis

When a programmer is given a problem to prepare for solution by computer, he must determine precisely what the problem involves and the best method of solving it. This step is called *analysis.*

Flowcharting

After it has been determined exactly what the problem is and just how to solve it, a diagram (or flow chart) is made of the logic of the solution (see Fig. 5-2).

The process of *flowcharting* is discussed in Chapter 10.

Coding

Coding is the writing of instructions in a form (code) which the computer can accept. The code is written to correspond to the logic and steps of a previously prepared flow chart.

Most installations employ keypunch operators to punch the

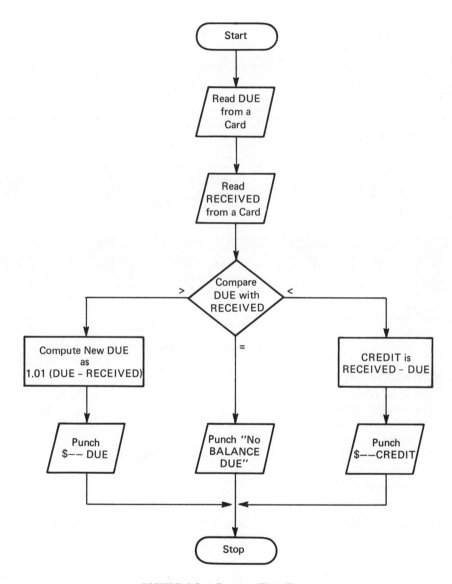

FIGURE 5-2. A Program Flow Chart.

programmers' codes into cards. The handwritten characters 2 and Z, 0 and O, 1 and I, and 5 and S closely resemble one another and can be misunderstood. The programmer should indicate to the keypunch operator how he distinguishes between them in his coding. One convention is:

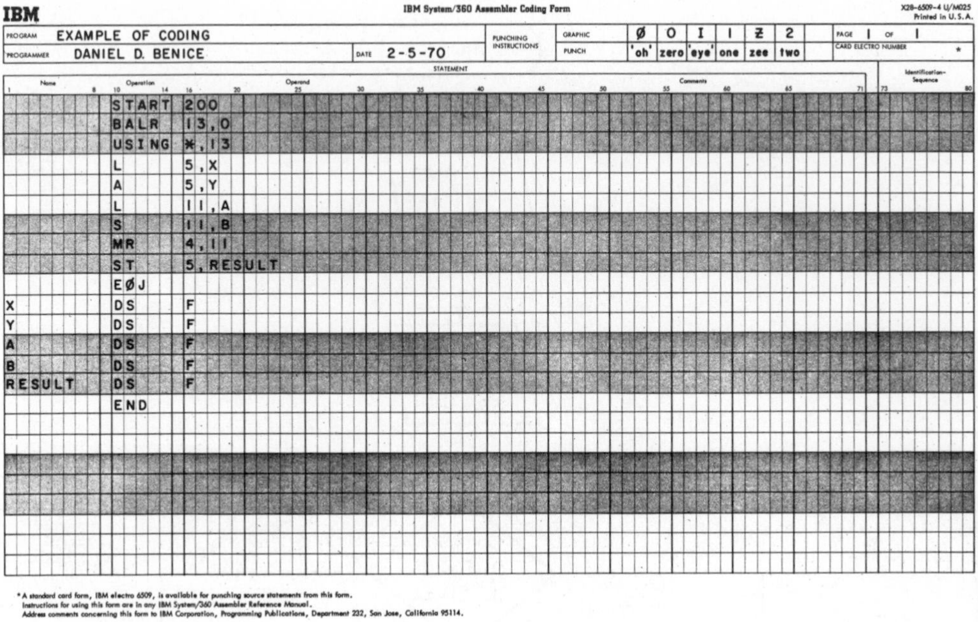

IBM — IBM System/360 Assembler Coding Form — X28-6509-4 U/M025 Printed in U.S.A.

PROGRAM: EXAMPLE OF CODING
PROGRAMMER: DANIEL D. BENICE — DATE: 2-5-70
PUNCHING INSTRUCTIONS — GRAPHIC: Ø 0 I 1 Ƶ 2 — PUNCH: 'oh' zero 'eye' one zee two
PAGE 1 OF 1 — CARD ELECTRO NUMBER *

Name	Operation	Operand	Comments	Identification-Sequence
	START	200		
	BALR	13,0		
	USING	*,13		
	L	5,X		
	A	5,Y		
	L	11,A		
	S	11,B		
	MR	4,11		
	ST	5,RESULT		
	EØJ			
X	DS	F		
Y	DS	F		
A	DS	F		
B	DS	F		
RESULT	DS	F		
	END			

* A standard card form, IBM electro 6509, is available for punching source statements from this form.
Instructions for using this form are in any IBM System/360 Assembler Reference Manual.
Address comments concerning this form to IBM Corporation, Programming Publications, Department 232, San Jose, California 95114.

FIGURE 5-3. A Coding Form.

The numeral *two* 2
The letter *zee* Ƶ
The numeral zero 0
The letter *"oh"* Ø
The numeral *one* 1
The letter *"eye"* I
The numeral *five* 5
The letter *ess* S

We shall use this convention when writing on coding forms (see Fig. 5-3).

Debugging

Errors in logic can occur in the programming process, although coding errors are made more frequently.

When errors in logic are made, a computer run usually produces either no results or incorrect (misleading) results.

When coding errors are made, the computer run is usually cut short (or never started) and an error is indicated.

Errors are common. The process of finding and removing errors from a computer program and producing a tested and working form is called *debugging*.

Very often a programmer will request a *dump* when his program is not executing correctly. A dump (short for core storage dump) provides the programmer with the contents of various storage locations. The contents are often given in hexadecimal and must be translated by the programmer.

Documentation

Often a computer program written by one person is used by others. It may even be changed by someone other than the original programmer. Accordingly, after debugging your program you should produce *documentation* to go with it. Such documentation usually includes:

1. Title, author, date completed
2. Computer system and language
3. Brief statement of problem
4. Input/output requirements
5. Special operating instructions
6. Flow chart of program
7. Listing of the (program) code

Production

Preparing a complete and working computer program is a time consuming process for any but trivial problems, since all steps (analysis, flowcharting, coding, debugging, documentation) must be completed. Consequently, no one will program a problem which is only going to be solved *once* (that is, with only one set of data) unless it is unusually complex.

When a programmer debugs a program he uses test data or sample data. It is usually representative of the kind of data to be used in runs after the program is debugged. A run using real data with the intention of actually using the results is called a *production* run. We say that a completely debugged (and documented) program is in production status.

SUBROUTINES AND MACROS

Solutions to many problems of both business and science involve computation of square roots. Thus, the process of finding square roots occurs frequently in programs. If each time a square root computation is desired the programmer has to spend time coding the necessary instructions, there is much duplication of effort and wasted time.

Subroutines are used to avoid wasteful reprogramming, as in the square root example and many other situations. A separate program (called a subroutine) might be written to compute the square root of a number supplied to it. Such a subroutine would be a complete program, but any other computer program could reference it.

A *main program* which uses a square root will *call* the subroutine by its predetermined name (say SQRT) when it needs the square root computed. The call is by a special computer instruction used for referencing subroutines (see Fig. 5-4).

Closely resembling the subroutine is the *macro* instruction. The computer translates a macro into a series of simpler instructions before executing a program containing it. Use of macros permits the programmer to simplify his coding, avoid repetition, and reduce errors.

THE "THINKING" COMPUTER

Computers have been called "giant brains" and "thinking machines" partly because they can carry out sequences of logical and arithmetic operations with great speed and accuracy and can make seemingly instant decisions. But the decisions the computer makes are not its own. The computer is instructed (via computer programs) exactly what decision should be made under given conditions. The programmer does the thinking; the computer merely follows directions. And it must be told, at every step, specifically what to do next.

Any error in the coding of the instructions will "confuse" the computer; wrong results or no results will appear. For example, if the instruction to indicate addition is supposed to contain "ADD" as the operation code, then such codes as "A", "AD", "ADDE", or even "ADD." will be unacceptable. Stray commas, periods, letters, and digits confuse the computer. Also, the computer usually expects its instructions to be punched in specific (predetermined) columns of punched cards.

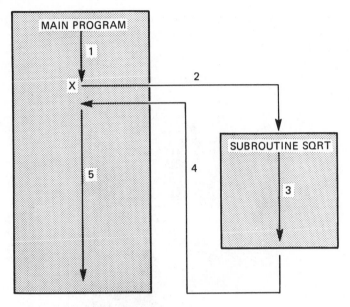

1. Begin main processing in main program.

2. Subroutine SQRT is called and transfer is made to it for computation of square root.

3. Square root is computed.

4. Return to main program (from subroutine) after computation.

5. Complete main processing.

FIGURE 5-4. Use of a Subroutine.

WHY WE USE COMPUTERS

There are several reasons why men of both business and science have turned to the computer to handle their data processing.

1. *Faster processing* and *fewer errors* usually result from computerizing data processing. However, lack of familiarity with a new computer system can slow down the mechanics of a process at first. Then too, keypunching errors can produce ridiculous mistakes, and the computer often gets the blame.
2. A combination of *rising clerical costs* and *shortage of clerical workers* necessitates computerizing any large scale operation.

3. Many phases of *research and development* in the sciences and engineering need the computer to handle otherwise impossible or impractical tasks.

For God's sake, man, can't you find something better to worry about than the effect on our real time system?

REAL-TIME COMPUTER SYSTEMS

A *real-time* computer system is one in which information can be processed fast enough so that the results can be used to affect the process under consideration.

Real-time systems are necessary for control of space probes, guided missiles, and interplanetary rockets. In some instances millions of calculations must be made every second, and the results of the calculations used to make course changes or corrections.

Many banks use real-time systems. They have terminals which are directly connected to a remote central computer.[1] Each customer's deposit or withdrawal request is processed, and his account updated, while he waits.

---

[1] A remote computer is one that is located at some distance from the input/output console, often several miles or more.

The airlines use real-time computer systems to handle their reservations. Your inquiry about the availability of seats on a given flight can be answered in seconds, after a check with the central computer system.

Some motel chains use a similar system to enable their guests to reserve accommodations in advance.

TIME-SHARING

Many computer manufacturers have established *time-sharing* computer systems. A time-sharing system may involve only one remote central computer system, yet allows many users to run programs "at the same time."

Connected to a remote computer are perhaps several hundred (user) consoles (or terminals). Each console is linked to the computer via telephone lines. A user simply dials the time-sharing phone number to "get on" the computer. Once on the user enters his program and data using the teletypewriter portion of the console (see Fig. 5-5).[2]

FIGURE 5-5. A Time-Sharing User at a Terminal. *Courtesy of General Electric Co.*

[2] Also popular are TV-like video displays with typewriter keyboards. They are described in Chapter 6.

The computer may work several seconds on one program, then several seconds on the next, and so on. Execution of *small* programs appears as "instant," and the programmer receives his results without apparent wait. However, when many users are on at the same time or the program is not a short one, the programmer may be told (by the computer) to "wait." The computer later signals "ready" before executing the program when able to.

The *users* are programmers from different installations. A small installation might have only one terminal; larger installations would have several. A console might be located in a user's office or work area. And if one terminal is being used he might use another located elsewhere in the same installation.

Another advantage of using time-sharing is the cost savings. Since many installations use the same computer the cost is shared. Each installation pays only for the time it uses the computer.

Perhaps the greatest advantage of time-sharing is that the programmer can debug or change his program while at the console, and he gets his results back immediately. This is in contrast to the long "turn around" time on systems which do not use time-sharing. Programmers might otherwise wait from several hours to over a day for results of one computer run. And how wasteful that is if the programmer merely omitted a comma from an instruction!

"I don't know the man personally . . . we share the same computer."
©DATAMATION

COMPUTER-ASSISTED INSTRUCTION

Computer-assisted instruction (CAI) involves the use of a computer as an individual instructor and tutor.

In one situation a student sits at a console (a "typewriter") which is directly connected (on-line) to a computer. The computer may give him several paragraphs to read and then ask him questions about the material. If he answers correctly, he can proceed with new material. If he answers incorrectly, he may be corrected or given additional information to help him understand what the correct answer should be (see Fig. 5-6).

Another method involves no reading material, just questions from the computer and answers by the student.

In still another situation the student may be permitted to ask questions as well as answer them.

Our examples above suggest that both the computer and the student *type* their responses. Other newer input/output (I/O) configurations are also possible, including voice and cathode ray tube (CRT) I/O. Voice I/O is useful for teaching languages, reading, and music appreciation. The CRT and light pen are valuable for presenting tables, maps, photos, and graphs. In some cases the student gives a drawn or graphic response using a light pen on the CRT.[3]

FIGURE 5-6. A Teletypewriter Terminal Can Be Used for CAI. *Courtesy of Teletype Corp.*

[3]CRT and voice I/O are discussed in Chapter 6.

The advantages of CAI are many.

1. The student progresses at his own rate.
2. The student is told instantly whether his answer is correct or incorrect.
3. No time is lost through diversions to material which is irrelevant.
4. The student is forced to give an answer (he must think!) rather than listen for others' answers, as might be done in a classroom.

MULTIPROGRAMMING

Multiprogramming is a technique by which two or more programs can occupy the same main storage unit and be executed "at the same time." While (lengthy) I/O operations of one program are being handled, the processor is essentially idle and can handle some (non I/O) processing of the second at the same time.[4]

OPERATING SYSTEMS

An *operating system* is a program consisting of an integrated set of routines (programs) used to control the overall operation of a computer system and hence speed up processing.

1. Use of an operating system increases the processing rate by running separate programs consecutively without interruption.
2. Operator participation is minimized in order to decrease the turn-around time.
3. Compilers (for FORTRAN, COBOL, PL/1, RPG) and assemblers are provided to facilitate programming.
4. A good balance is obtained between processor execution (of logical and arithmetic instructions) and separately handled input/output execution. This reduces processor idle time.
5. Utility programs are included to load a program into memory, provide memory dumps, and handle file-to-file conversions, (such as, tape to data cell, disk to tape, data cell to disk, card to tape, and others).[5]

[4] Such concurrent processing of several programs "at the same time" is called *parallel processing.*
[5] These input/output devices are described in the next chapter.

6. Debugging programs are available to assist the programmer who is trying to find and correct the errors in his program.[6]

---

[6]Debugging programs, utility programs, compiler programs, assembler programs and others are referred to as *software*; whereas the computer equipment itself (I/O devices, storage, etc.) is called *hardware*.

6

STORAGE AND
INPUT/OUTPUT

We learned before that it is the execution of a program of computer instructions which results in the processing of data by a computer. In order to be executed, such instructions must be stored within the computer. Thus a *storage* device is necessary to retain the computer program and the data which is to be processed.[1]

In addition, devices for handling input and output are necessary for communication with the computer's storage. In other words, we must have a way of getting our program and data into the computer and our results out (see Fig. 6-1).

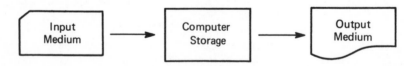

FIGURE 6-1. Communication with Storage.

Some devices which were originally intended for use as the internal storage of computers are now used for both storage and input/output (I/O). Similarly, some newer devices serve as both storage and I/O units. This chapter will explore both of these areas and their interrelationship.

---

[1] A given program is in storage long enough to be executed, but after execution it is replaced in storage by the next program to be executed.

MAGNETIC CORE

Magnetic core is the most widely used form of main storage. Such storage usually consists of hundreds of thousands of tiny ring-shaped magnetizable iron cores, each of which is about the size of the head of a pin (see Fig. 6-2).

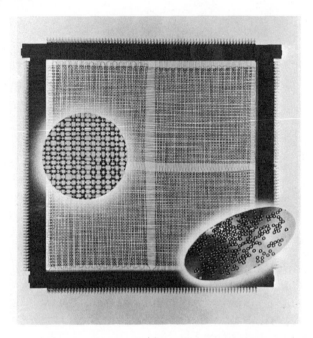

FIGURE 6-2. Magnetic Cores. *Courtesy of IBM Corp.*

The cores have wires passing through them and connecting them with other cores. They are magnetized by electric current which passes through the wires in one of two directions. The direction of the current determines the direction (or polarity) of the magnetism. Magnetism in one direction represents a one and magnetism in the opposite direction represents a zero. Hence, each core represents one binary digit (or *bit*) (see Fig. 6-3).

FIGURE 6-3. Polarity of Magnetic Cores.

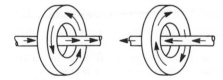

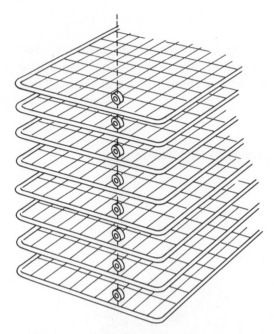

FIGURE 6-4. A Byte in Core Storage.

Magnetic cores are strung together in grids or planes, which are constructed so that only one core in each plane can be sensed (read from or written to) at any one time. But the basic data unit for the System/360 and other third generation computers is the *byte* (or character), and each byte consists of *eight* bits.[2] Thus, eight cores are needed to represent one byte, and eight core planes are needed for storage of data in bytes (see Fig. 6-4).

Magnetic core is the fastest (memory cycles of several hundred nanoseconds) and most compact form of storage in general use, Although it is also the most expensive, this disadvantage is offset by the fact that its speed allows more operations to be carried out in a given period of time.

Because of the high cost of core storage, computer systems usually contain auxiliary or on-line storage devices.[3] These less expensive memories are used when huge volumes of data are to be processed and extremely fast access to all data (or programs) is not needed at one time. Some of these auxiliary storages can be used directly, while others transfer data to main (core) storage for faster processing there.

Figure 6-5 shows a core storage unit.

[2] Two consecutive bytes (16 bits) are called a *halfword*. Four consecutive bytes (32 bits) are called a *fullword*.
[3] By *on-line* we mean directly connected to the central processing unit.

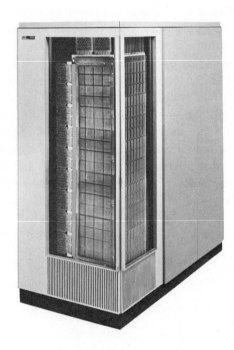

FIGURE 6-5. A Core Storage Unit.
Courtesy of IBM Corp.

MAGNETIC DRUM

Although the *magnetic drum* was once used as main storage, it is used in the most modern computer systems as auxiliary storage. Data or programs must be transferred from the magnetic drum to main (core) storage before they can be used in processing (see Fig. 6-6).

The drum is made of metallic coated steel, and can be magnetized. A magnetized area on the drum's surface represents a 1-bit, and an

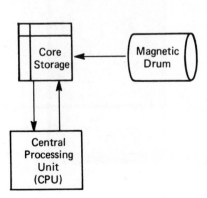

FIGURE 6-6. Transfer of Data from Drum to Core for Processing.

unmagnetized area represents a 0-bit. The drum is divided into channels with stationary read/write heads for each channel. The channels are further divided into sectors (see Fig. 6-7). The drum rotates at a constant speed, and reading or writing occurs when the specified sector of the given channel passes under the read/write head for that channel. *Writing* results in magnetizing some spots and leaving others unmagnetized. *Reading* is simply sensing the status of an area.

As an example, the IBM 2301 magnetic drum holds 4 million bytes and can transfer data to main storage at the high rate of over 1.2 million bytes per second. But before such transfer can begin the read/write head must wait for the rotating drum to position the desired data under it. This *access time* averages 8.6 milliseconds (see Fig. 6-8).

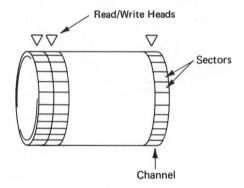

FIGURE 6-7. Schematic of a Magnetic Drum.

FIGURE 6-8. A Magnetic Drum. *Courtesy of IBM Corp.*

MAGNETIC DISK

Magnetic disk storage contains a stack of thin metal disks mounted on a vertical shaft. Read/write heads, placed on access arms, are positioned between the disks (see Fig. 6-9). When in operation, the disks rotate on the shaft at a constant speed and the access arms move to properly position the read/write heads for the reading (or writing) of data from the disk. The access arm between any two consecutive disks actually has two read/write heads, one for the bottom of the disk above it and the other for the top of the disk below it. Data is recorded as magnetic spots on the concentric, grooveless tracks of each disk. A disk might contain 500 such tracks on each side.

A magnetic disk file might have 25 or more disks and have a total capacity of over 100 million bytes or characters. Access time is less than 200 milliseconds and transfer rate is more than 150,000 bytes per second (see Fig. 6-10).

Disk files have also been developed which have stationary read/write heads positioned for each track of each disk. These head per track disks are much faster, since only the disk needs to move. Access time is about

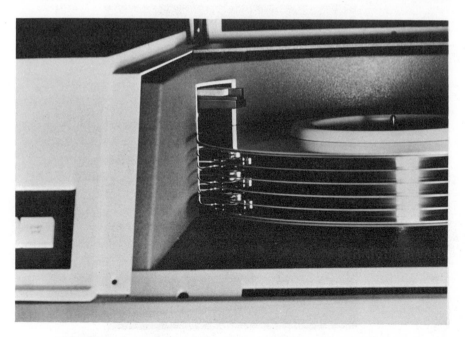

FIGURE 6-9. Magnetic Disk Storage Showing Access Arms and Read/Write Heads. *Courtesy of IBM Corp.*

FIGURE 6-10. A Magnetic Disk File. *Courtesy of IBM Corp.*

FIGURE 6-11. Head per Track Disk File. *Courtesy of Burroughs Corp.*

25 milliseconds and transfer rates to nearly 400,000 bytes per second are possible (see Fig. 6-11).

Disk drives with removable and replaceable packs are also available. One type of disk pack contains only six disks, yet has a capacity of over seven million characters. Average access time is 75 milliseconds and the transfer rate is over 150,000 bytes per second (see Fig. 6-12).

Figure 6-13 shows a typical disk pack.

FIGURE 6-12. Disk Drive with Removable Disk Packs. *Courtesy of RCA Corp., Information Systems Division.*

FIGURE 6-13. A Disk Pack. *Courtesy of Memorex Corp.*

RANDOM AND SEQUENTIAL ACCESS

The forms of input/output and storage which have been described thus far are all of the *random access* (or *direct access*) type. This means that a given item may be selected from anywhere in storage without scanning all other items which precede it. In other words, we can select any item at random, or directly. Processing using such I/O devices is called random access or *in-line* processing.

Such media as magnetic tape, paper tape, and punched cards (studied later) are *sequential access*; that is, a particular item can be read, but only by scanning additionally all items which precede it. Processing using such devices is most economically done with groups or batches of data, all of which are to be processed identically. Such processing is called *batch processing*.

Sequential access storage is *nonaddressable*; that is, you cannot refer to the contents of a particular storage address (location). Random access storage is *addressable*; reference can be made to the contents of any location by simply specifying that address or location.

Data stored in sequential access storage must be transferred to random access storage for processing. A common example of this is the reading of records from magnetic tape into core storage, processing, and then returning the updated records to magnetic tape.

DATA CELL

The *Data Cell Drive* is a device which uses a random access system of magnetizable tape and can store hundreds of millions of bytes.

Each cell is wedge-shaped and contains 20 subcells. The subcells contain 10 strips (each) of a wide 100-track tape. Such a cell can store 40 million bytes; and the complete Data Cell Drive contains a cylindrical formation of *ten* such cells (see Fig. 6-14).

The programmer controls the reading and writing process. The cell he specifies is positioned so that an individual subcell can be removed, and in turn a tape strip removed from the subcell. The selected strip is wound around a drum, passed by a read/write head, and returned to its subcell (see Fig. 6-15).

FIGURE 6-14. A Data Cell Drive. *Courtesy of IBM.*

Such storage is less expensive than magnetic disk storage, but is considerably slower. On the other hand, it is much faster than the ordinary sequential access magnetic tape (studied later) and is particularly suited to handling the huge volumes of data for which third generation computers are designed. The transfer rate is 55,000 bytes/second. Access time averages about 300 milliseconds.

CARD RANDOM ACCESS MEMORY (CRAM)

Card Random Access Memory (CRAM) uses large mylar magnetic cards to record and transfer large quantities of data at fairly high speeds (see Fig. 6-16).

The CRAM unit contains a cartridge of several hundred magnetic cards, any of which can be selected by program instruction, passed to a rotating drum for reading or writing, and returned (see Fig. 6-17).

The unit can hold 125 million bytes on its 384 CRAM cards. This storage provides a relatively low cost means for having the availability of huge volumes of data at one time. And like the disk pack, card cartridges are easily removed and replaced. The transfer rate is 100,000 bytes/second. Average access time is 125 milliseconds.

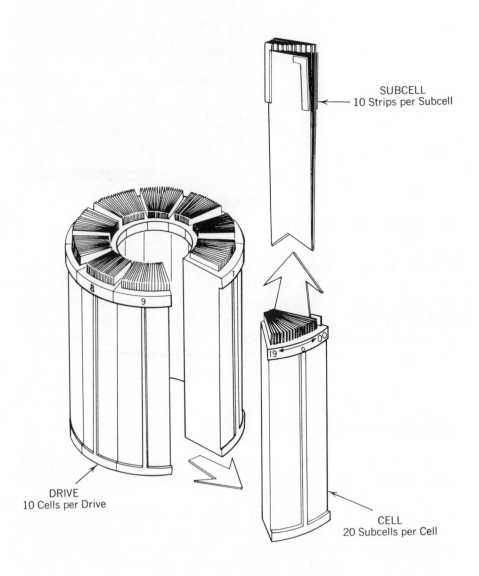

SUBCELL
10 Strips per Subcell

DRIVE
10 Cells per Drive

CELL
20 Subcells per Cell

FIGURE 6-15. Selecting a Cell, Subcell, and Strip.

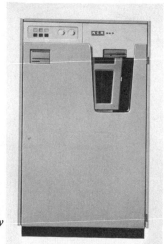

FIGURE 6-16. A CRAM Unit. *Courtesy of National Cash Register Co.*

THIN FILM

Thin film memory is essentially a miniaturized system of magnetic cores. The compact form provides a faster (access time in nanoseconds) and more reliable form of main storage. In some computers the main storage is composed of magnetic cores and thin film. One type of thin film consists of small dot-like metallic deposits on glass, plastic, or ceramic plates. The dots are connected by very thin wires, and they perform in the same way as do magnetic cores.

Woven plated wire memory is another type of thin film storage. Wires are plated with a magnetic thin film, and much thinner (insulated) wires are woven about them. A bit is formed at every intersection of a plated wire and an insulated wire (see Fig. 6-18).

CRYOGENICS

Attempts to make smaller and faster computers have lead to research toward the development of *cryogenic storage* devices. The metals used for such devices have very little resistance to the flow of electricity at temperatures near –450° F (absolute zero). Extremely fast and reliable

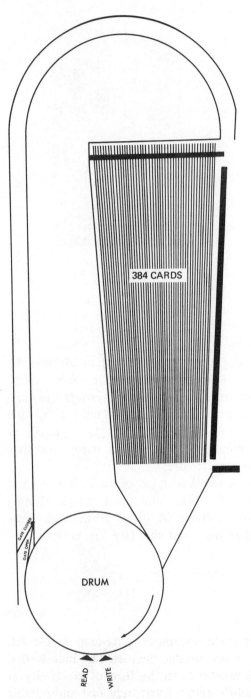

FIGURE 6-17. CRAM Operation. *Courtesy of NCR Co.*

INTERCONNECTIONS

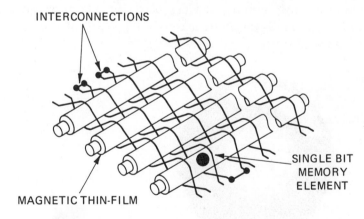

SINGLE BIT
MEMORY
ELEMENT

MAGNETIC THIN-FILM

BASIC MEMORY MATRIX

FIGURE 6-18. Woven Plated Wire Memory, a Thin Film. *Courtesy of Librascope, Singer—General Precision, Inc.*

memories have been based on this principle. Although the devices are themselves inexpensive, the cost of the necessary refrigeration is so great that such low temperature (cryogenic) storage devices are not practical.

NONDESTRUCTIVE STORAGE

It is important that the reader realize that storage devices studied here are *nondestructive,* in the sense that transferring (reading) data from one medium to another results in two copies; the original is not destroyed. For example, if data is read from either punched cards or magnetic disk into core storage, the original card or disk copy is left unaffected; it is merely duplicated in core. Similarly, if data is written from core storage to magnetic disk or punched cards, the copy in core is preserved. Note, however, that you can destroy (or replace) data in storage simply by writing other data "over it" in the identical place.[4]

MAGNETIC TAPE

One of the most popular devices used for recording information (data and programs) is *magnetic tape* (see Fig. 6-19). It is used for both input/output and storage.

FIGURE 6-19. A Reel of Magnetic Tape.
Courtesy of IBM Corp.

[4] All *magnetic* storage devices are reusable this way; however, paper tape and punched cards cannot be "erased" or used again.

The tape is made of a plastic material coated with particles which can be magnetized (polarized) in either of two directions. One polarity is used to represent binary one, the other binary zero. Each character is represented as a column of bits. On nine-channel tape each character contains nine bits. The coding scheme itself is discussed in Chapter 7.

The reel of magnetic tape is mounted on a tape drive to effect the reading or writing of data (see Fig. 6-20). Reading is the transferring of data from tape to the internal storage of the computer. This is done by sensing the already magnetized areas and copying them in storage. Such reading is nondestructive; that is, reading from the tape does not destroy the copy which is on the tape. Writing is the transferring of data from internal storage to magnetic tape. If there was any previous data on the portion which is being written on, it is automatically erased just before the new data is recorded.

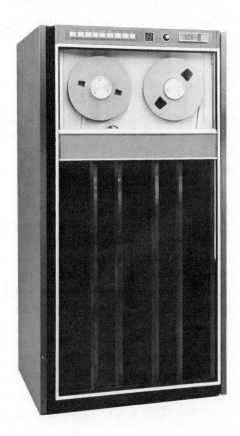

FIGURE 6-20. Magnetic Tape Unit.
Courtesy of Xerox Data Systems.

Data is read or written as the tape passes over a read/write assembly, which has a read/write head for each channel or track (see Fig. 6-21). The execution of a read or write program command results in the reading or writing of one or more records of data. A record contains one or more characters. A .6-inch *interrecord gap* (IRG) is left after each write has been completed. The gap serves to separate one record from another and allows distance for both stopping the tape after an operation and accelerating the tape to the proper speed when requested for the next operation. Reading continues until an IRG is sensed. The next read will read the next record in sequence (see Fig. 6-22). In order to save tape, and time, records can be *blocked*. This means that several records are grouped together between two IRGs, so that each read or write operation effects the reading or writing of several records, not just one.

To prevent the accidental writing of data on a tape which contains data to be saved, a *file protection ring* is used. On many systems the ring must be present to allow writing on a given tape. On other systems the presence of a ring opens a switch and therefore prevents writing (see Fig. 6-23).

Near the beginning of each tape is a reflective spot called a *load point*. It helps the operator position the tape he mounts on the tape drive, since the magnetic spots are invisible and he cannot otherwise tell where the data begins. Similarly there is an *end-of-reel marker* near the end of the tape. This is sensed by a photocell and prevents the tape from unwinding off the reel.

Although excellent as an input/output device, magnetic tape is not very good as a storage device unless you are doing batch processing. One problem is that data can only be accessed in the order in which it has been placed on the tape. Such sequential access means, for example, that one must read (scan) all of the first 1000 records when only the 1000th record itself is desired. Needless to say this wastes computer time.

When we compare magnetic tape with punched cards we find that punched cards are bulkier. A magnetic tape is ½ inch wide and its 2400-foot length is contained on a reel having a diameter of less than one foot. One tape can hold the equivalent of 400,000 punched cards, because of the high *density* with which characters can be stored on tape. Typical densities are 800 and 1600 characters per inch.

Magnetic tapes are read at speeds of 18.75, 37.5, 75, or 112.5 inches/second. This means that a tape of density 800 characters/inch

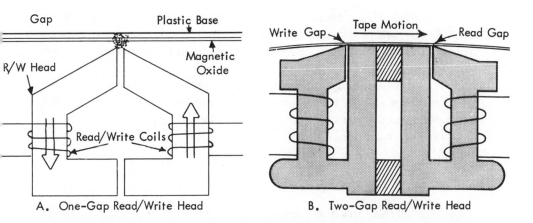

Gap   Plastic Base

R/W Head

Magnetic
Oxide

Read/Write Coils

A. One-Gap Read/Write Head

Write Gap   Tape Motion   Read Gap

B. Two-Gap Read/Write Head

FIGURE 6-21. The Magnetic Tape Read/Write Operation. *Courtesy of IBM Corporation.*

Gap   Record   Gap   Record   Gap   Record   Gap   Record

FIGURE 6-22. Records and Gaps on Magnetic Tape.

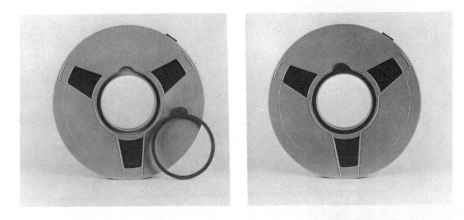

FIGURE 6-23. Magnetic Tape with File Protection Ring. *Courtesy of IBM Corp.*

which is read with a speed of 18.75 inches/second is read at the rate of 15,000 characters per *second*. On the other hand, punched cards are read at 1000/*minute* or 80,000 characters/*minute* or about 1300 characters/*second*.

Punched cards, of course, cannot be reused. On the other hand, magnetic tape can be reused, since data is recorded magnetically. Thus, magnetic tape will prove less expensive in the long run.

Hypertape

Also available are *hypertape* drives which use cartridge-contained magnetic tape and have extra high density and very high speeds. The IBM 7340 Hypertape Unit uses one-inch-wide tape with a density of 3022 characters/inch and a speed of 112.5 inches/second (see Fig. 6-24).

Converters

Since magnetic tape can be read much faster than can punched cards or paper tape, a conversion from these latter media to magnetic tape is

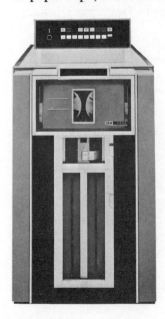

FIGURE 6-24. Hypertape Drive. *Courtesy of IBM Corp.*

common. For example, small computers or special (off-line) card-to-tape *converters* are used to increase input efficiency. Similarly, converters are used to speed output, since magnetic tape is faster for output than is the printer.

Magnetic Data Recorder

The *magnetic data recorder* is designed to eliminate the time consuming steps of card to tape and paper tape to magnetic tape conversion. The recorder is used to record data directly (by recorder operator) onto magnetic tape (or disk), just as a keypunch is used to record data on cards (see Fig. 6-25). Some devices provide a screen (optical verification) to show the operator just what she has recorded.

FIGURE 6-25. Magnetic Data Recorder. *Courtesy of Mohawk Data Sciences Corporation.*

PUNCHED CARDS

Punched cards can be read two ways.

1. Wire brushes contact a metal roller by fitting through holes in the cards.
2. Light is passed through holes in the cards and strikes photoelectric cells.

Cards are punched by punch dies, as indicated in Chapter 2.

Figure 6-26 shows a *card read-punch,* a machine which handles both reading and punching of data processing cards. Cards can be read at the rate of 1000/minute and punched at 500/minute.

PAPER TAPE

Data which is punched into paper tape is read by a *paper tape reader.* A *paper tape punch* is used to generate paper tape output (see Fig. 6-27).

Tape is read at over 1000 characters/second and punched at 300 characters/second. The coding scheme for paper tape is presented in Chapter 7.

FIGURE 6-26. Card Read-Punch. *Courtesy of Control Data Corp.*

FIGURE 6-27. Paper Tape Reader and Paper Tape Punch. *Courtesy of IBM Corp.*

PRINTERS

Printers are among the most popular output devices. This is natural, of course, since a printed page is easy to read and is excellent for reference.

There are many different kinds of printers, but most are basically either *character printers* or *line printers*. Character printers print one character at a time, somewhat like a very high speed typewriter. Line printers print an entire line at one time and are consequently much faster (see Fig. 6-28). Printers are available which print over 1000 lines/minute.

FIGURE 6-28. A Line Printer. *Courtesy of IBM Corp.*

DATA SYNCHRONIZERS/BUFFERS/CHANNELS

In most computer systems the central processing unit (CPU) can process data faster than input units can supply it. Also, information for output is supplied faster than output units can handle it. If this situation were accepted, then users would find themselves paying for an often-idle processor.

This problem was eliminated for second generation computers by using *data synchronizers* or *buffer storage*; that is, by using intermediate storage devices. The data is read into the buffer at the usual (relatively slow) rate. When all the desired data is in the buffer it is transferred to main storage at a much faster rate. Similarly, a buffer might be used between main storage and an output device (see Fig. 6-29).

Third generation computers introduced processing speeds which were too fast for the buffers. In other words, even with the use of buffers to speed up input/output the CPU would often remain inefficiently idle. Consequently, *channels* were introduced to handle all I/O operations separately from the CPU, so that I/O operations would have almost no effect on processing. With the use of channels (in place of buffers) there is a constant, gradual flow of data from input device to main storage

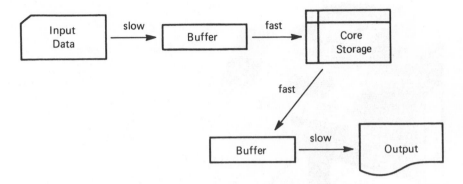

FIGURE 6-29. Use of a Buffer.

and from main storage to output device *at the same time* that processing is being carried out. This simultaneous operation of processing and I/O is called *overlap.*

ON-LINE TYPEWRITER

Computer systems have a "typewriter" directly connected to the processor. Using this device the operator can enter limited amounts of data and control messages. Additionally, the operator receives messages from the computer via the typewriter. This device prints at only 600-900 characters/minute.

The bulk of input and output is not handled by such a slow and limited medium. However, the typewriter is of great value as an aid to the operator who acts as intermediary between the programmer and the computer (see Fig. 6-30).

MICR (MAGNETIC INK CHARACTER RECOGNITION)

Some time ago the American Banking Association decided on data processing to handle the billions of checks which must be processed each year. The processing method which was developed is called *Magnetic Ink Character Recognition* (MICR).

FIGURE 6-30. An On-Line Typewriter. *Courtesy of RCA, Information Systems Division.*

Checks are imprinted with the bank's number and the customer's account number before being issued. After a check is cashed the bank cashing it imprints on it, in specially shaped characters, the amount paid (see Fig. 6-31).

The inked checks are magnetized and then read. Both operations are done by a magnetic character reader/sorter, which can sort, sequence check, select, *or* be directly connected (on-line) to a computer (see Fig. 6-32). When used on-line the reader/sorter provides input data (from the checks) for processing according to a computer program.

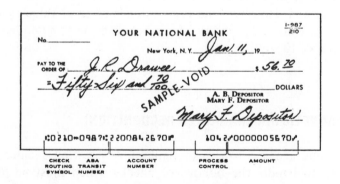

FIGURE 6-31. A Check with Magnetic Ink Characters. *Courtesy of IBM Corp.*

It is interesting to note that each character used is actually composed of 70 (7 by 10) small squares. Different characters have different patterns of magnetized and unmagnetized squares (see Fig. 6-33). Sensing the characters causes storage of a 0 (no magnetization) or a 1 (magnetization) for each of the 70 "parts" of each character.

FIGURE 6-32. Magnetic Character Reader/Sorter. *Courtesy of NCR Co.*

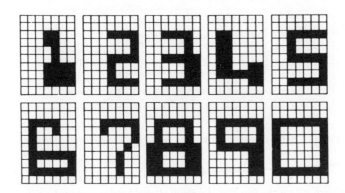

FIGURE 6-33. Matrix Patterns of MICR Characters. *Courtesy of IBM Corp.*

The advantages of such an MICR system are many. The original document (check) is actually used as input. No additional preparation of input is needed. Checks of different sizes can be processed together in the same batch. Bent or otherwise damaged checks can be processed unless the inked characters have been removed. And clerks can also read the inked characters on the checks.

OPTICAL CHARACTER RECOGNITION (OCR)

Optical scanners have been developed which can read letters, digits, and other symbols from paper documents. The documents are scanned by a light and the areas which do not reflect light are sensed. The nonreflecting areas are dark characters of different type fonts, such as those used on typewriters, high speed printers, and others (see Fig. 6-34).

Data from documents can be transferred directly to the computer's storage by scanners. This eliminates keypunching and verifying and thus increases the speed and accuracy of input.

Optical character recognition (OCR) is used by department stores, mail order houses, utilities, and most companies issuing credit cards.[5]

Enter partial payment below	MUNICIPAL WATER WORKS			
o o o o o	Account Number	Gross Amount	Net Amount	Last Day To Pay Net
: : : : :	RL45332	56 01	45 98	4 30 6-
: : : : :	DISCOUNT TERMS : IO DAYS			
: : : : :	Present Reading	Previous Reading	Consumption Gals.	E D JONES 745 CHESTNUT ST ANYTOWN USA
: : : : :	3255886	2369014	887	
: : : : :	PLEASE RETURN THIS WITH YOUR PAYMENT			

FIGURE 6-34. Optically Readable Characters. *Courtesy of IBM Corp.*

[5]And if it were not for the fact that *checks* get stamped and overprinted, OCR would undoubtedly be used instead of MICR. Magnetic characters are read accurately regardless of any overwriting, and that is why they are still used.

CATHODE RAY TUBE AND LIGHT PEN

The *cathode ray tube* (CRT) is very much like a TV picture tube (see Fig. 6-35). It is used to present data, designs, or graphs to a viewing clerk, manager, engineer, or scientist. The CRT provides quick response and can be used remotely; for example, in one's office or work area. Designs or data may be changed in the computer's storage by using the input capability of the CRT. There is a keyboard for entering data and commands and a *light pen* for indicating design changes by "writing" on the screen (see Fig. 6-36).

Cathode ray tubes and similar visual display devices are seeing considerable service in computer-assisted instruction (CAI). This concept is discussed in Chapter 5.

GRAPH PLOTTERS

Devices are available which plot graphs of data. Such *plotters* have a movable pen which is controlled both by program instruction and generated data (see Fig. 6-37). In many instances graphs may be the best form of output for interpreting results.

FIGURE 6-35. Cathode Ray Tube. *Courtesy of NCR Co.*

FIGURE 6-36. The Engineer in the Above Photo is Using a Light Pen to Make Changes in the Design of an Electronic Circuit. Both the Circuit and Components are Displayed on the Console of the New Control Data ® 274 Digigraphics System, Developed for Use with a Small-Scale Control Data ® 1700 Computer. The Digigraphics System Allows an Operator to Enter Data in Graphic Form Directly into an Electronic Computer for Processing, Storage and Retrieval. *Courtesy of Control Data Corp.*

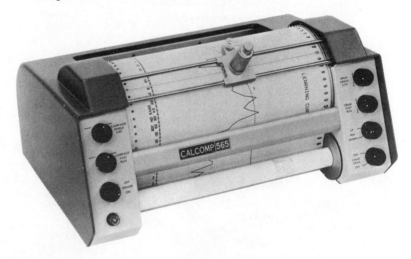

FIGURE 6-37. Graph Plotter. *Courtesy of California Computer Products, Inc.*

VOICE I/O

Computers exist that are able to accept a very limited vocabulary of input by voice. However, more popular is voice output, which is currently used to quote stock prices, information on accounts, and changes in telephone numbers. Such audio responses are prerecorded, and their selection is dependent on a computer's processing of input data.

DATA TRANSMISSION AND COMMUNICATION

It is often impractical to transport data from the point of its origin to a remote computer. Instead, data is transmitted using communications lines provided by the telephone and telegraph companies.

The input or output data to be transmitted is in the form of cards, paper tape, manual (keyboard), or magnetic tape. A *data transmission unit* changes the data to an intermediate form which is then acceptable to a *data set*. The data set converts the signals to a form which can be transmitted via a communications line (see Fig. 6-38).

At the other end of the communications line is another data set, another data transmission unit, and another I/O device (see Fig. 6-39).

FIGURE 6-38. A Data-Phone Data Set. *Courtesy of American Telephone and Telegraph Co.*

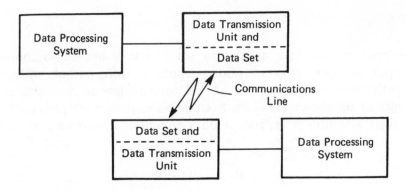

FIGURE 6-39. Data Transmission.

EXERCISES 6.1

1. Why are there both addressable and nonaddressable types of storage?

2. Why are there so many different kinds of addressable storage?

3. What is a bit? What is a byte?

4. Why are magnetic storage and I/O devices reusable; whereas nonmagnetic types are not?

7

REPRESENTING DATA: CODING SCHEMES

A computer is of no value to us if we cannot communicate with it. We give it data (input) and expect in return some useful information (output). We cannot talk to computers and expect them to understand us; nor can we write a letter and have a computer read and understand it.[1] Instead we must write our messages on special forms and in special codes which the computer can understand.

The internal storage facility of the computer uses two-state magnetic devices for recording data, as do many external storage and input/output devices. Consequently the codes associated with these various media (for most computers) are based on the binary number system.

PUNCHED CARDS

We have already seen the coding scheme used for representing data on punched cards. The codes for letters and digits are illustrated once again so that we can compare them with the codes used for representing data in the computer, on magnetic tape, and on paper tape (see Fig. 7-1).

[1]Technically speaking, however, some computer systems have been developed which accept a very limited vocabulary of clearly spoken words.

Character	Card Punches
0	0
1	1
2	2
3	3
4	4
5	5
6	6
7	7
8	8
9	9
A	12 - 1
B	12 - 2
C	12 - 3
D	12 - 4
E	12 - 5
F	12 - 6
G	12 - 7
H	12 - 8
I	12 - 9
J	11 - 1
K	11 - 2
L	11 - 3
M	11 - 4
N	11 - 5
O	11 - 6
P	11 - 7
Q	11 - 8
R	11 - 9
S	0 - 2
T	0 - 3
U	0 - 4
V	0 - 5
W	0 - 6
X	0 - 7
Y	0 - 8
Z	0 - 9

FIGURE 7-1. The Punched Card Code.

STRAIGHT BINARY

We have already seen how to convert decimal numbers to binary for representation in the computer's storage. For positive whole numbers this binary equivalent is merely preceded by enough 0's to complete one halfword or fullword, whichever the case may be. Representation of negative numbers and floating-point (fractional) numbers is more complicated.

EXAMPLE 7-1. Show the representation of $(58)_{10}$ as a straight binary halfword and as a fullword.

halfword: 00000000 00111010
fullword: 00000000 00000000 00000000 00111010

BINARY CODED DECIMAL (BCD)

The straight binary representation of data is excellent for computations, and is therefore most popular for engineering and scientific uses.

On the other hand, commercial data processing often involves the use of numbers for purposes other than computation. For example, social security numbers, street addresses, part numbers, and serial numbers are used in processing; but we don't add them or multiply them!

You can see that it would be convenient to be able to use a number like 58 as two "chunks" of bits (one chunk representing 5, the other chunk representing 8) rather than as an inseparable string of binary digits, 111010.

The system for such representation is a simple one. Each of the decimal digits 0 through 9 is represented by its binary equivalent, and four bits are used in all cases. Such representation is called *binary coded decimal (BCD)*.

decimal	*binary coded decimal* (BCD)
0	0000
1	0001
2	0010
3	0011
4	0100
5	0101
6	0110
7	0111
8	1000
9	1001

Now the decimal number 58 is represented as

0101   1000

5   8

in BCD, and the decimal number 9063 is simply 1001 0000 0110 0011.

It should be clear that such a BCD code would be still more valuable if it were *extended* to include letters and special characters. Such *extended BCD* codes do exist and are widely used. Two such codes are described next.[2]

EXTENDED BINARY CODED DECIMAL INTERCHANGE CODE (EBCDIC)

As you know, the IBM System/360 and other 3rd generation computers can store whole numbers as 32-bit fullwords, where the bits represent the equivalent of the decimal number being stored.

Recall that each 32-bit word can also be considered as four eight-bit bytes. If we use each *byte* to represent one *character* (letter, digit, special character), then we have a convenient way of representing names, addresses, and other strings of alphanumeric characters.

One code which uses eight bits to represent each character is called *Extended Binary Coded Decimal Interchange Code*, or *EBCDIC*. The digits:

Character	EBCDIC (binary)
0	1111 0000
1	1111 0001
2	1111 0010
3	1111 0011
4	1111 0100
5	1111 0101
6	1111 0110
7	1111 0111
8	1111 1000
9	1111 1001

Note that the binary equivalent of each digit appears as the last four bits of the byte representation. However, all eight bits are necessary since all characters must be the same size, and for the 360 that size is one byte or eight bits.

[2]Data that consists of letters, digits, and/or special characters is called *alphanumeric*.

In the chart above the bit configuration is shown for each character as two sets of four bits each. This is done here to make the code easier to read. Additionally, this leads to the use of hexadecimal shorthand: one hex digit for every four binary digits, two hex digits for each eight-bit character.

Character	EBCDIC (binary)	EBCDIC (hex)
0	1111 0000	F0
1	1111 0001	F1
2	1111 0010	F2
3	1111 0011	F3
4	1111 0100	F4
5	1111 0101	F5
6	1111 0110	F6
7	1111 0111	F7
8	1111 1000	F8
9	1111 1001	F9

Of course, if all we ever intended to represent were numeric characters, then we could use a four-bit code and agree that each byte would represent two numeric characters. This, however, is not what we want. Instead we find it useful to represent letters and special characters as well as digits, and we need more than four bits to code all digits (10), letters (26), and special characters.

The code for the letters is shown in Fig. 7-2. The relationship between the EBCDIC code and the code used for punched cards should be clear. In EBCDIC the first four bits serve as "zone" bits.

AMERICAN STANDARD CODE FOR INFORMATION INTERCHANGE (ASCII)

The *American Standard Code for Information Interchange,* or *ASCII,* is an attempt to provide a standard for the interchange of coded information among computing equipment.[3] Figure 7-3 shows a comparision of ASCII and EBCDIC for letters and digits. Note that the

[3] The need for such a standard 'ias been emphasized by the development and great use of data transmission to and from remote terminals.

Character	EBCDIC (binary)	EBCDIC (hex)
A	1100 0001	C1
B	1100 0010	C2
C	1100 0011	C3
D	1100 0100	C4
E	1100 0101	C5
F	1100 0110	C6
G	1100 0111	C7
H	1100 1000	C8
I	1100 1001	C9
J	1101 0001	D1
K	1101 0010	D2
L	1101 0011	D3
M	1101 0100	D4
N	1101 0101	D5
O	1101 0110	D6
P	1101 0111	D7
Q	1101 1000	D8
R	1101 1001	D9
S	1110 0010	E2
T	1110 0011	E3
U	1110 0100	E4
V	1110 0101	E5
W	1110 0110	E6
X	1110 0111	E7
Y	1110 1000	E8
Z	1110 1001	E9

FIGURE 7-2. EBCDIC Code for Letters.

ASCII code for the letters A thru Z is a continuous code, from A1 to BA in hexadecimal; whereas the EBCDIC code compares with the zone-numeric code of the punched card.

ASCII has been adopted as the standard for all computers and related equipment in federal agencies. Consequently it has also become the standard for many government contractors, universities, local and state governments, and others.

PARITY

The internal storage of the 360 computer keeps data in the form of eight-bit bytes. Associated with each byte is an additional (ninth) bit, a *parity bit*. The parity bit is used to check against any internal change in the bit configuration, since a machine error (and they don't occur often!) could change a bit from 0 to 1 or 1 to 0.

As the byte is stored, an extra (parity) bit is determined and set. The

Characters	EBCDIC (hex)	ASCII (hex)
A	C1	A1
B	C2	A2
C	C3	A3
D	C4	A4
E	C5	A5
F	C6	A6
G	C7	A7
H	C8	A8
I	C9	A9
J	D1	AA
K	D2	AB
L	D3	AC
M	D4	AD
N	D5	AE
O	D6	AF
P	D7	B0
Q	D8	B1
R	D9	B2
S	E2	B3
T	E3	B4
U	E4	B5
V	E5	B6
W	E6	B7
X	E7	B8
Y	E8	B9
Z	E9	BA
0	F0	50
1	F1	51
2	F2	52
3	F3	53
4	F4	54
5	F5	55
6	F6	56
7	F7	57
8	F8	58
9	F9	59

FIGURE 7-3. ASCII vs. EBCDIC.

bit is set to 1 or 0, whichever will make the total number of 1-bits *odd*. After the parity bit has been set the byte is checked every time it is used. If the total number of 1-bits becomes even, a *parity error* is indicated to the operator at the computer's console.

EXAMPLE 7-2. The EBCDIC code uses odd parity.[4] The code for the letter A is C1 (hex) or 1100 0001 (binary). Since the total number of 1-bits (3) is odd, the parity bit is a *zero*. Thus the code, including parity bit, is 0 1100 0001, where the first zero is the parity bit.

[4]There is even parity, in which case the total number of 1-bits (including parity bit) is even.

EXAMPLE 7-3. The letter E is C5 or 1100 0101. Since the total number of 1-bits (4) is even, the parity bit is a *one* to make the total number of 1-bits odd. The representation then is 1 1100 0101, where the first one is the parity bit.

PAPER TAPE

Data is recorded in paper tape as various combinations of punched holes. The holes are punched in parallel channels and, as with punched cards, a character is represented by the punches in a given column (see Fig. 7-4).

In addition to holes punched to represent data, there is also one horizontal row of small holes across the entire tape. These are the feed holes, which are used to transport the tape during punching. The tape is moved in the same way that a bicycle chain is moved by a rotating driving wheel which fits into holes in the chain.

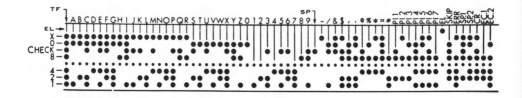

FIGURE 7-4. Eight-Channel Paper Tape. *Courtesy of IBM Corp.*

Eight-Channel Paper Tape

One type of paper tape has eight channels for recording punches. Each character is represented by some combination of eight punches and/or no-punches.

Numeric characters (0-9) are recorded in the bottom four channels. The bottom channel represents 1 *if punched.* The channel above it represents 2, the next channel 4, and the next 8. Thus, the digit 9 would appear as

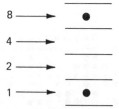

if we examined only the punches in the bottom four channels.

Near the top of the tape are the X and O channels (see Fig. 7-4). These are used together to form a "zone" punch. Thus, various combinations of X-0-8-4-2-1 produce the digits 0-9, the letters A-Z, and the special characters.

A through I	are recorded as	X-0-1 through X-0-8-1
J through R	are recorded as	X-1 through X-8-1
S through Z	are recorded as	0-2 through 0-8-1
0 through 9	are recorded as	0 through 8-1

To check for proper recording, each character is made to contain an odd number of holes. If necessary, an extra *check hole* is added (automatically punched) to make the total of punched holes odd.

Five-Channel Paper Tape

Five-channel paper tape uses a five-bit code which has no obvious pattern or scheme. No check hole is used.

With five channels only 32 different representations are possible. Thus, in some cases the same code must be used to represent two different characters, say a letter and a digit. In order to tell them apart a special LETTERS code punch automatically precedes the use of alphabetic punches and a FIGURES punch precedes the use of digits (see Fig. 7-5).

MAGNETIC TAPE (EBCDIC)

Data are recorded as magnetized spots on the horizontal tape channels. The spots represent bits, and a character is a combination of *nine bits*, one from each of the parallel horizontal tracks (see Fig. 7-6).

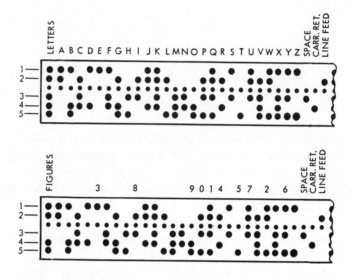

FIGURE 7-5. Five-Channel Paper Tape. *Courtesy of IBM Corp.*

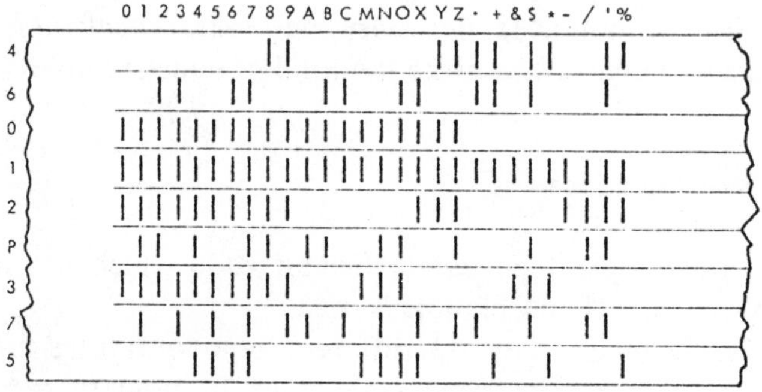

FIGURE 7-6. Nine-Track Magnetic Tape.

The P-track indicates the parity bit. Even parity is used on magnetic tape.

Tracks 0 and 1 indicate the type of character represented. For digits and capital letters both the 0 and 1 tracks are used.

Tracks 2 and 3 are used to indicate the zone, or first digit, in the two-digit EBCDIC representation. Digits (zone F) use both 2 and 3. The letters A through I (zone C) use neither. The letters J through R (zone D) use 3 and S through Z (zone E) use 2.

Character	9-Track EBCDIC Code
0	0-1-2-3
1	P-0-1-2-3-7
2	P-0-1-2-3-6
3	0-1-2-3-6-7
4	P-0-1-2-3-5
5	0-1-2-3-5-7
6	0-1-2-3-5-6
7	P-0-1-2-3-5-6-7
8	P-0-1-2-3-4
9	0-1-2-3-4-7
A	P-0-1-7
B	P-0-1-6
C	0-1-6-7
D	P-0-1-5
E	0-1-5-7
F	0-1-5-6
G	P-0-1-5-6-7
H	P-0-1-4
I	0-1-4-7
J	0-1-3-7
K	0-1-3-6
L	P-0-1-3-6-7
M	0-1-3-5
N	P-0-1-3-5-7
O	P-0-1-3-5-6
P	0-1-3-5-6-7
Q	0-1-3-4
R	P-0-1-3-4-7
S	0-1-2-6
T	P-0-1-2-6-7
U	0-1-2-5
V	P-0-1-2-5-7
W	P-0-1-2-5-6
X	0-1-2-5-6-7
Y	0-1-2-4
Z	P-0-1-2-4-7

FIGURE 7-7. Nine-Track EBCDIC Tape Code.

Tracks 4,5,6, and 7 are used to indicate the second digit of the two-digit EBCDIC code. The values of tracks 4, 5, 6, 7 are 8, 4, 2, 1 *in that order.* Tracks are chosen so that the sum of the values (8, 4, 2, 1) add up to that digit.

As an example, the digit 9 has an EBCDIC hex representation of F9. The EBCDIC tape code is

$$0\text{-}1\text{-}2\text{-}3\text{-}4\text{-}7,$$

since 2-3 is the "zone" for digits and 4-7 indicates 9 (8 and 1). Figure 7-7 gives the EBCDIC tape codes for all digits and letters.

A comparable code is used to represent characters using ASCII.

THE 96-COLUMN CARD

In 1969, IBM introduced a 96-column miniature punched card to go
with a new computer (called System/3) designed for small business.

The card is one-third the size of the standard 80-column card yet can
record 96 characters. It has three rows of 32 columns (characters) each.
Each character is represented by a pattern of six punches and/or
no-punches in a given column. The punches themselves are small round
holes (see Fig. 7-8).

The code for letters and digits closely resembles that of eight-channel
paper tape, except the zones are called B and A instead of X and O, and
there is no check hole. Compare Fig. 7-8 with Fig. 7-4.

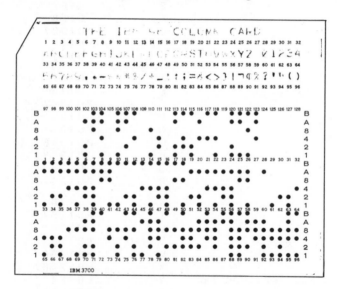

FIGURE 7-8. System/3 Card (Actual Size).

EXERCISES 7.1

*1. Represent $(123)_{10}$ in straight binary, in EBCDIC, and in ASCII.

*2. Represent in EBCDIC binary and EBCDIC hexadecimal: (a) CS101
(b) MJC (c) 75.

*3. Same as exercise 2, except use ASCII.

4. Translate from EBCDIC to ASCII: C5 E7 C5 D9 C3 C9 E2 C5.

5. Translate from ASCII to EBCDIC: A8 A1 B2 A4 B7 A1 B2 A5.

6. Represent the word COMPUTER in EBCDIC binary, including parity bits.

8

THE CENTRAL
PROCESSING UNIT

In this chapter we shall see how program instructions are selected and how they are executed. This job of selecting, interpreting, and carrying out instructions is handled by the *central processing unit* (CPU). The CPU serves to

1. select instructions from storage
2. decode selected instructions
3. fetch needed data from storage
4. perform arithmetic, logical, or I/O operations specified
5. store results of operations
6. control sequencing of instruction selection.

GENERAL REGISTERS

The IBM System/360 has 16 *general purpose registers*. They are located in the CPU. One of their functions is to hold the results of logical and arithmetic operations. They are also used to hold data which will be used during such logical and arithmetic operations. These uses and others will be seen in detail in Chapter 11.

SEQUENTIAL EXECUTION OF INSTRUCTIONS

Program instructions are executed in the order in which they are stored, which is the same order as originally coded by the programmer—one right after the other (see Fig. 8-1).

PROGRAM STATUS WORD

The information needed to correctly execute the instructions of a given program is contained in the *program status word* (PSW). This 64-bit special register of the CPU is divided into many sections, each of which contains information needed for program execution.[1]

Instruction Address

The instruction address portion of the PSW indicates the location in storage of the next program instruction to be executed.[2]

Not all instructions are the same size. Some occupy one halfword, some two halfwords, and others three halfwords. While an instruction is being carried out, that number (1, 2, or 3) is added to the instruction address portion of the PSW. This produces the address, called the *updated instruction address*, of the next instruction to be executed.

Order of Coded Instructions		Order of Instructions in Storage
First Instruction	⟶	First Instruction
Second Instruction	⟶	Second Instruction
Third Instruction	⟶	Third Instruction
•		•
•		•
•		•
Last Instruction	⟶	Last Instruction

FIGURE 8-1. Sequential Execution of Instructions.

[1] A word is 32 bits. The PSW (64 bits) is actually a "double word."
[2] The expressions *storage address* and *storage location* will be used interchangeably.

Instruction Length Code

When an instruction is fetched from storage for execution the number of halfwords which it occupies (1, 2, or 3) is determined and placed in the *instruction length code* portion of the PSW. It is then added to the address in the PSW to produce the updated address as mentioned above. This updated address will then be used to fetch the next instruction (see Fig. 8-2).

Halfword Locations of Instructions	Instructions
X	First instruction, say of length 2
X + 2	Second instruction, say of length 1
X + 3	Third instruction, say of length 2
X + 5	Fourth instruction, say of length 2
X + 7	Fifth instruction . . .

.
.
.

a. When the first instruction (at location X) is being executed the instruction length code is 2, since the first instruction is two halfwords in length.

b. This code (2) is added to the address where this instruction came from (X) to produce the address of the next instruction to be executed (X + 2).

c. When it is time to execute the second instruction, it is fetched from location X + 2, as determined in step b (above). Then its length (1) is added to its location (X + 2)   to produce the location of the next instruction (X + 3).

And so on.

FIGURE 8-2. Use of Instruction Length Code.

OTHER REGISTERS IN THE CPU

In order to execute an instruction, the CPU must fetch the instruction from storage and bring it into the CPU. The operation code must be decoded and the proper circuitry set up to carry out the indicated operation. Any data involved must be fetched. Results must be saved. Special registers in the CPU are used to hold either the locations or values of such numbers (data, results).

DECODING AN INSTRUCTION

Each instruction has an operation code (to indicate addition, reading, branching, or whatever), and associated with each operation code is circuitry for performing that operation. For example, one type of "add" has binary operation code 01011010. By *decoding* we mean determining the circuitry to be used to carry out an instruction.

THE CYCLE

We now list the steps in the *execution cycle (control cycle)* of a program instruction.

1. Fetch instruction indicated by instruction address in PSW.
2. Increase instruction address by indicated instruction length code so that next instruction can be fetched after current instruction has been executed.
3. Decode current instruction.
4. Fetch data needed for execution of the instruction.
5. Carry out operation using fetched data.
6. Store result as indicated.

BRANCHING

Program instructions are executed in the order stored unless a *branch* instruction is met. Branching instructions cause transfers out of normal sequence if certain conditions have been satisfied. For example, a "branch on zero" instruction will cause a transfer out of the normal sequence if the result of the previous arithmetic operation was zero. If the result was not zero, then no transfer is made and the next instruction in sequence is taken. In Chapter 11 we shall see the role of the PSW in branching.

INTERRUPTS

It sometimes becomes necessary to temporarily suspend the execution of a program. Such *interrupts* are handled by an automatic interrupt program called the interrupt supervisor.

Interrupts occur for various reasons. Program errors, unacceptable input, machine errors, and completion of input/output instructions are some of the circumstances which lead to interrupts.

Each interrupt leads to a corrective action by a prescribed routine; and after that routine has been completed the system resumes execution of the interrupted program.

"Log it as a system interrupt."

Old and New PSW

In order to allow a return to conditions prior to interrupt, a copy of the PSW prior to the interrupt must be saved. Such a copy is called an *old PSW*. Thus, whenever an interrupt occurs the *current PSW* is stored for future reference as the *old PSW*. Then the current PSW is replaced by a special *new PSW* which is determined by the kind of interrupt occurring. When the interrupt routine has been completed the old PSW replaces the current PSW and execution of the regular program is continued (see Fig. 8-3).

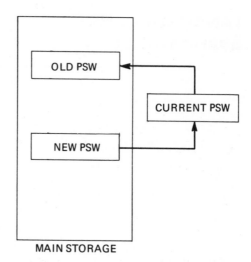

FIGURE 8-3. PSW Replacement at Interrupt.

MAIN STORAGE

EXERCISES 8.1

1. Why does a computer have a central processing unit?

2. What special registers are contained in the CPU, and what are their functions?

3. How many bits of the 64-bit PSW would be needed to represent the instruction length codes? What would these representations probably be?

4. If the 360's storage has 16,777,216 addressable locations, how many PSW bits are needed to represent any location from 0 to 16,777,215? Explain.

5. Explain the complete control cycle.

6. What functions of the PSW are mentioned in this chapter?

9

LANGUAGES AND
APPLICATIONS

This chapter serves two purposes: to present brief descriptions of some of the common programming languages and to describe a few general areas in which computers and languages are applied.

ASSEMBLER LANGUAGE

Assembler languages are called *lower-level* because they resemble the language of the computer (machine language) rather than the language of business, science, or of a particular type of problem. Consider, for example, this sequence of assembler language instructions:

```
L    7,A
A    7,B
S    7,C
ST   7,X
```

All of this code merely results in the computation (and storage of the result) of

$$X = A+B-C.$$

One instruction causes *one* computation or *one* movement of data. Although the actual use of such instructions will not be explained in detail in this chapter, you should note the following:

L	7,A	*l*oads A into a register (number 7)
A	7,B	*a*dds B to A, producing A+B
S	7,C	*s*ubtracts C from (A+B), producing A+B-C
ST	7,X	*st*ores the result as X, for future reference

Assembler languages vary from manufacturer to manufacturer. Compatability exists within a given system of computers produced by one manufacturer.[1]

COMPILER LANGUAGES

Higher-level languages, such as FORTRAN, resemble the problem language rather than the basic language of the machine. Compare the assembler language coding above with the FORTRAN coding

$$X = A+B-C$$

for computing

$$X = A+B-C.$$

This *one* FORTRAN statement does the same thing as *four* assembler language instructions. This exemplifies the many-for-one nature of statements coded in *compiler languages*.

Such compiler languages are essentially machine independent. This means that a FORTRAN program is written the same whether it is to be run on an IBM, XDS, or UNIVAC computer, for example.[2]

A list of several popular compiler languages follows.

---

[1] Second generation computers produced by the same manufacturer generally lacked compatability. There were no second generation systems of computers.

[2] There are some minor differences in specifications.

FORTRAN

FORTRAN stands for FORmula TRANslation. It is used mostly by those solving problems of science and engineering. However, it is occasionally used in commercial data processing.

COBOL

COBOL is the COmmon Business Oriented Language. It is used primarily for programming commercial data processing problems because of its descriptive nature and its adaptability to handling the file processing problems of business data processing.

PL/1

Programming Language One (PL/1) was introduced with third generation computers. It uses fully the hardware features available, which makes it equally valuable as a commercial or scientific programming language. PL/1 includes the features of COBOL and FORTRAN and may replace them eventually.

RPG

Report Program Generator (RPG) is used to produce reports, especially for management. An RPG program will generate reports or documents using the input supplied.

The processing functions of RPG are those of the EAM equipment and are discussed in a later chapter on RPG.

BASIC

BASIC is the Beginner's All-purpose Symbolic Instruction Code. It resembles several compiler languages, especially FORTRAN. BASIC lacks some of the capability available in the complete FORTRAN language, but it can be learned much faster. Consequently, BASIC is popular among nonprogrammers who seek a quick introduction to programming and computing. It is a popular time-sharing language.

ALGOL and JOVIAL

ALGOL, the ALGOrithmic Language, resembles FORTRAN and PL/1 and is intended to handle problems which are mathematical or numerical in nature. JOVIAL, Jules' Own Version of the International Algebraic Language, is similar to ALGOL.

FORMAC

FORMAC, or FORmula MAnipulation Compiler, is an extension of FORTRAN. The additional capabilities of FORMAC permit direct computation, manipulation, and use of functions of advanced mathematics which can only be done indirectly and approximately in FORTRAN.

MAD

MAD is the acronym for the Michigan Algorithmic Decoder. The language resembles FORTRAN and is useful in programming problems of numerical mathematics.

SNOBOL and Other List Processing Languages

SNOBOL, LISP, SLIP, COMIT, and IPL-V are designed for string manipulation or list processing. The structure of the languages is a set of rules, or statements, each of which aids in processing strings of characters. The collections (strings or lists) of characters are processed as *symbols*, not as algebraic or numeric quantities.

SIMSCRIPT

SIMSCRIPT is a FORTRAN-like language designed for programming simulations.[3] The language is event-oriented. This means that it can be used to reduce complex mathematical models to a series of interrelated smaller components. Decisions can be made by noting the alternatives presented when changes are made.

OPERATIONS RESEARCH

Operations research (OR) involves the application of mathematics and statistics to scientific decision-making. We shall look at several methods of operations research, including linear programming, game theory, simulation, and PERT.

The computer is a powerful tool for implementing the methods of operations research.

Linear Programming

In *linear programming*, mathematical techniques are used to determine the optimum (best) allocation of resources. Mathematics such as algebra, matrices, and probability is used to avoid the impractical consideration of each possible allocation.

The following is a typical linear programming situation. Design a shipping schedule that will minimize the total cost involved in accepting (from distributors) known quantities of merchandise. The merchandise will be shipped as directed to your warehouses; however, the warehouses have limited capacity and are hundreds of miles apart. The cost of shipping varies from warehouse to warehouse, since each is a different distance from the distributor.

In linear programming *one* decision is made. If the program requires a number of interrelated decisions to be made in some *sequence*, then the problem is suitable for solution using the methods of *dynamic programming*.

---

[3]The concept of *simulation* is discussed later in this chapter.

Game Theory

Decision-making can be complicated by competition. Consider as examples a chess game and a football game. A good move by an opposing chess player can be damaging to you or force you to change your intended move. Similarly, in football a good defensive play thwarts the offense.

Mathematical techniques of *game theory* can be applied by management to "similar" problems of business and science, where competition must be considered before decisions can be made.

Simulation

A street map is only a model of actual streets; yet it is (at first) a more useful guide to a driver who is lost than are the actual streets.

Similarly, a mathematical *model* of a war-game is valuable to military personnel, since they cannot start a war just to test weapons and strategy.

There are many problems which are either impossible or impractical to solve without forming mathematical models. *Simulation* involves construction and use of a model.

PERT

*P*rogram *E*valuation and *R*eview *T*echnique (PERT) was developed as a tool for effective project management, especially in the areas of construction, aerospace, and defense.

Let us think of a project as a series of interdependent tasks, activities, or events. To apply PERT techniques we determine the proper sequence and interdependence of the events. Then we chart the events as a PERT diagram (see Fig. 9-1) and determine three time estimates (optimistic, realistic, pessimistic) for each activity.

The computer uses statistical methods to determine an *expected duration* and variance for each activity. It then arranges the activities in the order in which they must occur and computes an expected completion date for each activity along the path. Next, *latest dates* (to allow completion on time) are calculated for each activity. Also

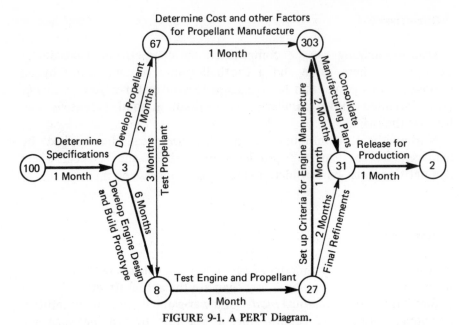

FIGURE 9-1. A PERT Diagram.

determined is the *critical path;* that is, the sequence of activities between the start and finish which will require the longest time to complete.[4]

There are several reasons why PERT has been both widely used and successful.

1. Construction of a PERT diagram requires disciplined planning and usually prevents omissions.
2. The diagram provides a clear picture of the scope of the project.
3. Progress can be checked at any time, and alternate plans can be considered and evaluated.

SYSTEMS ANALYSIS AND DESIGN

The *systems analyst* studies a complete operation or system. He describes and evaluates the equipment, its use, and the people who use it. Such studies and evaluations are made with the intention of making

---

[4] Methods of this type, which deal with critical paths, are called *critical path methods,* or *CPM.*

changes in the design of the system. The new design is suggested by a *systems designer* using the results of the analysis.

There are several reasons for using systems analysis and design.

1. Management may be dissatisfied with the present operation.
2. Changes in technology may suggest a better and more economical system, even though the present system is satisfactory.
3. Changes in the economy may suggest corresponding changes in the system.
4. The system may not yet exist; that is, analysis and design are used to originally develop a system as well as change or replace one.

10

PROGRAM
FLOWCHARTING

INTRODUCTION

In Chapter 5 we listed the steps in solving a problem with the aid of a computer. The current chapter concentrates on one of these steps, flowcharting.

A *flow chart* is a diagram showing the steps that a computer will carry out to solve a given problem. There are many reasons why flow charts are used, especially when the program being written involves more than a few simple calculations.

1. There is a huge gap between the original written statement of a problem and the code which the programmer writes to direct the computer to solve the problem. The flow chart fills the gap by providing a clear problem definition and a logical outline of the solution.

2. The chart provides the programmer with an opportunity to check the logic of his solution. He can determine whether he has considered all possibilities or whether he has duplicated any considerations.

3. The flow chart is a coding guide for the programmer, providing him with a clear picture of the proper sequence of operations. This sequence, of course, would be difficult to determine from just the statement of the problem, in any but very simple problems.

4. The use of flow charts gives the programmer a chance to experiment with several different approaches to solving a problem

without coding each one and comparing the code. He merely compares flow charts to determine the best approach.

5. Programs occasionally need to be modified, and it is simpler to change a program by looking at the flow chart than by looking at the actual code. You just cannot see the overall picture, and all the changes that might be necessary, by looking at the actual coded instructions. This is especially true if much time has passed since the original code was written.

6. In connection with (5) above, the chart is useful for problem discussions involving several people, perhaps a group including programmers and nonprogrammers.

7. One or more flow charts (detailed, general) is usually included in the writeup or documentation of a program.

THE SYMBOLS

Terminal

The beginning or end of a program is indicated by the symbol

Thus

will be used to indicate the beginning of a program, and

will be used to indicate the end of a program.

Input/Output

The reading of data into primary storage, from punched cards, paper tape, or magnetic tape, and the writing of data from storage to any of these media and others is indicated by the symbol

Input is indicated by putting the word "Read" inside the symbol. Output is specified by using "Write" or possibly "Print" or "Punch."

Decision

It is often desirable to transfer out of sequence to another part of the program, if a certain condition is satisfied. We indicate such a *conditional transfer* or *conditional branch* by using the symbol

The condition for branching is written inside the symbol, and the choices of where to transfer and under what conditions are indicated by directed lines leading from the decision symbol. Examples of its use will be given later in the chapter.

Processing

We chart actual program processing, such as computation and movement of data in storage, by using the symbol

For our purposes we can say that the rectangular processing symbol is used for any process other than input/output, start/stop, or decisions.

FLOWCHARTING EXAMPLES

Arrows

We use arrows to connect the blocks of our flow chart and thus indicate the direction of flow of the logic of the processing.

EXAMPLE 10-1. Show the flow chart for a program to read (from a card) a value for a variable named x, *compute* y = x + 5, *and print the values of* x *and* y.[1]

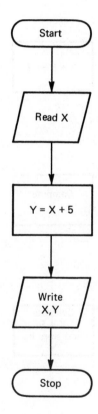

[1]We shall use capital letters for variables in flow charts, since we code (from the flow chart) in capital letters. Recall that the punched card alphabet contains only capital letters.

Although there is general agreement on what flowcharting symbols to use for various types of operations, there are different opinions on what *text* should go inside the symbols to indicate specifically what is happening. For example, the computation $y = x + 5$ (above) was charted as

$$Y = X + 5$$

but some might prefer

$$X + 5 \rightarrow Y$$

or

Compute
$$Y = X + 5$$

or

Compute
$$X + 5$$
and store in
Y

or

Add 5 to X
and store
in Y

or still other similar statements. Similarly,

may be charted as simply

or very precisely as

If we know, for example, that all data is read from cards, then it is not necessary to indicate "card" in the flow diagram, although many prefer including this information. On the other hand, if more than one form of input is possible at your installation, or someone elsewhere may read and use your program, then it is better to include the input medium in the block.

We usually find that those involved in business or commercial programming use *descriptive* flow charts; that is, each box contains a brief statement. On the other hand, scientific programmers avoid statements and use formulas involving letters and mathematical symbols. Their flow charts are *symbolic*.

EXAMPLE 10-2. Students taking a course receive grades of S (satisfactory) or U (unsatisfactory). The grade is determined by adding the scores obtained on three tests (TEST1, TEST2, TEST3). If the sum is greater than 180, a grade of S is assigned. A U is given if the sum is less than or equal to 180. Consider the following flow charts for reading three test scores and writing the grade.

A descriptive flow chart:

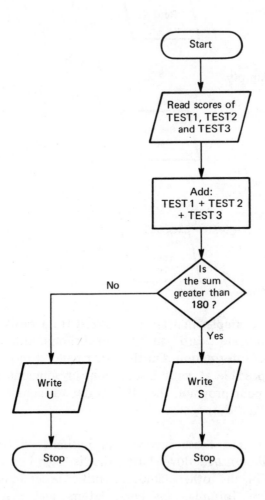

A symbolic flow chart:

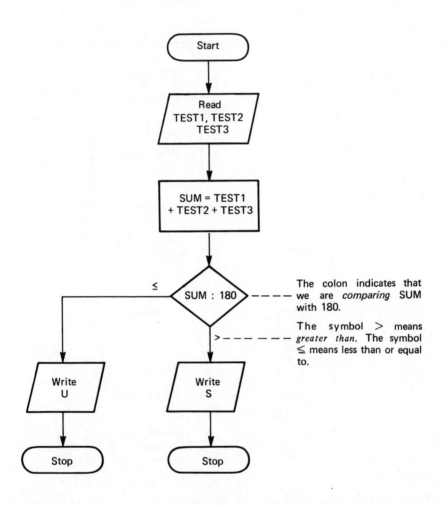

The colon indicates that we are *comparing* SUM with 180.

The symbol $>$ means *greater than*. The symbol $\leq$ means less than or equal to.

There is no reason to write the "Stop" twice. Instead this chart could be:

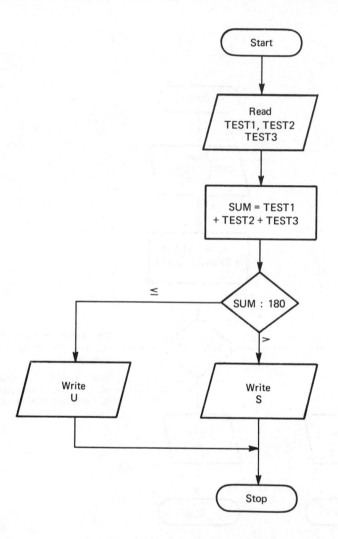

EXAMPLE 10-3. Two cards are read. The first contains the amount DUE as the result of one or more purchases. The second contains the amount RECEIVED from the customer. These two numbers are compared. If they are the same, then the customer has paid his bills and owes nothing. If the amount received is greater than the amount due (this rarely happens, but then you never know!) the customer is given credit toward his account and has a balance in his favor. However, if the amount received is less than the amount due, then the new amount due is computed by adding a 1% service charge (on the amount not paid) to the unpaid amount. This then is the new balance.

The descriptive flow chart in Fig. 10-1 shows the outline of this process, including output.

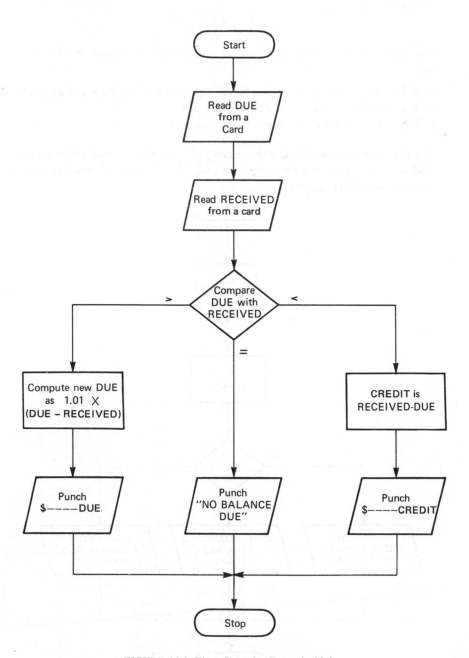

FIGURE 10-1. Flow Chart for Example 10-3.

EXAMPLE 10-4. Determine the nature of the roots of a quadratic equation.

A quadratic equation (that is, one of the form $ax^2 + bx + c = 0$) can be solved by using the formula

$$x = \frac{-b \pm \sqrt{b^2 - 4ac}}{2a}$$

The *nature* of the solution is dependent on the value of the *discriminant, $b^2 -$ 4ac*.

a. If $b^2 - 4ac$ is negative, the roots of the equation are imaginary and unequal.
b. If $b^2 - 4ac$ is zero, the roots are real and equal.
c. If $b^2 - 4ac$ is positive, the roots are real and unequal.

The flow chart below indicates the reading of *a, b,* and *c,* computation and test of the discriminant, and the output in each case. The actual solutions, *x,* are not determined in examples.

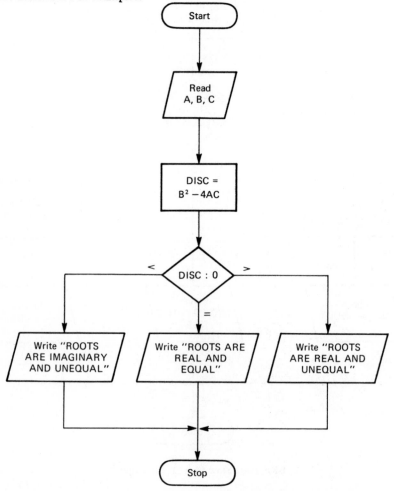

EXAMPLE 10-5. *If it is desirable to repeat a procedure, such as the one in the previous example, the flow chart can be changed to indicate this.*[2] *Consider a flow chart for 100 executions of the program of the previous example.*

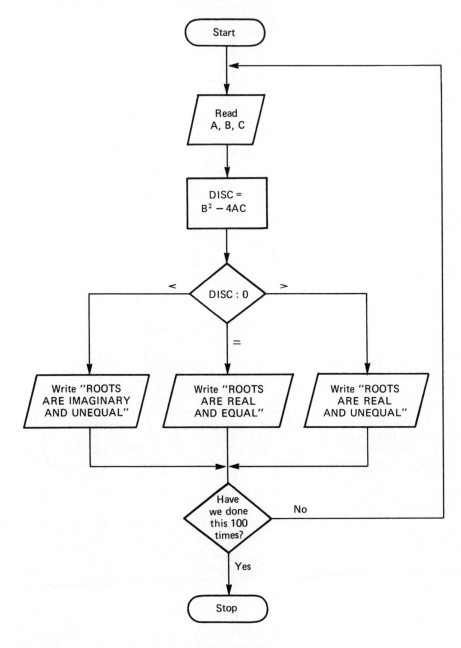

[2] A procedure which is repeated is called a *loop*.

The chart above may seem unappealing because of the line connecting the "No" of the test with the "Read" at the top. This can be changed as indicated below, using the small circular *connector* symbol.[3]

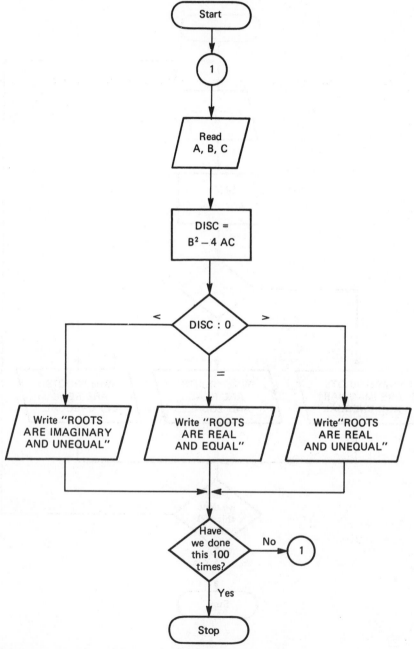

[3]If a connector is used to link two portions which are on different pages, we use off-page connectors (⬠).

Still another choice is to use connectors to "receive" arrows. This use is indicated by the connector "2" below.

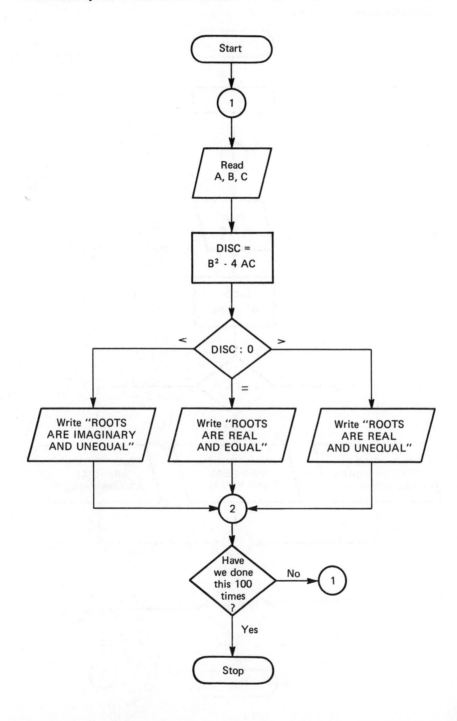

Finally, we show the use of a *counter,* which is set, tested, and incremented. This flow chart form for loops is particularly adaptable to program writing; that is, coding from a flow chart.

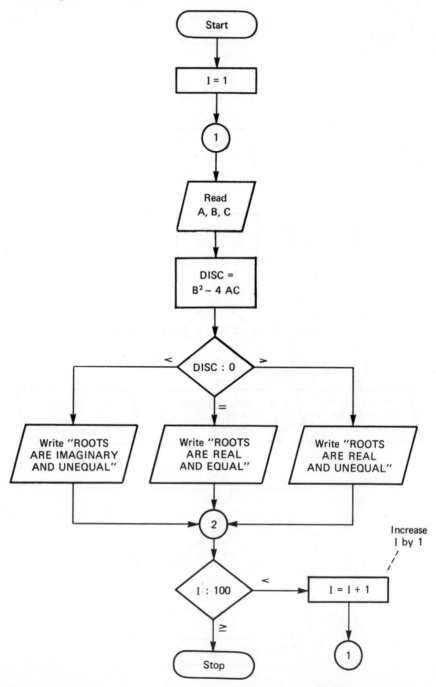

EXAMPLE 10-6. Draw a flow chart to read 50 numbers, say $x_1, x_2, x_3, \ldots,$ x_{50}, compute their average, and write all the x_i's and the average.
We shall use:

x_i to indicate any of the numbers from x_1 to x_{50}. When we assign i a particular value we are referring to a particular x_i. For example, if $i = 15$, the reference is to x_{15}.

SUM   indicates the sum which we shall accumulate in order to compute the average. Recall

$$\text{Average} = \frac{\text{sum of items}}{\text{number of items}} = \frac{x_1 + x_2 + x_3 + \cdots + x_{50}}{50}$$

AVG   indicates the average; that is,

$$AVG = \frac{SUM}{50}.$$

The Plan

We shall compute the sum of the x_i's by using a loop. We call the sum *SUM*. SUM is set to zero first.

SUM $\boxed{0}$

Next, x_1 is added to SUM. This gives us

SUM $\boxed{0 + \underline{x_1}}$

Next, x_2 is added to SUM. This gives us

SUM $\boxed{0 + x_1 + \underline{x_2}}$

Next, x_3 is added to SUM, producing

SUM $\boxed{0 + x_1 + x_2 + \underline{x_3}}$

And so on, until we finally add x_{50} to SUM to get

SUM $\boxed{0 + x_1 + x_2 + x_3 + x_4 + \cdots + \underline{x_{50}}}$

Such computation is indicated symbolically in flow charts as

$$SUM = SUM + x_i,$$

which is read as

SUM *is replaced by* SUM plus x_i.

In other words, add x_i to the old value of SUM to get the new value of SUM.

The index, i, is set initially at 1 ($i = 1$), so that x_1 is added to the SUM first. We then increase i by 1 ($i = i + 1$), so that x_i will be x_2 next, and so on.

The computation of SUM will be finished once x_{50} has been added to SUM to produce the final new SUM.

Then AVG is computed simply as

$$AVG = \frac{SUM}{50}.$$

See Fig. 10-2. for the flow chart.

GUIDES TO FLOWCHARTING

Consider the following guides when you make your own flow charts:

1. Use only vertical and horizontal straight lines. Do not use diagonal lines or curved lines.
2. Do not allow lines to cross one another. Use labeled connectors to avoid such situations.
3. Only one line should be directed *into* a particular symbol. Use connectors if necessary (the last example demonstrates this use of connectors).
4. All lines used in a chart should be connected to some symbol. There should be no lines which are not connected.
5. Flow charts are usually designed to be read from top to bottom or from left to right.
6. All text which is placed within the symbols of the chart should be neatly printed. The number of words used as an explanation should be kept small.
7. All possibilities must be considered, regardless of how remote.
8. Avoid using codes which apply only to some computers. For example, addition may be indicated by using "+" or the word "add," whereas computer codes such as A, AH, AL, AR, etc. should be avoided. Remember, your chart should be understandable to anyone reading it. A programmer should be able to program from it regardless of what programming languages he knows. This means additionally that the flow chart must be a complete and unambiguous outline of the solution to the problem.
9. When the problem is a complex one, it is advisable to first make a *general* flow chart of the overall process, and then make a *detailed* chart. However, by detailed we do not mean *every* instruction. Such minute detail, of course, will be available after the program is coded.

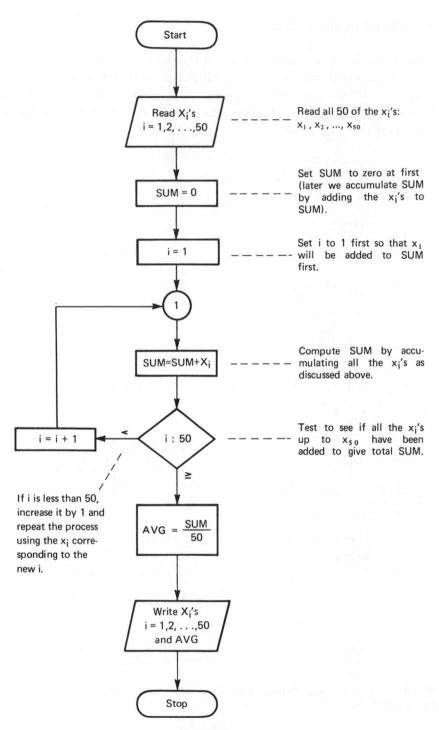

Start

Read X$_i$'s
i = 1,2, . . .,50   ------ Read all 50 of the x$_i$'s:
                                  x$_1$, x$_2$, ..., x$_{50}$

SUM = 0   ------ Set SUM to zero at first
                                  (later we accumulate SUM
                                  by adding the x$_i$'s to
                                  SUM).

i = 1   ------ Set i to 1 first so that x$_1$
                                  will be added to SUM
                                  first.

1

SUM=SUM+X$_i$ ------ Compute SUM by accu-
                                  mulating all the x$_i$'s as
                                  discussed above.

i = i + 1   <   i : 50   ------ Test to see if all the x$_i$'s
                                  up to x$_{50}$ have been
                                  added to give total SUM.

                ≥

If i is less than 50,
increase it by 1 and
repeat the process   AVG = $\dfrac{SUM}{50}$
using the x$_i$ corre-
sponding to the
new i.

Write X$_i$'s
i = 1,2, . . .,50
and AVG

Stop

FIGURE 10-2

AUTOMATIC FLOWCHARTING

Software has been developed which enables the computer to accept a program *as input* and produce as output a printed flow chart of the program. These computer-produced flow charts are excellent for inclusion in program documentation and can also be useful in debugging (see Fig. 10-3).

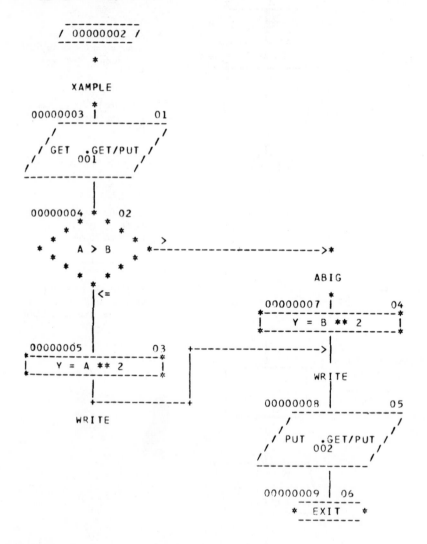

FIGURE 10-3. A Computer-Produced Flow Chart. *Courtesy of Applied Data Research, Inc.*

EXERCISES 10.1

Draw a flow chart for each problem below.

1. Read from a card two values: the AMOUNT of money invested and the RATE of interest paid on the investment. Compute DIVIDEND = RATE · AMOUNT. Then write RATE, AMOUNT, and DIVIDEND.

2. Read values for a, b, c, d, e, f, and x. Compute

$$SUM = a + b + c + d$$

$$PROD = d \cdot e \cdot f$$

$$QUO = \frac{a + b + c + d}{d \cdot e \cdot f}$$

$$XSUM = x + a + b + c + d$$

Write the values SUM, PROD, QUO, and XSUM.

3. Do the following 500 times: Read from a card two values (the PRICE of an item and the NUMBER of items sold at that price), compute TOTAL = NUMBER · PRICE, write NUMBER, PRICE, and TOTAL.

4. Same as problem 3, except first read a value for n. This value of n determines how many cards (500 in the problem above) should be processed.

5. Read values for a, b, c and *solve* $ax^2 + bx + c = 0$ (using the formula given in Example 10-4), unless the discriminant is negative. Write the roots (if solved) or "roots are complex" (if not solved).

6. Read a and b. Determine which is larger and write it. Can you do it with only one "Write" in your chart?

7. Read a value for n and do all of the following n times: read x, y, and z, compute $a = (x + y) z$, and if $a \neq 0$ also compute

$$b = \frac{x}{(x + y)z}$$

(in either case write the result or results).

8. Find the sum of the odd integers $(1, 3, 5, 7, \ldots)$ from 1 to 40. Write the sum.

9. Change the flow chart of Example 10-6 so that a value of n can be read. The n is followed by n x_i's $(x_1, x_2, x_3, \ldots, x_n)$. The average of these n x_i's should then be computed.

10. Read a value for n and compute the sum of the integers (whole numbers) from 1 to n. (For example, if n is 5, compute $1 + 2 + 3 + 4 + 5$.) Then write n and the sum.

11. Read a value for n and compute the product of the integers from 1 to n. Write n and the product.

12. Read $x_1, x_2, x_3, \ldots, x_{100}$ and compute $SUM1 = x_1 + x_3 + x_5 + \cdots + x_{99}$. If $SUM1 > 0$ also compute $SUM2 = x_2 + x_4 + x_6 + \cdots + x_{100}$. Write all results.

11

SYSTEM/360
ASSEMBLER LANGUAGE
PROGRAMMING

The IBM System/360 is not *a* computer, but rather a whole system of different size computers; for example, 360 model 30, 360/40, and 360/65. The entire line of 360's includes small, medium, and large-scale computers. The larger the model number the larger the computer, and hence the greater its capability. A unique feature of the 360's is that they are upward compatible; that is, programs written for one model can also be run on most larger models. And this was not true of computers preceding System/360. Another important feature of this system is that a given model handles commercial and scientific problems with equal ease.

In this chapter we shall study program writing for the 360. Specifically we will treat *assembler language coding.*[1] Subsequent chapters will explain FORTRAN, COBOL, PL/1, and RPG.

INTRODUCTION

Instructions to the computer and data to be used and processed are stored as *bytes* or groups of bytes in main storage. A byte is eight consecutive binary digits (bits).

[1]Other third generation computer systems have similar assembler languages.

175

byte: | 1 | 0 | 0 | 1 | 1 | 1 | 0 | 0 |

For discussions it is often helpful to number the bits from 0 to 7.

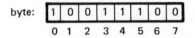

byte: | 1 | 0 | 0 | 1 | 1 | 1 | 0 | 0 |
        0   1   2   3   4   5   6   7

The 360's storage can be thought of as a long string of bytes. The first byte is identified as (byte) location 0, the second as location 1, the third as location 2, and so on.

Ist byte   2nd byte   3rd byte

storage: | 8 BITS | 8 BITS | 8 BITS | • • •

location 0   location 1   location 2

The location or address refers to the leftmost (most significant) bit of the byte. We shall assume that we have 32,000 bytes (32K) of main storage. Such a storage is common in smaller models of the 360.

Two consecutive bytes are called a *halfword*. Thus, a halfword is 16 bits.

halfword: | 1 | 0 | 0 | 0 | 1 | 1 | 0 | 0 | 1 | 0 | 0 | 0 | 1 | 0 | 0 | 1 |
        0   1   2   15

Care must be taken when referencing (that is, addressing) halfwords in storage. The first halfword is at location 0, but the second is at location 2. This is because all references to storage addresses are to *byte* addresses.

1st halfword   2nd halfword   3rd halfword

| 1 byte | 1 byte | 1 byte | 1 byte | | • • • |

0   1   2   3   4   6

Halfword locations must be multiples of two; that is, 0, 2, 4, 6, 8, 10, ...

A *word* or *fullword* is four consecutive bytes. This, of course, is also two halfwords or 32 bits.

fullword:

| 1 | 1 | 0 | 1 | 0 | 0 | 1 | 0 | 1 | 0 | 0 | 0 | 0 | 1 | 0 | 1 | 1 | 1 | 0 | 1 | 1 | 0 | 0 | 0 | 0 | 1 | 0 | 0 | 0 | 1 | 1 | 1 |
0   1   2   31

The first fullword of core storage is at (byte) location 0, the second is at location 4, and the third is at location 8.

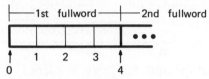

It should be clear that fullword locations must be multiples of four; that is, 0, 4, 8, 12, 16, 20, ...

There are 16 *general purpose registers*. They can be used to hold the results of arithmetic operations of addition, subtraction, multiplication, and division. These registers can also be used to help construct loops or cycles.

Each general register holds 32 bits or one fullword. The bits are numbered 0, 1, 2, 3, . . . , 31. For discussions we shall refer to the registers as R0, R1, R2, R3, . . . , R15; but when they are actually used with instructions they will be designated simply as 0, 1, 2, 3, . . . , 15.

FIXED-POINT NUMBERS

To simplify matters we shall use only one type of data: whole numbers. Such numbers are called *fixed-point numbers* or integers. They can be recorded in storage as halfwords or as fullwords.

If a number is recorded as a halfword, then bit position 0 holds the sign of the number and bits 1-15 indicate the magnitude. We sometimes label the 0th bit "s," for *sign*. If a number is positive the s-bit is 0. A negative number has a 1 s-bit.

EXAMPLE 11-1.   *Show how (19)$_{10}$ looks as a halfword in the 360's storage.* The first bit is a 0 since the number is positive. Bits 1-15 are the binary equivalent of the base 10 number 19, and since $(19)_{10} = (10011)_2$, the halfword is

$$\boxed{0000000000010011}$$
S1   15

EXAMPLE 11-2.   *What base 10 number is represented by the binary halfword*

$$\boxed{0000000000111010} \quad ?$$
S1   15

The sign bit is 0, so the number is positive. Also, $(111010)_2 = (58)_{10}$. Thus, the number is simply 58.

If a number is recorded as a fullword, then bit position 0 holds the sign of the number and bits 1-31 indicate the size of the number. Thus, the $(19)_{10}$ of Example 11-1 is represented as the word

```
00000000000000000000000000010011
```
S1   31

in the storage of the 360. Similarly, the word

```
00000000000000000000000000111010
```
S1   31

represents $(58)_{10}$.

TWO'S COMPLEMENT AND NEGATIVE NUMBERS[2]

For the purpose of discussion let us consider a hypothetical four-bit register. There is no such register in the 360, however. Suppose now that the register contains the four bits 1011.

four-bit register: | 1   0   1   1 |

By the *1's complement* of the number in this register we mean the number which when added to 1011 produces 1111. Clearly this is just 0100. Similarly, the 1's complement of 0101 is 1010.

$$
\begin{array}{cccccl}
0 & 1 & 0 & 1 & \leftarrow & \text{number} \\
1 & 0 & 1 & 0 & \leftarrow & \text{1's complement} \\
\hline
1 & 1 & 1 & 1 & \leftarrow & \text{sum is all 1's}
\end{array}
$$

It should be obvious that the 1's complement of a binary number is determined by forming a number which has 1-bits where the original has 0-bits and 0-bits where the original has 1-bits.

Consider what happens when 1 is added to 1111 in a four-bit register.

```
| 1 1 1 1 |
```
```
        1
```
1 | 0 0 0 0 |

---

[2] No continuity is lost if this section is omitted; however, its inclusion is necessary for an understanding of the representation of negative integers in the 360.

Since the register holds only four bits, the result is "0" and the carried 1 is lost. Thus, we have shown that

$$\boxed{\text{NUMBER} + 1\text{'S COMPLEMENT} + 1 = 0}$$

The number formed by adding 1 to the 1's complement is called the *2's complement*.

EXAMPLE 11-3

Number:	1	0	0	1
1's complement:	0	1	1	0
2's complement:	0	1	1	1

Number:	1	0	0	1
1's complement:	0	1	1	0
Sum:	1	1	1	1

Number:	1	0	0	1
2's complement:	0	1	1	1
Sum: 1	0	0	0	0

We conclude that

$$\boxed{\text{NUMBER} + 2\text{'S COMPLEMENT} = 0}$$

This means that the 2's complement is the negative (or opposite) of the number. Recall from algebra

$$5 + (-5) = 0$$
$$x + (-x) = 0$$

EXAMPLE 11-4. Represent 3 and –3 using a four-bit register.

3:	0	0	1	1
1's complement:	1	1	0	0
2's complement:	1	1	0	1

So –3 is 1 1 0 1, since –3 is the 2's complement of 3.

Check.

3		0	0	1	1
–3		1	1	0	1
0	1	0	0	0	0

The extension of this concept to 16-bit storage registers (halfwords) and 32-bit storage registers (fullwords) should be clear.

EXAMPLE 11-5. Represent 25 and –25 as halfwords.

25:	0000000000011001
1's complement:	1111111111100110
2's complement:	1111111111100111
–25:	1111111111100111

EXERCISES 11.1

1. Identify each: bit, byte, halfword, fullword.

*2. The computer we are discussing has 32,000 bytes of storage. How many halfwords is this? How many fullwords is it?

*3. Which of the following are acceptable as halfword addresses: 1, 19, 40, 150, 673?

*4. Which of the following are acceptable as fullword addresses: 1, 19, 40, 150, 160, 326, 400, 656, 1000?

5. Represent as binary halfwords: 12, 73, 205.

6. Represent as binary fullwords: 12, 73, 205.

*7. Represent as binary halfwords: –12, –73, –205.

THE INSTRUCTIONS

As you know, a program is a list of instructions. What instructions make up the program depends, of course, on what the program is supposed to accomplish.

Most 360 instructions indicate three things:

1. *What operation is to be carried out*; for example, multiply, subtract, read, write, halt, transfer. The operation is indicated by a mnemonic operation code.

2. *Where the data to be used can be found*. This is indicated by a register number or a storage location.

3. *Where the result (if any) is to be placed.* This too is indicated by a register number or a storage location.[3]

The instructions we shall study are of two types. Instructions of one type occupy two bytes each. Each instruction is introduced in the form of an example, rather than in general form. The generalization is obvious in each case.

The actual translation (*assembly*) of instructions into machine executable binary code is discussed later in the chapter.

RR-TYPE INSTRUCTIONS

All **RR**-(register-to-register) type instructions have the following basic properties:
1. Each occupies two bytes (one halfword) of storage.
2. Each references two general registers. Storage is not referenced or used.

LR 5,8 (Load Register)

When executed this instruction will cause the number (fullword) in register 8 to be loaded into register 5, thus replacing the previous contents of register 5. The contents of register 8 do not change.

Suppose, for example, that we have the following numbers in registers 5 and 8 originally:

R5 2974   R8 12

Suppose additionally that "LR 5,8" is executed. The result is

R5 12   R8 12

The choice of registers 5 and 8 was arbitrary. They could just as well have been 10 and 6, or any other two of the registers 0 through 15.

---

[3]The contents of locations such as those mentioned in (2) and (3) are called *operands.*

AR 7,3 (Add Registers)

The number in R3 is added to the number in R7. The result is placed in R7, thus replacing what was in R7 before the addition took place. The contents of R3 are unchanged.

EXAMPLE 11-6. Assume

$$R7 \quad \boxed{29}$$

$$R3 \quad \boxed{15}$$

After execution of "AR 7,3" we have

$$R7 \quad \boxed{44}$$

$$R3 \quad \boxed{15}$$

SR 5,8 (Subtract Registers)

The number in R8 is subtracted from the number in R5. The result is placed in R5. The contents of R8 are unchanged.

EXAMPLE 11-7. Assume

$$R5 \quad \boxed{50}$$

$$R8 \quad \boxed{20}$$

After execution of "SR 5,8" we have

$$R5 \quad \boxed{30}$$

$$R8 \quad \boxed{20}$$

MR 8,5 (Multiply Registers)

Multiplication is somewhat more complicated than addition or subtraction.

1. The first register mentioned in any use of the multiply instruction must be an *even* numbered one, but the register actually used is the *odd* one which is next in order numerically.
2. The second register may be either an even or an odd one; it doesn't matter. Thus, two examples of acceptable multiply instructions are:

    MR 8,5 and MR 8,12.

3. Since the product of two fullwords *could* occupy more than one register, the computer's circuitry is set up to always allow *two registers for the product.* The two registers used to hold the product are:
   (a) The first (even) register specified by the instruction. This is "8" in the examples above.
   (b) The (odd) register which is next in order. This is "9" in the examples above, since 9 is the first odd register after 8.

Although the result of multiplication takes up two registers when two are needed, usually only one register is needed to contain the result; and the result of multiplication is always right justified. This means that for common numbers *the result appears entirely within the odd-numbered register.*[4] Thus

MR 8,5

multiplies the number in $R9$ by the number in R5 and leaves the result in R8 and R9; but unless the product is very large it appears only in $R9$. And this will be an assumption we make for simplicity.

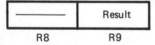

Thus, the even register will contain all zeros if the result is positive or else all ones if the result is negative.[5]

We need an instruction to stop the processor after execution of all program instructions has been completed.

EOJ (End Of Job)

The nature of program organization for the System/360 indicates no specific "stop" or "halt" instruction. Instead a supervisor program runs the computer between programs and a macro instruction, EOJ, is used

[4] For numbers less than 2,147,483,648 (or 2^{31}) the result is contained completely in the odd-numbered register.
[5] See Exercise 6.

to call the supervisor to indicate that execution of the current program has been completed, and that the next program should be loaded for execution.

EXAMPLE 11-8. Write a program which will multiply the numbers in R7 and R1 and add to this product the number in R8. The final result should be placed in R15.

At this point we note that program instructions must be in storage before they can be executed. Instructions are stored in the sequence written. Let us assume that they are stored beginning at byte location 200.

We present the program in a special format.

byte location	instruction	comment
200	MR 6,1	$c(R1) \cdot c(R7)$ in R7[6]
202	AR 7,8	product + $c(R8)$ in R7
204	LR 15,7	move result to R15
206	EOJ	stop

Note that since RR-type instructions occupy two bytes each, their byte addresses are 200, 202, 204, and 206.

The format above includes a location field, an instruction field, and a comment field. Comments are not required but are helpful to the programmer when he is writing, debugging, or altering his program (especially months or even years later). They are usually used more sparingly than in the examples presented in this chapter.

RX-TYPE INSTRUCTIONS

It is natural to wonder if there are instructions that can process the data that is in the main storage. After all, there are only 16 general registers. Clearly we cannot process much if we are restricted to the use of only these registers.

The **RX**-type instructions (register-to-storage) handle the communication of data between the general registers and storage. They have the following properties:

1. Each occupies four bytes (one fullword) of storage.
2. Each specifies one register and one (byte) location of a fullword, in that order.

---

[6] $c(R1)$ means the contents of R1; that is, the number in register 1.

L 3,400 (Load)

The number (fullword) at location 400 is loaded into R3, replacing its previous contents. The contents of location 400 are unchanged.

EXAMPLE 11-9. If we have

R3 $\boxed{14}$

400 $\boxed{293}$

and then "L 3,400" is executed, the result is

R3 $\boxed{293}$

400 $\boxed{293}$

A 1,444 (Add)

The number at location 444 is added to the number in R1. The result appears in R1, and the contents of location 444 are unchanged.

EXAMPLE 11-10. Suppose we have

R1 $\boxed{28}$

444 $\boxed{350}$

and then "A 1,444" is executed. The result is

R1 $\boxed{378}$

444 $\boxed{350}$

Let us examine Example 11-10 in terms of binary digits and storage.

| before: | R1 | $\boxed{00000000 \quad 00000000 \quad 00000000 \quad 00011100}$ |
| | 444 | $\boxed{00000000 \quad 00000000 \quad 00000001 \quad 01011110}$ |

| | 444 | 445 | 446 | 447 |

after: R1 | 00000000 00000000 00000001 01111010 |

                444 | 00000000 00000000 00000001 01011110 |

The point is that the *fullword* at location 444 is the number 350.
However, the *byte* at location 444 contains only zeros. For fixed-point
numbers stored in fullwords, the address is the address of the leftmost
byte of the word, but the number has its (imaginary) decimal point at
the right end of the rightmost (fourth) byte. Thus

fullword at 444 | 00000000 00000000 00000001 01011110 |

halfword at 444 | 00000000 00000000 |

byte at 444 | 00000000 |

ST 14,800 (Store)

The number in R14 is stored in the fullword at location 800. The
contents of R14 are unchanged.

EXAMPLE 11-11. Assume

R14 | 3007 |

800 | 1230 |

After execution of "ST 14,800" we have

R14 | 3007 |

800 | 3007 |

*EXAMPLE 11-12. Write a program to add the numbers (fullwords) in locations
1500 and 1672 and store the sum in location 1000. Begin storing instructions
at location 200.*

location	instruction	comment
200	L 5,1500	c(1500) to R5
204	A 5,1672	c(1500) + c(1672) in R5
208	ST 5,1000	store sum at loc. 1000.
212	EOJ	stop

The locations of the instructions are sequenced 200, 204, 208, 212 because these are RX instructions. Each occupies *four* bytes.

S 11,1500 (Subtract)

The fullword at location 1500 is subtracted from the number in R11. The result appears in R11, and the fullword at location 1500 is unchanged.

EXAMPLE 11-13. If we have

R11 | 100 |

1500 | 30 |

and we execute "S 11,1500" we then have

R11 | 70 |

1500 | 30 |

The RX multiply is essentially like the RR multiply. The only difference is that the second number refers to a storage location.

M 8,612 (Multiply)

The number in R9 is multiplied by the number in location 612. The result is placed in R9. The contents of location 612 are unchanged. R8 contains either all zeros or all ones, depending on whether the product is positive or negative, respectively.[7]

EXAMPLE 11-14. Assume

R8 | 0 |

R9 | 4 |

612 | 5 |

---

[7]Recall (compare with MR instruction) that the specified register must be an even numbered one, and that the result will appear in the next sequentially numbered odd register.

Then execution of "M 8,612" produces

R8 $\boxed{0}$

R9 $\boxed{20}$

612 $\boxed{5}$

EXAMPLE 11-15. Write a program to perform the following computation and store the result at location 1000: $(x + y)(a - b)$, where a is the fullword at location 500, b is the content of 504, x is in 508, and y is in 512.

location	instruction	comment
200	L 5,508	x in R5
204	A 5,512	$x + y$ in R5
208	L 11,500	a in R11
212	S 11,504	$a - b$ in R11
216	MR 4,11	$(x+y)(a-b)$ in R5
218	ST 5,1000	$(x+y)(a-b)$ in 1000
222	EOJ	

Note that the MR instruction only occupies two bytes, and therefore the ST instruction begins at location 218 rather than 220. Also, although the ST is an RX instruction and occupies four bytes it need not be a fullword in the strictest sense. In other words, the ST need not begin at a location which is a multiple of four, but it does occupy four consecutive bytes. The "multiple of four" restriction is only for "data," and we shall see this in more detail later.

Example 11-15 points out advantages of mixing RR arithmetic instructions with RX arithmetic instructions. In fact, it justifies the existence and use of RR arithmetic. For example, if we did not use the "MR 4,11" then we would have had to use instead something like

```
ST 11,600      Location 600 is any (temporary) storage location.
M  4,600
```

That is, we would have had to write two instructions instead of one. There are several reasons we avoid writing more instructions than needed.

1. We save machine execution time by executing fewer instructions.
2. Storage capacity is limited. It is especially important on larger programs that we try to minimize the number of instructions written, since each occupies two or four bytes of storage.

3. We save time coding fewer instructions. Also, we risk fewer clerical errors.

HALFWORD PROCESSES

To save space in storage, relatively small integers may be stored as halfwords (two bytes) rather than as fullwords (four bytes).[8] The load, store, add, subtract, and multiply instructions are basically the same as for fullwords. The differences are listed.

1. We use the mnemonic operation codes LH, STH, AH, SH, and MH rather than L, ST, A, S, and M.
2. The location specified in the instruction is the location of the first byte of a halfword rather than that of a fullword.
3. The halfwords are right justified in the fullword-size general registers. This means that they occupy the rightmost 16 bits of the 32-bit registers.

FLOATING-POINT NUMBERS

For most computations in science and engineering it is necessary to use numbers involving fractions or decimals. Such numbers are called floating-point numbers. Each floating-point number is represented in storage as a binary fraction with an appropriate binary exponent. The exponent is the power of 2 by which the fraction is multiplied. Figure 11-1 shows the form of a floating-point number and an actual example, without explanation.

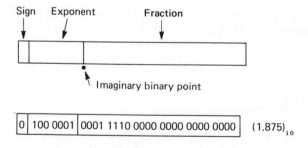

FIGURE 11-1. Floating-Point Representation.

[8]Numbers less than 32,768 (or 2^{15}) may be stored as halfwords.

CHARACTERS

Many commercial data processing problems require the use of characters (letters, digits, special characters) for dates, employee numbers, addresses, and codes rather than for computation. For such applications each character is represented as one byte using the EBCDIC or ASCII code.[9] Special instructions are available for use in programming these problems.

EXERCISES 11.2

1. What are the differences between the RR instructions and the RX instructions? Are both types really necessary? Why or why not?

2. Why is it usually desirable to minimize the number of instructions in a given program?

*3. Write a program to compute $(a + bc + d)e$, where a, b, c, d, and e are the numbers (fullwords) in locations 620, 624, 628, 632, and 636, respectively. Store the result in location 640. Begin the program at location 200.

4. Assume that b, q, r, and w are the numbers in locations 440, 444, 448, and 452. Write a program to compute and store the following:
   (a) $q + r$
   (b) $(b - q)r + w$
   (c) $(b - w)(q + r)$.
   Place the results in fullword locations 1000, 1004, and 1008. Begin the program at location 200.

*5. In Example 11-15 we used MR 4,11 instead of the combination of ST 11,600 and M 4,600. How many bytes of storage did we save by doing this?

6. Show by using binary numbers and registers that if $(50)_{10}$ is in R5 and is multiplied by $(12)_{10}$, the product is contained completely in R5.

SYMBOLIC CODING

The version of 360 programming language presented so far uses symbolic or mnemonic operation codes, such as A or AR to indicate "add" and L or LR to indicate "load," and others. However, the storage locations specified are absolute rather than symbolic. That is, if

[9] See Chapter 7 on coding schemes.

we want to load $\dot{x}$ we use an instruction such as L 4,500, where we "know" that the number in location 500 is a value of x. Such coding is not truly symbolic.

To use more of the tools of symbolic assembly language we include symbolic addresses with the symbolic operation codes. In this section we explain how to use this facility.

An example will serve to introduce the new ideas. Specifically, let us take Example 11-15:

$$(x + y)(a - b) \;\to\; \text{location 1000.}$$

The code was

200	L 5,508	x in R5
204	A 5,512	$x + y$ in R5
208	L 11,500	a in R11
212	S 11,504	$a - b$ in R11
216	MR 4,11	$(x + y)(a - b)$
218	ST 5,1000	
222	EOJ	

When written in truly symbolic code this program might appear as

	START 200	
	BALR 13,0	
	USING *,13	
	L 5,X	
	A 5,Y	$(x + y)$ in R5
	L 11,A	
	S 11,B	$(a - b)$ in R11
	MR 4,11	
	ST 5,RESULT	$(x + y)(a - b)$ to RESULT
	EOJ	
X	DS F	
Y	DS F	
B	DS F	
A	DS F	
RESULT	DS F	
	END	

An explanation of the code follows.

START 200

The reader will immediately note that no byte locations appear to the left of the operation codes. One advantage of this more symbolic form of coding is that the programmer does not have to keep track of the locations of instructions. Instead, a START instruction is used to indicate the location of the first instruction. The assembler determines the other locations automatically.

Thus, the "START 200" results in the first instruction being loaded at location 200.

BALR 13,0 and USING *,13

This combination causes the location of the next instruction to be executed to be placed in R13. This is needed to cause the "L 5,X" to be executed. R13 (in this example) is called the *base register* for this program and should not be used for computations or temporary storage. The combination

```
BALR  15,0
USING *,15
```

would make R15 the base register for a program in which it appeared.

DS and X, Y, A, B, RESULT

In symbolic coding if we want to add x and y we merely load one of them and add the other to it. We do not specify the numeric (or absolute) locations where values of x and y are stored; we simply use *symbolic addresses* such as X and Y. Additionally, when a symbolic address is used this way in a program (whether once or fifty times) it must appear exactly once in the program to the left of a "DS" instruction.[10] Such DS instructions merely reserve storage locations and are not executed when the program is run. They are placed after the EOJ instruction.

[10] DS stands for *define storage*.

As indicated in the program above, each complete DS instruction consists of the operation code "DS" followed by the letter "F." The F indicates that a fullword of storage is being reserved for the number (H would be used if the numbers were to be halfwords).

Each DS is preceded by a *name* X, Y, A, B, or RESULT. The name, of course, depends on what variables are being used in the program. And each variable which is used in the program must be so defined. Any name can be used, as long as it *begins with a letter* and contains *seven or fewer additional letters and/or digits*. Thus, Q, R71, ABC123, and X1Y235B5 are all acceptable names (or symbolic storage locations).

END

An assembler language program cannot be executed in the form in which it is written. Although the computer will accept it (as input) in the coded form, it can only execute *binary* instructions. A large program, called an *assembler*, is used to translate the code.[11]

The END instruction is simply a signal to the assembler that there are no more symbolic program instructions to follow. After receiving this signal, the assembler can proceed to translate the program which it has been given.

It should be clear that the END must be physically the last instruction in the program.

DC   (Define Constant)

Suppose, for example, that in our program above we know that *x* will always have a value of 10. We can generate a "10" in storage by writing

                    X   DC   F'10'

instead of

                    X   DS   F

---

[11] The assembler is discussed later in more detail.

The DS merely sets aside a location named X. This assumes that a value for X will be read in or computed and later stored in location X.

On the other hand, the DC defines a constant value for the name which precedes it. The DC example above defines a value of 10 for the name X, so that when X is used throughout the program we are always using (for it) the constant 10.

Figure 11-2 presents the symbolic program example on a standard coding form. Each line of code will be punched into one card, so that each punched card will contain one instruction (see Fig. 11-3).

Comments are indicated by skipping one or more spaces after an instruction; the comment is then written, but it may not extend beyond column 71. If you choose to make an entire line a comment, then place an asterisk (*) in column 1 and the comment anywhere in columns 3 through 71.

Some of the advantages of using this more symbolic form of the assembler language are clear.

1. We do not have to keep track of the locations of the program instructions. We simply specify where the first one should be placed.
2. Code can be written which more closely resembles the problem. This makes programs easier to write, easier to follow, and easier to correct or update.

Although it appears that using a more symbolic form of assembler language wastes storage by using more instructions, this is not really the case. The START, USING, and END instructions are only instructions to the assembler. Their execution occurs during the assembly process. Consequently, they are not loaded into storage for program execution. The results of DS and DC take up one fullword each; but if these were not used, then other locations would be used similarly to store values for variables used in the program.[12] The symbolic program uses X, Y, A, B, and RESULT; the less symbolic program used 500, 504, 508, 512, and 1000.

---

[12]DC and DS may also be used to define or reserve bytes (characters), halfwords, and doublewords.

IBM — IBM System/360 Assembler Coding Form — X28-6509-4 U/M025 Printed in U.S.A.

PROGRAM: EXAMPLE OF SYMBOLIC PROGRAM

PROGRAMMER: DANIEL D. BENICE — DATE: 2-5-70

PUNCHING INSTRUCTIONS							
GRAPHIC	Ø	O	I	I	Ƶ	2	
PUNCH	'OH'	ZERO	'EYE'	ONE	ZEE	TWO	

PAGE OF — CARD ELECTRO NUMBER *

STATEMENT: Name (1–8), Operation (10–14), Operand (16–), Comments (–71); Identification-Sequence (73–80)

```
         START 200
         BALR  13,0
         USING *,13
         L     5,X
         A     5,Y            (X+Y) IN R5
         L     11,A
         S     11,B           (A-B) IN R11
         MR    4,11
         ST    5,RESULT       (X+Y)(A+B) TØ RESULT
         EØJ
X        DS    F
Y        DS    F
B        DS    F
A        DS    F
RESULT   DS    F
         END
```

* A standard card form, IBM electro 6509, is available for punching source statements from this form.
Instructions for using this form are in any IBM System/360 Assembler Reference Manual.
Address comments concerning this form to IBM Corporation, Programming Publications, Department 232, San Jose, California 95114.

FIGURE 11-2. Symbolic Coding on a Coding Sheet.

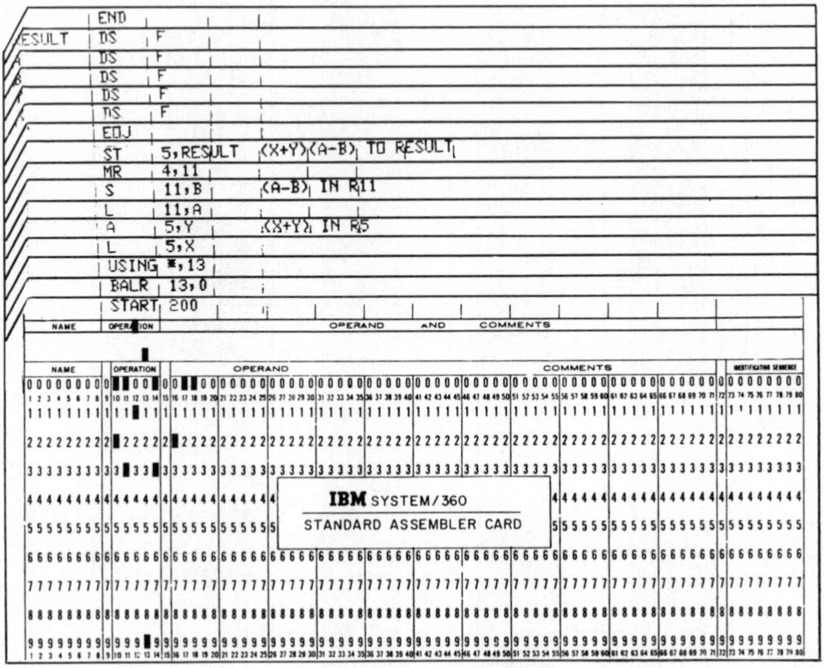

FIGURE 11-3. Symbolic Coding on Punched Cards.

EXAMPLE 11-16. Write a program to compute   PER = 2(l + w).

```
              START   200
              BALR    13,0
              USING   *,13
              L       7,L
              A       7,W
              M       6,TWO
              ST      7,PER
              EOJ
    L         DS      F
    W         DS      F
    PER       DS      F
    TWO       DC      F'2'
              END
```

EXERCISES 11.3

For 1-9 write programs to carry out the indicated computations. Use
the symbolic methods introduced in this section.

1.   DIST = RATE · TIME

2. $PER = 2l + 2w$
   $AREA = lw$
   $VOL = lwh$

*3. $r = a + bc$
    $s = (a + bc - d)e$

*4. $z = 5x + 10y$

5. $y = mx + b$

6. $y = ax^2 + bx + c$

7. $i = prt$
   $A = p + prt$

8. $PER = 4e$
   $AREA = e^2$
   $VOL = e^3$

9. $A_1 = (x - y)(p + q)$
   $A_2 = 17A_1 + 6$
   $A_3 = A_1 + A_2$

*10. Which are unacceptable names for symbolic locations?
     X, NAME, LOOP3, A15, 15A, 19, B17.3, EXERCISE2, X12345

11. Why must the END be physically last? Why not the EOJ, since the EOJ causes termination of execution?

*12. Show the binary contents of location A as a result of

```
A     DC    F'39'
```

*13. Show the binary contents of location X as a result of

```
X     DC    F'-20'
```

14. Find the errors in the program below. It is supposed to compute $w = t + 9$ and $x = 5y + z$.

```
        START   200
        BALR    13,0
        USING   *,13
        L       8,T
        A       8,NINE
        ST      8,W
        L       11,Y
        M       10,5
        A       10,Z
        EOJ
T       DS      F
X       DS      F
```

Y	DS	F
Z	DS	F
NINE	DC	F'9'

INPUT/OUTPUT

Input/output with System 360 assembler language is very complicated. A complete discussion of I/O is beyond the scope of this text. But rather than omit I/O completely, a simplified version is presented.

All input data will be read from 80-column punched cards. An IBM-2501 card reader will be used to handle this input (see Fig. 11-4).

Output will be on printed pages. An IBM-1403 printer, with 132-character-per-line capability, will be used (see Fig. 11-5).

FIGURE 11-4. The IBM-2501 Card Reader. *Courtesy of IBM Corp.*

Input Instructions

The sequence

X	DTFCD	BLKSIZE = 80
		DEVICE = 2501
	OPEN	X
	GET	X A,B,C

causes one value for A, one value for B, and one value for C to be read from *80*-column punched cards by the *2501* card reader.

FIGURE 11-5. The IBM-1403 Printer.
Courtesy of IBM Corp.

The **DTFCD** macro instruction is used to define the input file. In this case it is the IBM-2501 card reader, which reads 80-column cards. A name (X was arbitrarily chosen) precedes the DTFCD. This means that this particular device can be referred to elsewhere in the program by using that name (X). The name, of course, can be any combination of eight or fewer letters and/or digits, beginning with a letter.

The **OPEN** macro instruction is used here to initialize the input device so that reading (input) can take place. Hence, the device labeled X is the one that is "opened."

The **GET** macro instruction indicates where the values are to be stored when they are read into storage from the device labeled X. In this case the first value read is stored in symbolic location A, the next is stored in B, and the last in C.

In order to simplify data handling, we shall insist that each number on the card be preceded by its symbolic location name (and an = sign). Each entry must be separated from the others by a comma and the last one must end with a semicolon. The order of the data on the card does not matter, since each value is named on the card.

EXAMPLE 11-17. Acceptable card input.

N1 = 153,   M = 206,   X = 17, Q – 15,   YNUM = 0;

EXAMPLE 11-18. If the card of Example 11-17 is read by

```
READ1          DTFCD   BLKSIZE = 80
                       DEVICE = 2501
               OPEN    READ1
               GET     READ1      N1,M,X,Q,YNUM
```

then we have in storage

$$N1 \quad \boxed{153}$$

$$M \quad \boxed{206}$$

$$X \quad \boxed{17}$$

$$Q \quad \boxed{-15}$$

$$YNUM \quad \boxed{0}$$

assuming that each of N1, M, X, Q, and YNUM is defined later in the program with a DS instruction.

Output Instructions

The sequence

```
Y              DTFPR   BLKSIZE = 132
                       DEVICE = 1403
               PUT     Y    A,B,C
               CLOSE   Y
```

causes the printing of the current values of *A*, *B*, and *C* on a printed page. The page is *132* characters wide and the printer is the *1403*.

The **DTFPR** macro instruction defines the output file. In this example it is the IBM-1403 printer, which prints 132 characters per line. The name (Y) which precedes the DTFPR is used elsewhere in the program when reference is made to the named device.

The **PUT** macro instruction indicates what values are to be printed by the device named Y. In this example the first number printed is the current (stored) value of A. The second is the current value of B. The last is the value of C.[13]

_____

[13] If the values of A, B, and C are 2, 7, and 0, the output would appear as
A = 2 B = 7 C = 0.

The **CLOSE** macro instruction is used to indicate the end of input/output operations. Here the device named Y is the one which is "closed."

Note. *All* input/output devices must be "opened" before using and "closed" before the program stops. Thus, a card reader must be closed as well as opened, and a printer must be opened as well as closed.

EXAMPLE 11-19. Write a program to read values for v_0, g, and t from cards, compute $v = v_0 - gt$, and print the result. Call the card reader (symbolically) READ. Call the printer WRITE.

	START	200
READ	DTFCD	BLKSIZE = 80
		DEVICE = 2501
WRITE	DTFPR	BLKSIZE = 132
		DEVICE = 1403
	BALR	13,0
	USING	*,13
	OPEN	READ,WRITE
	GET	READ VO,G.T
	L	5,G
	M	4,T
	L	8,VO
	SR	8,5
	ST	8,V
	PUT	WRITE V
	CLOSE	READ,WRITE
	EOJ	
G	DS	F
VO	DS	F
T	DS	F
V	DS	F
	END	

Note 1. Both the input and output files must be opened, and this can be done with *one* OPEN. Similarly, both files must be closed, and this can be done with *one* CLOSE.

Note 2. The DTFCD and DTFPR are placed together before any of the processing instructions. This is done because the "DTF's" are *referenced* by instructions which are executed (the OPEN, GET, PUT, and CLOSE), but are not themselves executed (in the usual sense).

In the next example we use two GET's and two PUT's to demonstrate how such a situation should be handled. A file needs only one description (DTF) and need only be opened and closed once!

EXAMPLE 11-20. Write a program to read values for a, b, and c from cards, compute and print $x_1 = (a + b)c$, then read values for p, r, and w, compute $x_2 = p + r - w$ and print x_2. Use symbolic file names INFILE for the card reader and OUTFILE for the printer.

```
          |  START   200
INFILE    |  DTFCD   BLKSIZE = 80
          |          DEVICE = 2501
OUTFILE   |  DTFPR   BLKSIZE = 132
          |          DEVICE = 1403
          |  BALR    13,0
          |  USING   *,13
          |  OPEN    INFILE,OUTFILE
          |  GET     INFILE    A,B,C
          |  L       7,A
          |  A       7,B
          |  M       6,C
          |  ST      7,X1
          |  PUT     OUTFILE    X1
          |  GET     INFILE    P,R,W
          |  L       9,P
          |  A       9,R
          |  S       9,W
          |  ST      9,X2
          |  PUT     OUTFILE    X2
          |  CLOSE   INFILE,OUTFILE
          |  EOJ
A         |  DS      F
B         |  DS      F
C         |  DS      F
X1        |  DS      F
P         |  DS      F
R         |  DS      F
W         |  DS      F
X2        |  DS      F
          |  END
```

EXERCISES 11.4

Write complete programs for exercises 1-5.

1. Read values for a, b, c, d. Compute $P = a + b + c + d$. Print a, b, c, d, P. Also, show a data card and printed output for a, b, c, d having values 5, 3, 7, 4, respectively.

*2. Read I and R. Compute $E = IR$ and $P = I^2 R$. Print I, R, E, P.

3. Read four numbers (say A, B, C, D). Compute $(A - B - C)D$ and print the result.

4. Read five numbers, form the sum of the first three and the product of the fourth and fifth. Print all seven numbers.

*5. Read values for a, b, c and compute $d = b^2 - 4ac$. Then read a value for x and compute $y = ax^2 + bx + c$. Print a, b, c, d, x, and y.

6. Find the errors in the program below. It is supposed to read values for a, b, c, d, and e, compute $f = (a + b)c + 5(d - e)$, and write f.

```
              START   200
       X      DTFCD   DEVICE = 1403
       Y      DTFPR   DEVICE = 2501
              OPEN    X,Y
              READ    X
              L       6,A
              A       6,B
              M       6,C
              L       8,D
              S       8,E
              A       8,6
              ST      8,F
              WRITE   Y
              EOJ
       A      DS      F
       B      DS      F
       C      DS      F
       D      DS      F
       E      DS      F
       X      DS      F
       Y      DS      F
```

LOOPS

We introduce this section with an example.

EXAMPLE 11-21.   Write a program which will read two numbers (values for x and y), form their sum, and print the result. However, write the program so that it will do the cycle of "read-compute-print" three times.

```
           START  200
RD         DTFCD  BLKSIZE = 80
                  DEVICE = 2501
WR         DTFPR  BLKSIZE = 132
                  DEVICE = 1403
           BALR   14,0
           USING  *,14
           OPEN   RD,WR
----------+------------------------------------------
           GET    RD    X,Y      read values for x and y
           L      10,X           x to R10
           A      10,Y           x + y to R10
           ST     10,SUM         x + y to SUM
           PUT    WR    SUM
----------+------------------------------------------
           GET    RD    X,Y      read 2nd set of x,y values
           L      10,X
           A      10,Y
           ST     10,SUM
           PUT    WR    SUM
----------+------------------------------------------
           GET    RD    X,Y      read 3rd set of x,y values
           L      10,X
           A      10,Y
           ST     10,SUM
           PUT    WR    SUM
----------+------------------------------------------
           CLOSE  RD,WR
           EOJ
X          DS     F
Y          DS     F
SUM        DS     F
           END
```

The dashed lines emphasize that much of the coding is merely repetition. If the problem had indicated *50* cycles of the same instructions, the code would be a ridiculous repetition and wasteful of storage. To avoid the waste and repetition we use a very important and powerful tool of programming--the *loop*.

If we want to write a program to do the processing of the above example, but do it *50* times rather than three times, then we want the simplest code which can be written to agree with the flow chart of Fig. 11-6.

In order to write the desired code we use two new instructions.

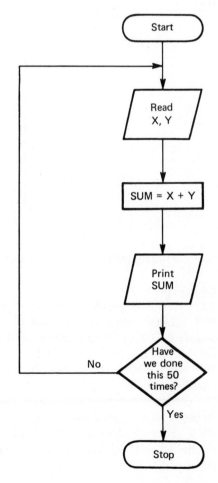

FIGURE 11-6. Flow Chart for 50 Cycles of Read-Compute-Print.

LA 5,50 (Load Address)

The actual number *50* is placed in *R5*. Any register can be used, and any constant can be placed in that register.

BCT 5,LOOP (Branch on Count)

Decrease the contents of *R5* by 1. If the contents of R5 (after decreasing) are not 0, transfer is made to the instruction labeled *LOOP*. Otherwise, the next instruction in sequence is taken.

EXAMPLE 11-22. The code

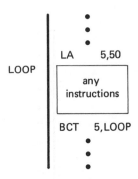

causes all instructions in the box to be executed 50 times. This is the case since

1. LA 5,50 places a 50 in R5
2. All of the instructions in the box are then executed.
3. BCT 5,LOOP causes the contents of R5 (set at 50 by LA 5,50) to be decreased by 1, to 49. Since this is not 0, transfer is made back to LOOP.
4. Now all the instructions in the box are executed a second time.
5. The BCT 5,LOOP is executed again, leaving 48 in R5. This is still not 0, so transfer is again made to LOOP.
6. The process is continued until the instructions in the box have been executed 50 times. At that point the execution of the BCT decreases the contents of R5 by 1 for the 50th time. In other words, c(R5) = 0. So control is *not* transferred to LOOP. Instead the next sequential instruction *after* the BCT is executed.[14]

[14]Use of the name LOOP was arbitrary. Any name can be used. R5 was also an arbitrary choice. Any register can be used.

EXAMPLE 11-23. The program to carry out the procedure of Example 11-21 50 times might be coded as

```
            | START  200
RD          | DTFCD  BLKSIZE = 80
            |        DEVICE = 2501
WR          | DTFPR  BLKSIZE = 132
            |        DEVICE = 1403
            | BALR   14,0
            | USING  *,14
            | OPEN   RD,WR
- - - - - - - | - - - - - - - - - - - - - - - - - - - - - - - - - - - -
            |
            | LA     7,50        put 50 into R7
LOOP        | GET    RD    X,Y
            | L      10,X
            | A      10,Y
            | ST     10,SUM
            | PUT    WR    SUM
            | BCT    7,LOOP
- - - - - - - | - - - - - - - - - - - - - - - - - - - - - - - - - - - -
            | CLOSE  RD,WR
            | EOJ
X           | DS     F
Y           | DS     F
SUM         | DS     F
            | END
```

The corresponding flow chart is shown in Fig. 11-7.

EXERCISES 11.5

Draw flow charts and write programs for each of exercises 1-11. Input data is assumed to be on one card unless otherwise stated or implied.

1. Do the following 100 times: Read five numbers, compute their sum, and print the result.

*2. Do the following 75 times: Read v_0, and g, compute $v = v_0 - gt$, and print v_0, g, t, and v.

3. Same as exercise 2, except first read a value for n. This value of n will determine the number of times that the read-compute-print cycle should then be carried out.

4. Do the following 250 times: Read values for hourly WAGE and

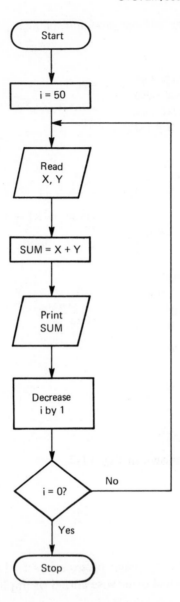

FIGURE 11-7. Flow Chart for Example 11-23.

HOURS worked, compute PAY = WAGE · HOURS, and print WAGE, HOURS, and PAY.

*5. Same as exercise 4, except first read a value for NUMBER. This NUMBER will determine the number of times that the read-compute-print cycle should then be carried out.

*6. Read a value for x and compute $y = x^7$. Print x and y. Use a loop.

7. Read values of n and x. Compute and print $y = x^n$.

8. Read a value for x, compute $y = x^{100} + 5$, and print x and y.

9. Read a value for CARDS. This number (CARDS) will determine how many *pairs* of additional cards must be read. Each such pair has a balance DUE on the first card and an amount RECEIVED on the second. For each pair compute the balance due, DUE – RECEIVED, and print values of DUE, RECEIVED, and balance due.

10. Read values for a, b, c. Then compute and print $y = ax^2 + bx + c$ for $x = 1$, $x = 2$, and $x = 3$.

*11. Read values of m and b. Print m and b. Then compute $y = mx + b$ for $x = 1, 2, 3, 4, 5, 6, 7, 8, 9, 10$. Print x and y after each computation. Be sure to use the same m and b for all x-values.

12. What is the difference between the LA and L instructions?

13. Can exercise 1 be done without the LA instruction? In other words, is there another way of getting the number 100 into a general purpose register? Explain.

SHIFTING

There are instructions which can be used to shift the contents of a general register left or right a specified number of bit positions. Before introducing the instructions let us see just what this means.

EXAMPLE 11-24. Illustrate what happens if R5 (below) is shifted left two positions.

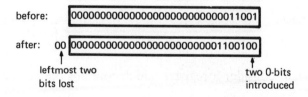

The result is that the leftmost two bits are shifted out of the register and lost. Introduced on the right are two 0-bits.

EXAMPLE 11-25. Suppose we shift R5 of the previous example right three positions.

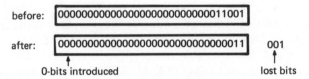

Again, the bits shifted out of the register are lost. The process is the same regardless of the original contents of the register: any bits shifted out of the register are lost, and 0-bits are introduced at the other end. And any register may be shifted.[15]

Consider a register which contains the binary equivalent of $(16)_{10}$.

$$00000000000000000000000000010000$$

If the register is shifted *right* one position we have

$$00000000000000000000000000001000$$

which is $(8)_{10}$.

If the register is shifted right one more position we have

$$00000000000000000000000000000100$$

which is $(4)_{10}$.

We might conclude that *a right shift of one position is equivalent to division by 2 (or multiplication by ½).*

The statement is true as long as the original number is *even*. If the number is odd the shifted result represents the *integer* portion of half the number. In other words, the fractional part is lost (truncated).

EXAMPLE 11-26. Suppose R8 contains $(5)_{10}$ and is shifted right one position.

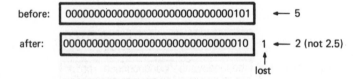

Let us again consider a register which contains the binary equivalent of $(16)_{10}$.

$$00000000000000000000000000010000$$

---

[15] We shall assume that all numbers are positive and are small compared to the register's capacity.

If the register is shifted *left* one position we have

```
000000000000000000000000000100000
```

which is $(32)_{10}$.

We conclude that a *left shift of one position is equivalent to multiplication by 2*. And this is true whether the original number is even or odd.[16]

We now introduce the instructions used to shift registers.

SRL 9,1 (Shift Right)

Shift the contents of R9 *right* one bit position. In general, any register may be used, and it may be shifted any number of positions.

EXAMPLE 11-27. Show a partial program to compute $c = \frac{1}{2}(a + b)$ and $y = \frac{1}{4}x$.

```
        .
        .
        .

    L       12,A
    A       12,B              ⎧ right shift of one
    SRL     12,1              ⎨ is the same as
    ST      12,C              ⎩ multiplication by ½
        .
        .
        .

    L       10,X              ⎧ right shift of two
    SRL     10,2              ⎪ is the same as
    ST      10,Y              ⎨ multiplication by ¼
        .                     ⎩ since  ½ · ½ = ¼
        .
        .
```

There is no reason to use DCs to define ½ and ¼, since these *numbers* were not used. We merely shifted the contents of registers.

SLL 6,1 (Shift Left)

Shift the contents of R6 *left* one bit position. In general, any register may be used, and it may be shifted any number of positions.

[16]See exercise 7.

EXAMPLE 11-28. Show a partial program to compute c = 2a − 8b.

		•
		•
		•
L	5,A	
SLL	5,1	multiply by 2
L	6,B	
SLL	6,3	multiply by 8 = 2 • 2 • 2
SR	5,6	
ST	5,C	
		•
		•
		•

EXERCISES 11.6

Write complete programs for each of exercises 1-6 below.

*1. Read m, v. Compute $E = \frac{1}{2}mv^2$. Print m, v, E.

2. Read b_1, b_2, h. Compute $A = \frac{1}{2}h(b_1 + b_2)$. Print b_1, b_2, h, A.

3. Read a, l, n. Compute $S = \frac{n}{2}(a + 1)$. Print a, l, n, S.

*4. Read a, b, c. Compute $x = 2a + 4b − 8c$. Print a, b, c, x.

5. Do the following 100 times: Read v_0, g, and t, compute $s = v_0 t − \frac{1}{2}gt^2$, and print v_0 g, t, and s.

6. Read x. Compute $y = x^{15}/8$. Print x and y.

7. Show, using bits, that shifting an odd number (use 9) *left* one position will multiply it by 2 *exactly*. Show that a *right* shift of one position produces 4, not 4.5.

8. Could we have coded Example 11-28 without using the SLL instruction? Explain.

*9. Suppose R5 contains the binary equivalent of $(31)_{10}$. If SRL 5,4 and SLL 5,3 are executed, what is the final contents (in base 10) of R5?

OTHER BRANCHING

You may recall that one portion of the *program status word* (PSW) is used to specify the location of the next instruction to be executed. Another portion is used to indicate a *condition code*. Such condition codes are set in the PSW by execution of certain instructions (such as A, S, AR, SR) and can be tested by using a "branch on condition" instruction. The codes, as used by the programmer:

binary	decimal for use	condition
1000	8	zero
0100	4	negative
0010	2	positive
0001	1	overflow[17]

BC 8, NAME (Branch on Condition)

If the condition specified by the PSW is zero, transfer to NAME for the next instruction. Otherwise take the next instruction in sequence. Note that 8 is not a register number. The 8 is the programmer's code for a zero, as listed above.

EXAMPLE 11-29   BC 2, YBIG

If the condition is positive transfer to YBIG. Otherwise proceed in normal sequence.

We can use the BC instruction for conditional branching within a program.

EXAMPLE 11-30.   Write a program which reads A and B and computes SUM = A + B. If SUM is negative, also compute PROD = A · B; otherwise just stop. Be sure to write the result(s) in either case.

```
                |START   200
        READ    |DTFCD   BLKSIZE = 80
                |        DEVICE = 2501
        WRITE   |DTFPR   BLKSIZE = 132
                |        DEVICE = 1403
                |BALR    14,0
                |USING   *,14
                |OPEN    READ,WRITE
```

---

[17]Overflow will be explained later in this section.

```
              GET     READ     A,B
              L       8,A
              A       8,B
              ST      8,SUM
              BC      4,MULTAB              branch if result is negative
              PUT     WRITE    SUM
              CLOSE   READ,WRITE
              EOJ
MULTAB        L       7,A                   begin computation of PROD = A • B
              M       6,B
              ST      7,PROD
              PUT     WRITE    SUM,PROD
              CLOSE   READ,WRITE
              EOJ
A             DS      F
B             DS      F
SUM           DS      F
PROD          DS      F
              END
```

Note how the branching is handled, and that the "PUT, CLOSE, EOJ" combination appears in each branch. However, only one branch is taken for a given set of data; thus only one such combination is actually executed per program run. Putting an instruction in a program does not mean that it will be executed each time the program is run.

In the example above, a branch was made if the result of an addition was negative. Suppose instead that a branch was desired if the result were either positive or zero. This is the opposite of the condition in the example, but might be used in another program to save an instruction or fit better with the logic. The condition codes

0010 for greater than zero

and   1000 for equal to zero

can be combined (added) as 1010, greater than or equal to zero.

The instructions would be

```
    BC     10, _____   (branch on greater than or equal to zero; 2 + 8 = 10).
```

Other such combinations of condition codes are permitted; for example,

```
    BC     12, _____   (branch on less than or equal to zero; 4 + 8 = 12)
    BC      6, _____   (branch on greater than or less than zero; 2 + 4 = 6).
```

Overflow

Although the general registers can hold very large fixed-point numbers, it is possible to perform an addition or subtraction which will produce a number containing more bits than one register can hold. Such a condition is called *overflow*. When overflow occurs the leftmost bit is lost and the condition code 1 is set. Testing for overflow (BC 1,___) causes transfer to a named part of the program, if overflow has occurred.

It is often desirable to transfer unconditionally to another part of a program; that is, transfer regardless of the results of any operation. An instruction for such an unconditional transfer exists.

BC 15, COMP6 (Branch Unconditionally)

Branch unconditionally to the instruction labeled COMP6 for execution next. Condition *15* is the combination $(8 + 4 + 2 + 1)$ of conditions 8 (zero), 4 (negative), 2 (positive), and 1 (overflow). Thus, BC 15,___ is a branch on *any* condition; that is, an unconditional branch.

EXERCISES 11.7

Flowchart and code exercises 1-5.

*1. Read q. If q is negative compute $p = q^2$; otherwise $p = q + 5$. Write q and p.

2. Read a and b. Compute $w = 10a + \frac{1}{4}b$. Also, if $w = 0$ compute $z = 7ab$. Write all results.

*3. Read x. If x is greater than 10, compute $y = x^2$; otherwise $y = 9x$. Write x and y.

4. Do 25 times: Read R, compute $Q = R^2 + 15$, and write R and Q. *Use BC rather than BCT.*

5. Read r and s. Determine which is larger and write it.

6. Explain in words what each does:

(a) BC 6,X   (c) BC 12,COMPUTE   (e) BC 14,LOOP2
(b) BC 15,A   (d) BC 10,Q

ASSEMBLER LANGUAGES

The programming language studied in this chapter is an *assembler language*. Each instruction is written in a symbolic code which has mnemonic value to the programmer. For example, the operation code for a branch on condition is BC. Also, if the data used are values for *x*, *y*, and *z* they can be so named (X, Y, Z) in the code.

But the 360 computer works only with binary code, so the symbolic instructions which are presented to the computer must be translated into binary before the program can be executed. It is the *assembler program* which performs the translation of each instruction into its binary equivalent. Such an assembler is written using binary instructions. (Actually it is written in hexadecimal, which is easily converted to binary).

If the program is punched on cards, the assembly process may be pictured as

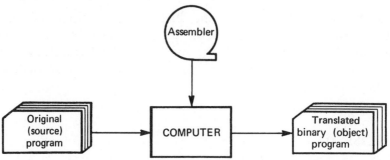

The original (*source*) program deck is returned in addition to an executable binary (*object*) form.[18] An additional product of assembly is a *listing* of the program instructions as written, and next to them is their hexadecimal equivalent and the actual storage locations (in hex) used to hold the translated form (see next page).

Figure 11-8 shows an assembled listing of a program containing errors. The assembler can indicate many errors in coding via *diagnostic messages*. Needless to say, these diagnostics are useful for debugging. For example, the first diagnostic message indicates an "incorrect register specification" in the statement numbered (by the assembler) 9. You should see the error immediately: An odd register is used with the (M) multiply. The second diagnostic indicates an "undefined symbol" in statement 10. This is because location X has not been defined (by a DS).

---

[18] An object program can be returned on cards, magnetic tape, disk, or drum.

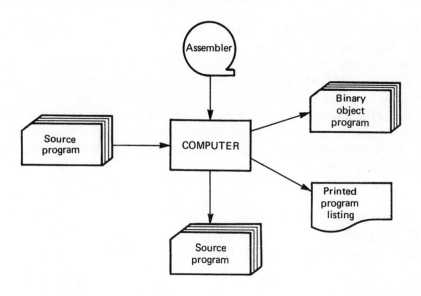

```
              PROGRAM WITH ERRORS

    LOC    OBJECT CODE     ADDR1 ADDR2   STMT      SOURCE STATEMENT

0000C8                                     4              START  200
0000C8  05D0                                5              BALR   13,0
0000CA                                      6              USING  *,13
0000CA  5850 D012            000DC          7              L      5,A
0000CE  5A50 D016            000E0          8              A      5,B
0000D2  0000 0000            00000          9              M      5,C
           *** ERROR ***
0000D6  0000 0000            00000         10              ST     5,X
           *** ERROR ***
                                           11              EOJ
0000DC  00000005                           14  A           DC     F'5'
0000E0  00000002                           15  B           DC     F'2'
0000E4  00000003                           16  C           DC     F'3'
                                           17              END
                                                    CROSS-REFERENCE

SYMBOL      LEN    VALUE   DEFN

A          00004  0000DC  00014     0007
B          00004  0000E0  00015     0008
C          00004  0000E4  00016     0009
X                                   0010
                                                     DIAGNOSTICS

STMT   ERROR CODE     MESSAGE

   9   IJQ010         INCORRECT REGISTER SPECIFICATION
  10   IJQ024         UNDEFINED SYMBOL

  2 STATEMENTS FLAGGED IN THIS ASSEMBLY
```

FIGURE 11-8. Listing of Program with Errors.

Figure 11-9 shows an assembled listing of a program which has no errors caught by the assembler.

The assembly process is quite complicated, and a full explanation is beyond the scope of this book. As a final note, however, the reader should realize that the binary translation produced by the assembler is not simply a translation of each letter and digit to its binary equivalent using straight binary and EBCDIC codes. Operation codes, for example, have binary equivalents which the assembler assigns by looking them up in a table of codes.

```
                    PROGRAM WITHOUT ERRORS


        LOC   OBJECT CODE    ADDR1 ADDR2  STMT    SOURCE STATEMENT

     0000C8                                 4           START 200
     0000C8  05D0                           5           BALR  13,0
     0000CA                                 6           USING *,13
     0000CA  5850  D012      000DC          7           L     5,A
     0000CE  5A50  D016      000E0          8           A     5,B
     0000D2  5C40  D01A      000E4          9           M     4,C
     0000D6  5050  D01E      000E8         10           ST    5,X
                                           11           EOJ
     0000DC  00000005                      14  A        DC    F'5'
     0000E0  00000002                      15  B        DC    F'2'
     0000E4  00000003                      16  C        DC    F'3'
     0000E8                                17  X        DS    F
                                           18           END



                                              CROSS-REFERENCE


     SYMBOL     LEN   VALUE   DEFN

     A          00004 0000DC  00014     0007
     B          00004 0000E0  00015     0008
     C          00004 0000E4  00016     0009
     X          00004 0000E8  00017     0010



     NO STATEMENTS FLAGGED IN THIS ASSEMBLY
```

FIGURE 11-9. Listing of Program without Errors.

CONCLUSION

The IBM System/360 has considerably more capability than has been implied so far in this chapter. We end by giving, without explanation, a list of some additional operations which are available with System/360 assembler language.

1. logical operations: AND, OR, and others
2. conversions: binary to decimal, decimal to binary
3. movements in storage: characters, numerics, zones
4. editing operations
5. additional input/output methods
6. floating-point arithmetic and additional fixed-point arithmetic
7. additional branches
8. packing, unpacking, and masking
9. character processing operations

12

FORTRAN
PROGRAMMING

FORTRAN is a *FOR*mula *TRAN*slating compiler language. It is used primarily for scientific programming because it resembles algebra. However, a number of commercial data processing problems are adaptable to FORTRAN, so it is used occasionally for commercial programming.

CONSTANTS

In algebra we call numbers such as +4, -6.72, 0, 4.0164, .066, and -37 *constants*. What we mean is that each has an explicit value which cannot change.

In FORTRAN such numbers are also called constants. They are separated into two types or *modes:* fixed-point and floating-point.

Fixed-point (or *integer*) constants are whole numbers which contain no decimal point. Such numbers as +62, -22000, 739, and 0 are fixed-point (or integer) constants. Plus signs are optional and commas are never allowed in such numbers.[1]

---

[1] There are limits to the size of fixed-point constants. We shall insist that integers be between -2147483647 and 2147483647, which is the maximum possible size using four bytes (or one fullword).

Floating-point (or *real*) constants are numbers which contain a decimal point. Examples include -29.6278, $1.$, $.9999999$, and -2.0. As with fixed-point constants, plus signs are optional and commas are not used.[2]

Fixed-point numbers and floating-point numbers have completely different binary representations in storage (see Chapter 11).

VARIABLES

In algebra we often use letters to represent numbers. This is generally done either because we don't know the value of the unknown we seek, or because the letter is a *variable* which may take on different values. For example, in $y = 3x + 5$, x and y are variables (and, of course, 3 and 5 are constants).

In FORTRAN we use variables for the same reasons we do in algebra. However, a FORTRAN variable can only have values of one mode; that is, *all* values of a particular variable must be fixed-point *or else* all values must be floating-point. The same variable cannot take on both fixed-point and floating-point values. For example, if a variable can have the values 51 and -3, etc. it cannot have as values such numbers as 14.3, -3.6, 5.79, etc., which are floating-point numbers.

There are rules for forming the names which we give to variables.

1. All variable names have *six or fewer* characters. The *first must be a letter.* The other five (or fewer) can be any combination of letters or digits or both. No characters other than letters or digits may be used.[3] Thus, such names as ABC, Q12345, X, I6QR, and AEIOUY are acceptable as variable names. However, such names as 5ABC (does not begin with a letter), Q1234A3 (more than six characters), and NUM+3 (contains a character which is neither a letter nor a digit) are illegal as FORTRAN variable names.

2. Names of variables which take on only *fixed-point* values *begin* with one of the letters I, J, K, L, M, N. (We shall denote this as [I,N] in the future.)

3. *Floating-point* variable names *begin* with any other letter; that is A through H or O through Z.

----

[2] Restrict their size to seven digits plus a decimal point.

[3] Actually, the symbol "$" is acceptable as a letter.

I6, K, M35R, and LABCDE are valid fixed-point variable names; A, B9, RSTUI5, Z5IJKL, and Q are valid names for floating-point variables.

It should be emphasized that the only restriction on names for fixed- and floating-point variables is on the *first* letter. The others don't affect the mode of the variable.

EXPRESSIONS

In algebra, an *expression* is a combination of constants and/or variables. They are combined using addition, subtraction, multiplication, division, and exponentiation. Thus 3, x, $x - 2$, $5y^2 + 2x$, $A + B$, and $x/y + 1$ are algebraic expressions.

In FORTRAN, the only difference is in some of the symbols used to indicate the arithmetic operations.[4]

The symbols are:

+   addition

-   subtraction

*   multiplication

/   division

**   exponentiation

Observe the use of these symbols in translating algebraic expressions into equivalent FORTRAN expressions.

Algebra	FORTRAN
$\dfrac{x}{y}$	X/Y
$7j$	7*J
$14 + n$	14 + N
a^3	A**3
$w + x - z$	W + X - Z

[4] And, of course, the programmer must code with capital letters.

Rule 1. Two operation symbols cannot appear next to each other.

EXAMPLE 12-1. X/-Y is not a valid expression.

Rule 2. Parentheses are used to indicate grouping as in algebra.

EXAMPLE 12-2. The expression in Example 12-1 can be correctly written as X/(-Y).

EXAMPLE 12-3. $(a + b)^2$ is written (A + B)**2. If you write A + B**2 you are representing $a + b^2$ rather than $(a + b)^2$. See Rule 3, below.

Rule 3. When parentheses do not completely specify the order of operations in an expression, then all exponentiations are performed first. Second, all multiplications and divisions are performed in the order they occur, from left to right. Last, all additions and subtractions are performed from left to right.

EXAMPLE 12-4

A + B * C	The algebraic interpretation is $a + bc$, since multiplication is performed before addition when no parentheses are used to indicate otherwise.
(A + B) * C	Here parentheses indicate that the addition is performed before the multiplication. The algebra is $(a + b)c$.
X/Y * Z	The result is $\frac{x}{y} \cdot z$ or $\frac{xz}{y}$, since the equal level operations are performed from left to right in the order they appear. Recall that Rule 3 specifies that multiplication and division are operations of the same level.
X/ (Y*Z)	The result is $\frac{x}{yz}$, since parentheses are used.
A − B + C	The result is $(a - b) + c$.
A − (B + C)	The result is $a - (b + c)$.

Rule 4. Fixed-point quantities (constants or variables) and floating-point quantities won't be used in the same expression (one exception: a floating-point base might have a fixed-point exponent).[5]

---

[5] Second generation FORTRAN IV does not allow any mixing of modes, except as indicated above. Third generation versions of FORTRAN IV permit mixing of modes at will. However, whenever fixed-point quantities and floating-point quantities are mixed in the same expression the result is floating-point.

EXAMPLE 12-5. X + Y + 4 involves both floating-point (X,Y) and fixed-point (4). To avoid mixing modes write this as X + Y + 4.0.

(I + J) + 5 * SUM mixes I, J, and 5 (all fixed-point) with SUM (floating-point). To avoid mixing modes we might use ISUM instead of SUM. Thus, we would have (I + J) + 5 * ISUM.

FUNCTIONS

In evaluating formulas it is often desirable to be able to determine the square root of a number. This, of course, is a fairly long series of arithmetic operations. However, FORTRAN contains a "function" for determining the square root of any *floating-point* number. The form is

$$\text{SQRT (floating-point expression)}$$

and the result is a floating-point number.

EXAMPLE 12-6

Algebra	FORTRAN
$\sqrt{x}$	SQRT(X)
$9\sqrt{5-q}$	9.0*SQRT(5. - Q)

Similarly we can use ABS( ) to obtain the absolute value of a floating-point expression. There are also functions to handle logarithms, trigonometric functions, and others.

EXERCISES 12.1

*1. Determine which are acceptable as constants, variables, or expressions, and which are unacceptable. Indicate the mode (fixed or floating) of each.

(a)	A	(b)	5J
(c)	(X + Y)(D + W)	(d)	2.3*ALPHA
(e)	DAY-OF-THE-WEEK	(f)	IOTA*BETA
(g)	98*ABC + 5.	(h)	EPSILON
(i)	W - X/Y - Z	(j)	2.99863*ABS(I + 2)
(k)	X**4 + 3.89	(l)	KAPPA*18
(m)	(A - B)	(n)	70 - SQRT(R - USUMX)
(o)	5*(A + B + C + D + E)	(p)	X**2.5

2. Write a FORTRAN expression for each algebraic expression.

*(a) $\dfrac{a+b}{c-d}$ (b) $x+y^2$

(c) $ab^x c$ (d) $27+5\,|\,3-ax\,|$

(e) πr^2 (f) $\left(\dfrac{a}{b}\right)^{k+1}$

(g) $17.2r+ct$ *(h) $a^{m+1}g$

*(i) $\left(\dfrac{x}{p+q}\right)^{x+1}$ (j) $(x+y)^2$

(k) $w+\dfrac{x}{y}+z$ (l) $\sqrt{\dfrac{c+d}{x}}$

(m) x^n (n) $10(x-y)$

                               *(o) $7(\alpha+\beta)$

STATEMENTS

A FORTRAN program is a list of statements. With this in mind, and with our knowledge of constants, variables, expressions, and functions, we begin a study of FORTRAN statements.

Arithmetic Statements

Arithmetic statements are used to perform computations. The general form is

$$\boxed{\text{VARIABLE = EXPRESSION}}$$

That is, there are three "parts" to the statement:

1. an equal sign: =
2. a *variable* to the left of the equal sign
3. an *expression* to the right of the equal sign.

The arithmetic statement is *not* an equation. It is instead a direction to the computer to *replace* the variable which appears on the left by the computed value of the expression on the right.

EXAMPLE 12-7

   I = 2

This statement can be understood as any of the following:
1. I takes on the value 2.
2. 2 replaces the previous value of I, so that I has the value 2 for future use and reference.
3. The value of I is replaced by 2.

EXAMPLE 12-8

   ISUM = I + J

The previous value of ISUM is replaced by the sum of the current values of I and J. Suppose, for instance, that we execute the statements

     I = 2
     J = 3

and *then* the statement

     ISUM = I + J

Then ISUM is replaced by the süm of 2 and 3. Hence, the previous value of ISUM is replaced by 5.

EXAMPLE 12-9

   I = I + 1

Execution of this statement increases the value of I by 1. That is, 1 is added to the current value of I and this new sum (I + 1) replaces the previous value of I (note that such an equation is nonsense in algebra, although it is a valid statement in FORTRAN).

EXAMPLE 12-10. The formula $y = ax + b$ is written in FORTRAN as Y = A * X + B. The value of Y becomes whatever results when A * X + B is computed from supplied values of A, X, and B. Thus

     A = 3.0
     B = 4.0
     X = 1.5
     Y = A * X + B

produces a value of 8.5 for Y.

Although we will not mix modes within the same expression, we might have different modes on opposite sides of the equal sign of an arithmetic expression. Thus, the statement Y = 7*I-K is acceptable in any version of FORTRAN. The expression on the right will be computed in fixed point since it is a fixed-point expression. But this computed fixed-point number is supposed to replace the previous value of Y, a floating-point variable. Y can only take on floating-point values, since it is a floating-point variable, so the computed fixed-point number is changed to floating-point before being stored as the value of Y. In terms of FORTRAN we say that a decimal point is added to the number (after the last digit), and Y is replaced by the newly formed floating-point whole number.

EXAMPLE 12-11

      I = 6
      K = 4
      Y = 7 * I + K

The right-hand side of Y = 7 * I + K is computed as 7 * 6 + 4 or 46, a decimal point is added, and 46.0 replaces the previous value of Y.

EXAMPLE 12-12. *What results from execution of I = 2.0 * X + 4.73?* Suppose that the value of X supplied at the time of execution is 5.12. Then the right-hand side has the value 14.97. However, the variable on the left is fixed point, so no decimal point (or digits after such a point) can appear. Thus, I is replaced by the value 14, with the decimal point and all digits after it dropped completely, *not rounded off.*

This process of dropping the decimal point and all digits after it is called *truncation.* Note that truncation will occur in computations like 7/2, since fixed-point computations leave fixed-point results. Thus 7/2 = 3 and 3.5.

EXAMPLE 12-13. The result of

      I = 2
      J = 3
      IDIV = I/J

is that IDIV will be replaced with 0, a fixed-point zero.

EXAMPLE 12-14. The result of

$$I = 2$$
$$J = 3$$
$$X = I/J$$

is 0. and *not* 0 or .6666666. The right side is fixed-point and is computed as such (thus producing a 0). The decimal point is "inserted" only before storage as a value for the floating-point variable X.

EXAMPLE 12-15. 1./3. * 3. gives (.3333333) * (3.) or .9999999, which is *not exactly* 1.0 (but usually close enough); whereas 1. * 3./3. gives 3./3. = 1.000000, which is exact!

It is important to be aware of this nature of FORTRAN (as pointed out in the examples above), and to program accordingly, so that misleading results are not produced.

EXERCISES 12.2

1. Write FORTRAN statements for each.

(a) $P = 2l + 2w$

(b) $A = \pi r^2$

(c) $V = \frac{4}{3}\pi r^2$

(d) $C = 2\pi r$

(e) $i = prt$

(f) $V = e^3$

(g) $F = \frac{m_1 m_2}{d^2}$

*(h) $s = \frac{1}{2}gt^2 + v_0 t$

*(i) $d_r = \sqrt{b^2 - 4ac}$

*(j) $a_0 = |x_1 - x_2|$

(k) $R = \frac{1}{R_1} + \frac{1}{R_2}$

(l) $y = ax^2 + bx + c$

(m) $s = \frac{1}{2}(a + b + c)$

*(n) $A = \sqrt{s(s-a)(s-b)(s-c)}$

(o) $T = 2\pi \sqrt{\frac{1}{g}}$

(p) $F = ma$

(q) $Z = \sqrt{R^2 + (X_L - X_C)^2}$

(r) $\omega = \frac{\theta}{t}$

*2. Write FORTRAN statements to indicate the following.

    (a) Increase n by 1.
    (b) Decrease i by 2.
    (c) Replace y by x.
    (d) Set j equal to 0.
    (e) Double x.

*3. For each computation indicate the value stored in the symbolic location I or X. Be sure to include a decimal point if the stored value is floating point.

    (a) $I = 1 + 2 + 3$ (b) $X = 1 + 2 + 3$
    (c) $I = 1 + 2*3$ (d) $X = 20.0/4.0*5.0$
    (e) $X = 9/10$ (f) $I = 9/10$
    (g) $X = 5*1/5$ (h) $I = (1/5)*5$
    (i) $I = 7.0/2.0 + 2.1$ (j) $X = 7.0/2.0 + 2.1$
    (k) $X = 1./3. + 1./3. + 1./3.$ (l) $I = 1./3. + 1./3. + 1./3.$
    (m) $X = 2*(1/2)$ (n) $I = 4 + 2/1 + 5$

INPUT/OUTPUT

There are several devices which can be used to handle input and several which can be used for output. For simplicity all programs and data shall be assumed to be originally on punched cards. This information is then put (off-line) onto magnetic tape or some other magnetic I/O device before it is read (on-line) by the computer. Similarly, output is first placed (on-line) on a magnetic I/O device before being printed (off-line).

Input

To read data into storage we use a **READ** statement. The data we read are values for specified fixed- or floating-point variables (or both). A READ statement indicates three things:

1. the number of the unit being used for input
2. the names of the variables for which values will be read
3. the format of each variable; that is, the number of card columns that each number occupies.

EXAMPLE 12-16. An example of a READ statement is

READ (5,100) MNT, NUM

where
1. the input data is on unit 5
2. the data being read are values for the variables MNT and NUM
3. the "100" indicates the number of a *FORMAT statement.* The FORMAT statement is used to indicate the mode (fixed or floating) and size (number of columns) of each variable.[6]

EXAMPLE 12-17. One FORMAT statement which could be used with the statement READ (5,100) MNT, NUM is

100 FORMAT(I5,I3)

where
1. The statement number 100 indicates that this FORMAT statement is associated with the READ which specifies "100."
2. The I5 indicates that any value read for the variable MNT must be fixed point or *in*teger (hence the I) and must be punched in the *first five* columns of the data card.
3. Similarly, the I3 indicates that any value of NUM shall be fixed point and in the *next 3* columns of the card.

When the READ and FORMAT statements of the previous examples are written together we have

READ(5,100)MNT, NUM
100 FORMAT(I5,I3)

Note again that the number (100) in the READ statement and (100) of the FORMAT statement agree. They can be any whole numbers, but they must be the *same.*

I5 is called the *format* of the variable MNT; the format of NUM is I3. The first format specified in the FORMAT statement corresponds to the first variable in the READ statement, and so on.

---

[6] A number which refers to or precedes a statement is called a *statement number.* In these examples, 100 is a statement number.

EXAMPLE 12-18.   Figure 12-1 shows a data card that could be read using

$$\text{READ(5,62)NUM1,NUM2,IJK}$$
$$\text{62 FORMAT(I4,I3,I4)}$$

The numbers on the card are 2000, 537, and 8712.

Although the data card in Fig. 12-1 is correct, it is not as easy to read as is the card in Fig. 12-2. But this new card will not work correctly with the given FORMAT statement, since the first number must appear in columns 1-4 (I4), the next in columns 5-7 (I3), and the last number in columns 8-11 (I4).

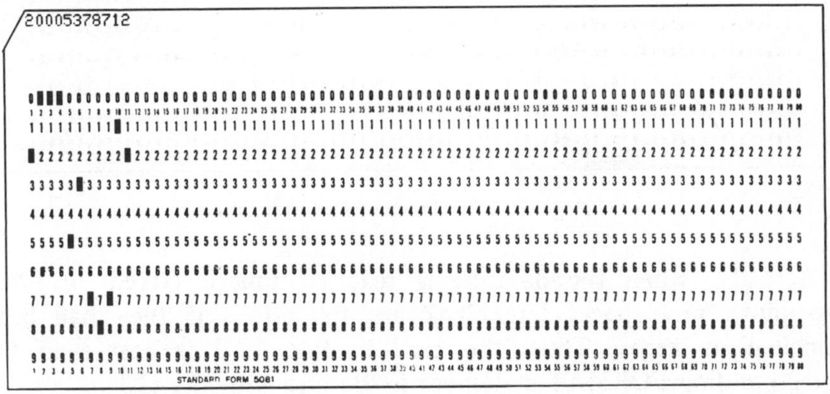

FIGURE 12-1. A Data Card for Example 12-18.

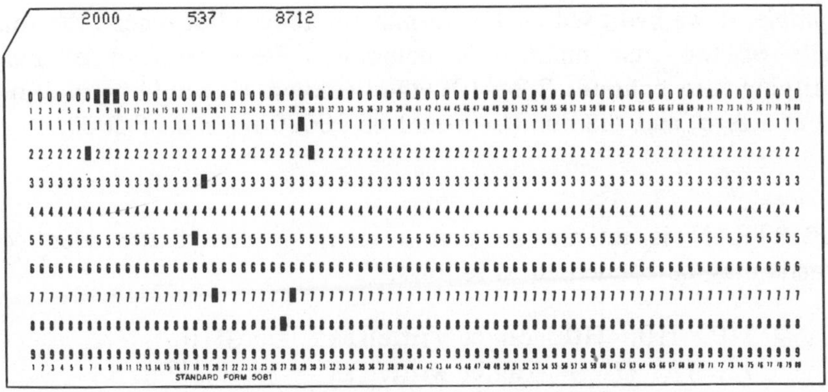

FIGURE 12-2. An Easier Card to Read.

We could put zeros before each number to fill in the blank spaces, and then change the formats to I10. The FORMAT statement would be

62 FORMAT(I10,I10,I10),

and the card seems easier to read than the original, anyhow (see Fig. 12-3).

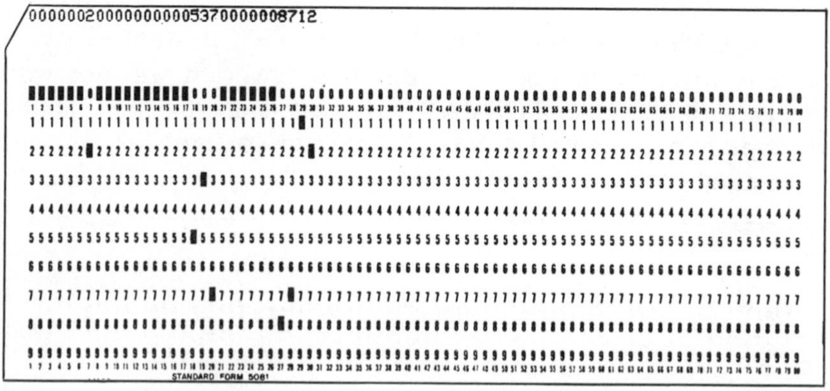

FIGURE 12-3. A "Compromise" Data Card.

Actually, when the data being read is numeric (fixed- or floating-point), any spaces left blank are treated as if they had been punched as zeros. Thus, the card in Fig. 12-2 is best (and the corresponding FORMAT statement is the one with the I10's).

All fixed-point numbers must be right justified on data cards. That is, all blanks must come before the actual digits of the number—no blanks should be left after the number *in its allotted space*. For example, if we had used an I10 format (as above) but placed the four digits of the first number in columns 6-7-8-9 (instead of right justifying into columns 7-8-9-10), then column 10 would be interpreted as a zero, and the number would be 20000 instead of 2000.

FORTRAN is set up so that a series of *consecutive* identical formats may be condensed as follows:

I10, I10, I10	can be written as	3I10
I2, I7, I7	can be written as	I2,2I7
I7, I2, I7	cannot be simplified.	

So far we have indicated only fixed-point numbers in our READ and FORMAT statements. When *f*loating-point values are read we use an *F*-format. The form is

　　　Fc.d

where

　　　c is the number of card columns used for the number, including the decimal point and sign, if any;

　　　d is the number of digits *after* the decimal point.

EXAMPLE 12-19. If the number -27.36 appeared in six columns of a card (the $-$ and . each take up one column since each is a character), the format would be F6.2; that is, six card columns including two digits after the decimal point. If this same number were in 10 columns we would use F10.2.

Floating-point data is better right justified on the card, although it is not necessary to do this since any blanks (zeros) resulting from failure to right justify appear *after* the decimal point and therefore do not change the value of the number. For example, 92.6 and 92.600 have the same value.

We can mix fixed- and floating-point data in the READ and FORMAT statements.

EXAMPLE 12-20. Indicate READ and FORMAT statements which can be used to read values for two fixed-point variables MX and JSUM, each of which occupies 7 columns on a card, and a floating-point variable, YBAR, which occupies 9 columns and has three digits after the decimal point.

　　　　　READ(5,318)MX,JSUM,YBAR
　　　　　318 FORMAT(2I7,F9.3)

Output

There are few differences between the statements used for output and those used for input.

1. We **WRITE** rather than READ.

2. We use output unit 6 rather than input unit 5.[7]

Also, you should think in terms of spaces on a page rather than columns on a card.

With the above in mind we can rewrite Example 12-20, assuming that we are writing the data on a page rather than reading it from a card.

```
        WRITE(6,318)MX,JSUM,YBAR
    318 FORMAT(2I7,F9.3)
```

EXERCISES 12.3

Answer all questions assuming that unit 5 is used for input and unit 6 for output. Write programs for exercises 3-7.

1. Determine the READ and FORMAT statements for each.
   *(a) Read two-digit numbers j, k, l (form xx).
    (b) Read y of form x.xxxx.
   *(c) Read a_1 and a_2 of form xx.x and the two-digit number i.
    (d) Read NUM1 and K25, each having five digits.
   *(e) Read p and r, each of which is of the form –xxx.x.

2. Determine WRITE and FORMAT statements for each.
   *(a) Write three-digit numbers i, k, JSUM and one-digit numbers n and m_1.
    (b) Write three values (i, j, k), each of which has a sign and two digits.
    (c) Write two numbers in the form xxxxx.xx.
   *(d) Write h and o in the form x.x and QVAL in the form .xxxxx.
   *(e) Write z in the form xx.x, i in the form xxxx, and q in form xx.x.

3. Read floating-point values for a, b, c (each between 0 and 99). Compute
   $$x_1 = \frac{-b + \sqrt{b^2 - 4ac}}{2a} \qquad x_2 = \frac{-b - \sqrt{b^2 - 4ac}}{2a}$$
   Write a, b, c, x_1, and x_2.

4. Read values for a and b (form xx.x) and n (one digit). Compute $y = (a + b)^n$. Write a, b, n, and y. Use form xxxx.xxx for y.

---

[7]We shall always use unit 5 for input and unit 6 for output. A computer system has several other units for such uses as holding binary and EBCDIC intermediate results, providing compilers and library programs, and checking the system's performance. Our choice of 5 and 6 is arbitrary.

5. Read values for r_1, r_2, r_3, r_4, r_5 (of form x.xxxxx). Compute ASUMR = $| r_1 + r_2 + r_3 + r_4 + r_5 |$. Write r_1, r_2, r_3, r_4, r_5 and ASUMR.

6. Read l and w (of form x.x). Compute $P = 2l + 2w$, A = lw, and DIAG = $\sqrt{l^2 + w^2}$. Write l, w, P, A, and DIAG.

7. Read a, b, c (of form x.x). Compute $s = \frac{1}{2}(a + b + c)$ and $A = \sqrt{s(s-a)(s-b)(s-c)}$. Write a, b, c, s, and A. Write A in the form xx.xxxx.

THE CODING FORM

Figure 12-4 shows the form which is used for writing FORTRAN programs before the statements are punched into cards. The columns of the coding form correspond to the columns of a card (see Figs. 12-4 and 12-5), and

1. Statement numbers can appear anywhere in columns 1-5; for example, the statement number 100 can appear in columns 1, 2, 3 or in 2, 3, 4 or else in 3, 4, 5.
2. Statements (excluding statement numbers) begin in column 7.
3. Spaces may be skipped (within statements) for readability.
4. If a statement is too long to fit entirely in columns 7-72, then it is continued in column 7 of the next line and a 1 is placed in column 6 of the continuation line. If a third line is needed, a 2 is written in column 6 of such a continuation line, etc.
5. Columns 73-80 are not used for FORTRAN statements.

We demonstrate the use of the FORTRAN coding form by coding a sample problem on the form.

EXAMPLE 12-21. Write a program which will read three floating-point numbers of the form xxxx.x, determine their sum, and write this result.

Since the numbers are of the form xxxx.x (no sign, five digits and a decimal point), the minimum format is F6.1; however, we shall use F10.1 to avoid crowding the data on the input card.

The numbers we are reading are values for three floating-point variables. We name the variables simply X, Y, Z. Since we form their sum and write it, we might call that result SUM. Figure 12-6 shows the program on a coding form and Figure 12-7 shows the program on cards.

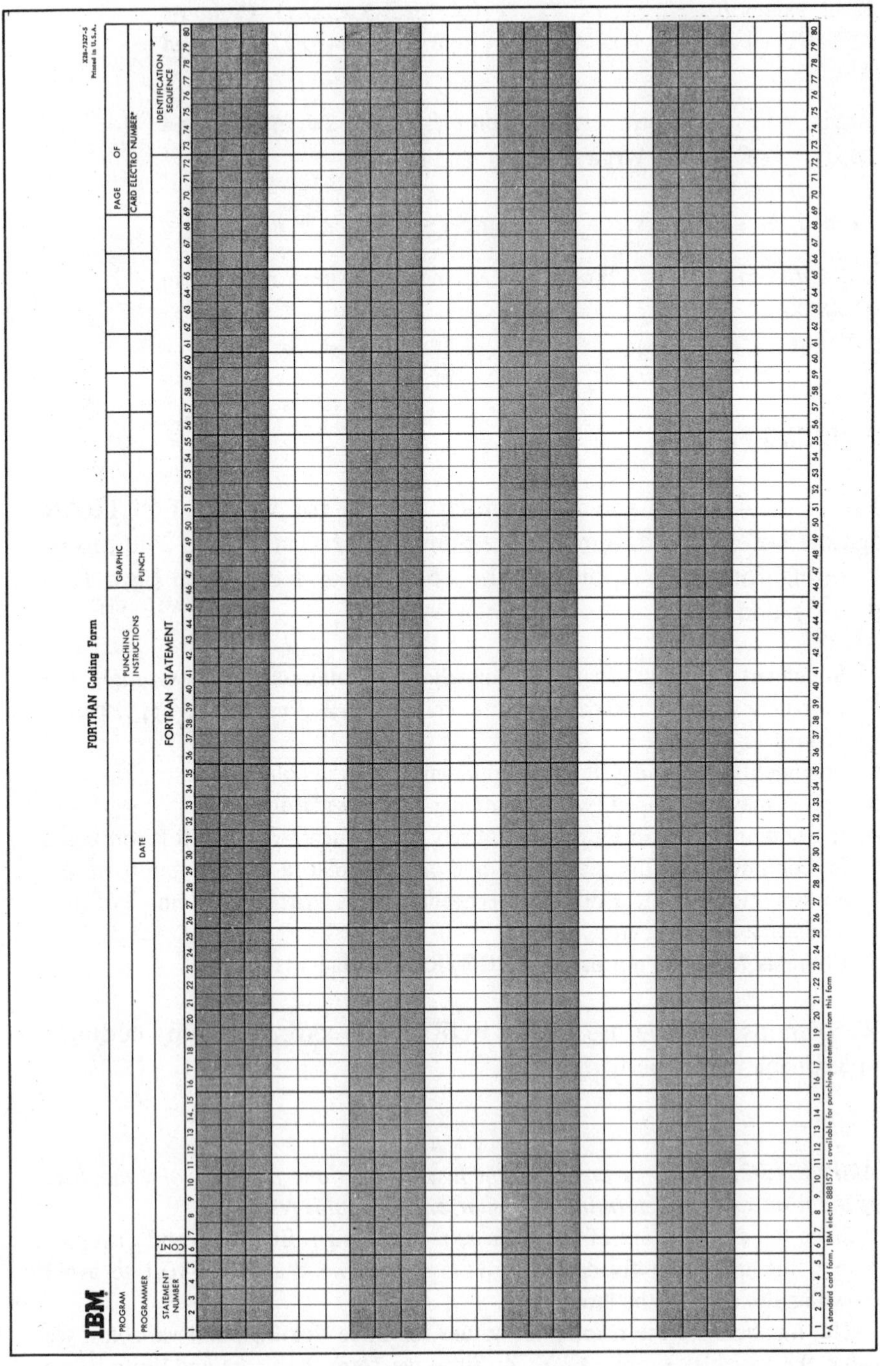

FIGURE 12-4. A FORTRAN Coding Form.

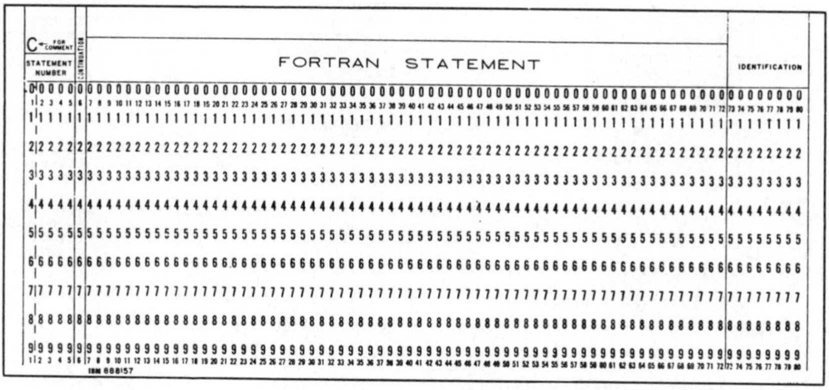

FIGURE 12-5. A FORTRAN Card.

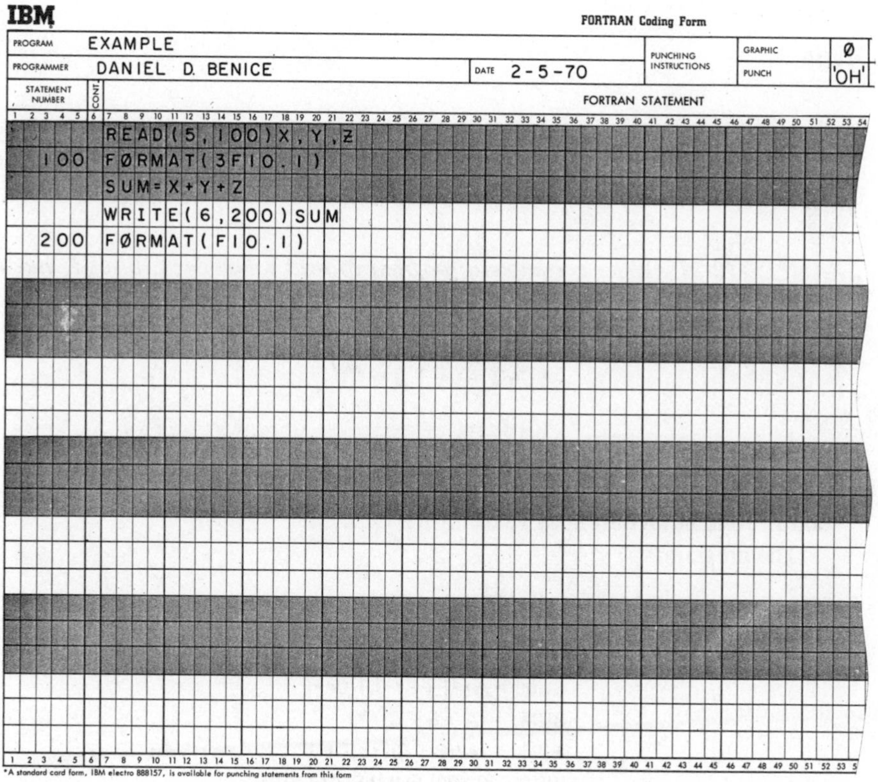

FIGURE 12-6. A FORTRAN Program on a Coding Form.

```
200 FORMAT(F10.1)
    WRITE(6,200)SUM.
    SUM=X+Y+Z
100 FORMAT(3F10.1)
    READ(5,100)X,Y,Z
```

FIGURE 12-7. A FORTRAN Program on Punched Cards.

STOP

To make any program complete there must be a statement which, when executed, causes the computer to terminate execution of the current job. The **STOP** is such a statement; its use is illustrated below.

EXAMPLE 12-22. Write a complete program to read values of A, B, C, I, and J. Compute

$$SUMI = A^I + B^I + C^I$$
$$SUMJ = (A + B + C)^J$$
$$EIPJ = \left(\frac{A}{B + C}\right)^{I+J}$$

and write the results. Assume input forms of F7.2 for A, B, and C and I5 for I and J. Assume all output to be of form F12.5.

The program:

```
      READ(5,100) A,B,C,I,J
  100 FORMAT(3F7.2,2I5)
      SUMI = A**I + B**I + C**I
      SUMJ = (A + B + C)**J
      EIPJ = (A/(B + C))**(I + J)
      WRITE(6,200) SUMI,SUMJ,EIPJ
  200 FORMAT(3F12.5)
      STOP
```

END

A FORTRAN program cannot be executed in the form in which it is coded. Although the computer will *accept* the FORTRAN cards, it can only *execute* binary instructions. A large *compiler* program is used to translate the FORTRAN into machine language.

The **END** statement is merely a signal to the compiler that there are no more FORTRAN statements to follow. The compiler can then proceed to translate the program which it has been given. The END statement must be physically the last statement in the program.

ARITHMETIC IF

The **IF** is a three-way branch. An expression is written in parentheses following the word IF. Three statement numbers are written after the expression in parentheses. When the statement is executed, the expression is evaluated and a decision is made.

1. If the value of the expression is *less than zero,* control is transferred to the statement whose number appears *first* after the expression in parentheses.
2. If the value of the expression is *zero,* transfer is made to the statement indicated by the *second* statement number.
3. If the expression is *positive,* transfer is to the statement indicated by the *third* number.

EXAMPLE 12-23. Consider what happens when the following statement is executed: IF(I + 5)105,219,142.

1. The expression (I + 5) is evaluated using the value that I has at the time this IF statement is executed.
2. A transfer is made to
   a. statement 105, if (I + 5) is negative, or to
   b. statement 219, if (I + 5) is zero, or else to
   c. statement 142, if (I + 5) is positive.

Statement numbers are *not* storage locations; their choice is arbitrary, and it does not matter in what order they appear in the program.

EXAMPLE 12-24.   Write a complete program which will read values for N, X1, X2,
and X3 and compute

   a. X1 + X2 + X3, if N is less than zero
   b. X1 · X2 · X3, if N is equal to zero
   c. (X1 + X2)/X3, if N is greater than zero.

The computed result should be called RESULT, and should be written. Assume
N is of form I5 and X1, X2, X3 are of form F10.2. Use F13.5 for the RESULT.
   A flow chart is shown in Fig. 12-8.

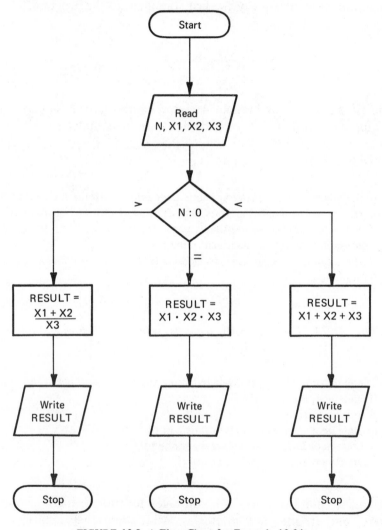

FIGURE 12-8. A Flow Chart for Example 12-24.

The code:

```
              READ(5,362)N,X1,X2,X3
          362 FORMAT(I5,3F10.2)
              IF(N) 53,12,79
           53 RESULT = X1 + X2 + X3
              WRITE(6,320)RESULT
          320 FORMAT(F13.5)
              STOP
           12 RESULT = X1*X2*X3
              WRITE(6,509)RESULT
          509 FORMAT(F13.5)
              STOP
           79 RESULT = (X1 + X2)/X3
              WRITE(6,752)RESULT
          752 FORMAT(F13.5)
              STOP
              END
```

FORMAT statements are *nonexecutable;* that is, although they are necessary for the use of READ and WRITE statements, they provide no commands to control and therefore are not actually executed.[8] Also, they have statement numbers to associate them with a particular READ or WRITE statement. With this in mind it should not be too surprising that

1. It doesn't matter where in the program you place the **FORMAT** statements.
2. If several **READs** or **WRITEs** use identical **FORMAT** statements, then it is only necessary to include the **FORMAT** once.

We can now rewrite the unnecessarily long and wasteful code of Example 12-24 as

```
              READ(5,362) N,X1,X2,X3
          362 FORMAT(I5,3F10.2)
              IF(N) 53,12,79
           53 RESULT = X1 + X2 + X3
              WRITE(6,200)RESULT
          200 FORMAT(F13.5)
              STOP
```

[8]The arithmetic (=) statement causes computation, the READ causes reading, the WRITE causes writing; but the FORMAT merely completes a READ or WRITE statement.

```
12  RESULT = X1*X2*X3
    WRITE(6,200) RESULT
    STOP
79  RESULT = (X1 + X2)/X3
    WRITE(6,200) RESULT
    STOP
    END
```

Two of the WRITE statements were changed so that all three refer (by statement number) to the same FORMAT statement.[9]

GO TO

Even with these changes, both the flow chart and the code still show the need for an *unconditional transfer* statement. That is, both the flow chart and the code can be simplified by avoiding the obvious repetition of WRITE and STOP statements.

The **GO TO** statement transfers control to the statement specified by the statement number after the words GO TO. Thus, execution of *GO TO 100* would cause the statement numbered 100 to be executed next.

Using the GO TO in the program above we get the simplified form:

```
     READ(5,362) N,X1,X2,X3
362  FORMAT(I5,3F10.2)
     IF(N) 53,12,79
53   RESULT = X1 + X2 + X3
     GO TO 500
12   RESULT = X1*X2*X3
     GO TO 500
79   RESULT = (X1 + X2)/X3
500  WRITE(6,200) RESULT
200  FORMAT(F13.5)
     STOP
     END
```

[9]Note that although more than one statement may refer to some other statement (by number), no two statements can be *preceded by* the same statement number. For example, there can be only one statement *numbered* 200.

The simplified flow chart is

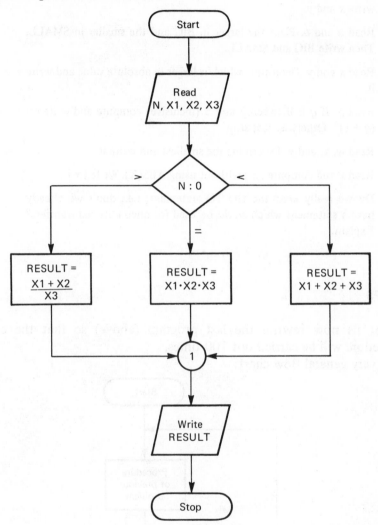

EXERCISES 12.4

Flowchart and write complete FORTRAN programs for exercises 1-7.

1. Read BALANCE. If BALANCE is negative change the value of BALANCE to (1.015) · BALANCE. Otherwise leave BALANCE unchanged. Write the new BALANCE.

*2. Read x. If $x \geqslant 0$ compute $y = x^3$. Otherwise compute $y = x^2$. Then write x and y.

*3. Read a and b. Place the larger in BIG and the smaller in SMALL. Then write BIG and SMALL.

4. Read x and y. Determine which is larger in absolute value and write it.

5. Read q. If q is between 3 and 5 (inclusive) compute and write $r = (q + 1)^3$. Otherwise just stop.

6. Read w, x, and y. Determine the smallest and write it.

*7. Read x and compute $|x|$ without using ABS(X). Write $|x|$.

8. Do we really *need* the GO TO statement; i.e., don't we already have a statement which *could* be used for unconditional transfers? Explain.

LOOPS

Let us now rewrite the last program (above) so that the entire procedure will be carried out 100 times.

A very general flow chart:

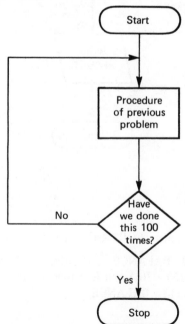

We shall use a variable, say *i,* to keep count of how many times we have performed the procedure. This counter, *i,* will be set to zero before the procedure has been performed, and increased by one after each performance. After the increment, we use an IF to test whether we have performed the procedure 100 times.

Figure 12-9 shows the flow chart (and loop construction). The code:

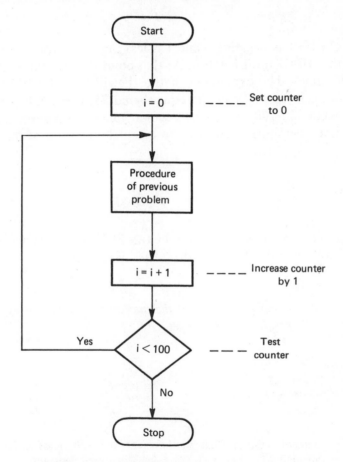

FIGURE 12-9. A Flow Chart Showing Loop Construction.

```
    I = 0
 50 READ(5,362) N,X1,X2,X3
362 FORMAT(I5,3F10.2)
    IF(N) 53,12,79
 53 RESULT = X1 + X2 + X3
    GO TO 500
 12 RESULT = X1*X2*X3
```

```
       GO TO 500
    79 RESULT = (X1 + X2)/X3
   500 WRITE(6,200) RESULT
   200 FORMAT(F13.5)
       I = I + 1
       IF(I - 100) 50,75,75
    75 STOP
       END
```

Since $(I-100)$ is negative while I is less than 100, transfer is made back to the READ until $I = 100$. At that point the procedure has been done 100 times. The expression in the IF will be $100 - 100 = 0$, so transfer is made to the statement numbered 75, the STOP. Although the expression $(I-100)$ can never become greater than zero, the third statement number must be supplied to complete the form of the IF.

DO-LOOPS

One of the most powerful tools in the FORTRAN language is the *DO-loop*. We shall introduce it with a series of examples.

EXAMPLE 12-25. Compute the sum of the integers from 1 to 100 by using a DO-loop.

```
       ISUM = 0
       DO 12  I = 1,100
    12 ISUM = ISUM + I
```

The **DO** statement indicates that all statements below it (and) as far as and including statement 12 (note: DO 12) will be executed first with $I = 1$, then again with $I = 2$, and so on until they are executed last with I having the value 100.

In this example, of course, only the statement ISUM = ISUM + I is executed repeatedly.[10]

---

[10] 12 is an arbitrary statement number.

EXAMPLE 12-26. *Compute the sum of the odd integers from 1 to 100 by using a DO-loop.*

```
      ISUM = 0
      DO 12 I = 1,100,2
   12 ISUM = ISUM + I
```

The only difference between this code and that of the previous example is the comma and 2 after the 100 in the DO statement. This causes the count to change by 2 rather than by 1. I is 1 the first time, 3 the second time, 5 the third time, and so on. I is 99 the last time. The statement in the loop is executed for I values not exceeding 100, only. In other words,

```
      DO 12 I = 1,100,2
      DO 12 I = 1,99,2
```

and
will have the same effect.

EXAMPLE 12-27. *Compute the sum of the even integers from 1 to 100 by using a DO-loop.*

```
      ISUM = 0
      DO 12 I = 2,100,2
   12 ISUM = ISUM + I
```

We want the sum $2 + 4 + 6 + \cdots + 100$, so we begin with 2 (rather than with 1, as before).

EXAMPLE 12-28. *Use a DO-loop to do the following 300 times: read a and b, compute $y = (a + b)^2$, and write a, b, and y.*

```
         DO 59 J = 1,300
         READ(5,2000) A,B
   2000  FORMAT(2F10.2)
         Y = (A + B)**2
      59 WRITE(6,3000) A,B,Y
   3000  FORMAT(2F10.2,F15.4)
         STOP
         END
```

We chose J for the index this time to point out that any fixed-point variable can be used.

The statement number 59 is placed in front of the WRITE rather than the FORMAT because the WRITE is the last statement which is *executed* each time. Recall that FORMAT statements are not executed.

Note that J is 1 the first time through the read-compute-write cycle, J is 2 the second time through, and J is 300 the last (300th) time through.

EXAMPLE 12-29. Do the same as in the last example, except first read a value for N to determine how many cycles of read-compute-write are desired.

```
        READ(5,1000) N
   1000 FORMAT(I3)
        DO 59 J = 1,N
        READ(5,2000) A,B
   2000 FORMAT(2F10.2)
        Y = (A + B)**2
     59 WRITE(6,3000) A,B,Y
   3000 FORMAT(2F10.2,F15.4)
        STOP
        END
```

This example shows the use of a (predetermined) variable as an upper limit in the DO.

LOGICAL IF[11]

When a two-way branch is needed (rather than a three-way branch) programmers often use the **Logical IF** statement. It is simpler to use and easier to read than is the Arithmetic IF. Our general form is

IF (expression) GO TO _____

where the expression in parentheses will be one which is *true* or *false*, as explained below, and

if true transfer is made to the statement whose number appears after the words GO TO
if false the next statement in sequence is executed.

The expression following the word IF *must* include one of the following abbreviations:

[11]The Logical IF is not available in all versions of FORTRAN IV.

.GT.	greater than
.LT.	less than
.EQ.	equal to
.NE.	not equal to
.GE.	greater than or equal to
.LE.	less than or equal to

The expression may additionally use the regular arithmetic operations: + – */**.

EXAMPLE 12-30

$$IF(1 + 1 .GT .5)GO TO 100$$

The statement says that if $(I + 1)$ is greater than 5 then statement 100 is taken next; otherwise the statement on the next line (that is, the next statement in sequence) is taken.

EXAMPLE 12-31

$$IF(SQRT(X) .EQ. Y) GO TO 6$$

If $\sqrt{x} = y$, then go to 6; otherwise continue in sequence.

EXAMPLE 12-32. The loop example coded from Fig. 12-9 can be changed to show a good use of the logical IF. Specifically, we can change the statement

$$IF(I - 100) 50,75,75$$

to

$$IF(I.LT.100) GO TO 50$$

which should have more appeal to the reader.

EXAMPLE 12-33. Write a complete FORTRAN program to read a value for N and compute and write N! (N! is read N-factorial. $5! = 5 \cdot 4 \cdot 3 \cdot 2 \cdot 1$ or $1 \cdot 2 \cdot 3 \cdot 4 \cdot 5$; $7! = 7 \cdot 6 \cdot 5 \cdot 4 \cdot 3 \cdot 2 \cdot 1$). Assume that N is less than 13 so that N! is less than 10 digits. The flow chart is given in Fig. 12-10. The code:

```
      READ(5,700) N
  700 FORMAT(I2)
      NFACT = 1
  100 NFACT = NFACT*N
      N = N – 1
      IF(N.GE.2) GO TO 100
      WRITE(6,300) NFACT
```

300 FORMAT(I10)
STOP
END

The reader should note that the program does not work if N = 0 (0! = 1, by definition). As an exercise rewrite the program to work for *all* N less than 13, including N = 0.

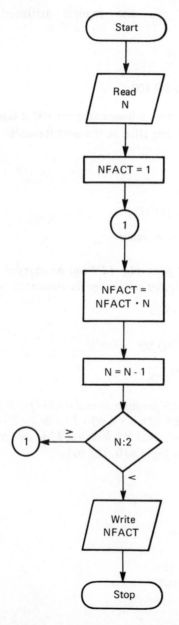

FIGURE 12-10. A Flow Chart for Example 12-33.

EXERCISES 12.5

Flowchart and write FORTRAN programs for each exercise.

*1. Do the following 100 times: read x, compute $y = x^2 + 1$, write x and y.

2. Do the following 250 times: read a, b, and c, compute $s = \frac{1}{2}(a + b + c)$ and $A = \sqrt{s(s - a)(s - b)(s - c)}$, and write a, b, c, s, and A.

3. Modify exercise 2 to read a value for n and carry out the procedure n times.

* Read m and do the following m times: read i, n, and P, compute $S = P(1 + i)^n$, and write i, n, P, and S.

5. Rewrite Example 12-33 (N-factorial) to work for all N less than 13, including N = 0.

6. How can the program in Example 12-33 be changed to allow the writing of N as well as N!? Note that as the program is written, computation of N! destroys N.

7. Read n and do the following n times:
   (a) read a, b, c
   (b) compute $b^2 - 4ac$
   (c) if $b^2 - 4ac$ is less than 0, write a, b, c
   (d) if $b^2 - 4ac$ is greater than or equal to 0, compute

   $$x = \frac{-b \pm \sqrt{b^2 - 4ac}}{2a}$$

   and write a, b, c, and the x's.

*8. Read a, b, and n. Compute $w = (a + b)^n + \sqrt{ab}$. Write a, b, n, and w.

9. Read NUM and form the sum of the integers from 1 to NUM. Write NUM and the sum. Use the logical IF.

*10. Read k and form the product of the integers from 1 to k. Write k and the product.

11. Compute the sum of the squares of the integers from 5 to M, for a value of M which is read. Then write M and the sum.

COMMENTS

The programmer can put remarks or comments throughout his program by preceding each card (or line) of comment by the letter "C" in column 1 of that card. The following are examples of acceptable comments:

```
C     USE COMMENTS WISELY
C (A + B)(C + D) IS OK AS A COMMENT
C
C                        COMMENTS CAN BEGIN IN
C                        ANY COLUMN AFTER COLUMN 1.
```

It is not necessary to have comments in programs, but they are generally helpful to both the programmer writing the program and to anyone who might later read or use the program.

The comment is *not* translated into binary. It is *not* executed, unlike most other FORTRAN statements we have studied. The comment is merely printed out as part of the listing of the program statements.

EXAMPLE 12-34. Rewrite the program of Example 12-33 with suitable comments.

```
C    THIS PROGRAM COMPUTES N-FACTORIAL.
        READ(5,700)N
     700 FORMAT(I2)
C    INITIALIZE BY SETTING NFACT = 1
        NFACT = 1
C    MULTIPLY THIS 1 BY N,N-1,N-2, . . .,2
C    SO THAT WE GET N-FACTORIAL.
     100 NFACT = NFACT*N
        N = N-1
C    TEST TO SEE IF WE HAVE MULTIPLIED BY ALL NUMBERS
C    FROM N DOWN TO 2.
        IF(N.GE.2) GO TO 100
        WRITE(6,300) NFACT
     300 FORMAT(I10)
        STOP
        END
```

The purpose of this example was to emphasize the use of COMMENTs within a program. In practice you might use comments less freely, although the choice is yours.

TYPE STATEMENTS

If we form the sum of several *fixed-point* numbers we might like to call the result SUM. However, instead we would choose ISUM, NSUM, or some other *fixed-point* name. Such a choice of a fixed-point name is made since we later combine it with other fixed-point quantities.

Insisting on fixed-point variables beginning with [I,N] only, and floating-point variables beginning with any other letter is a restriction which sometimes prevents us from using a name of excellent mnemonic value.

We can overrule the restrictions on variable naming by using the REAL and INTEGER *type statements.*

EXAMPLE 12-35. If we want the name SUM to be fixed-point (integer) rather than floating-point (real) then we write the statement

INTEGER SUM

at the beginning of the program.

EXAMPLE 12-36. We can make I, J, K, and NUM3 all floating-point (real) with the statement

REAL   I,J,K,NUM3

Although it is not necessary, some programmers put *all* variable names in REAL or INTEGER statements--even in cases where this is unnecessary.

THE FORTRAN COMPILER

FORTRAN is a compiler language. It is a language of statements which are easily written and understood by programmers. But computers work with binary code, so the FORTRAN statements must be translated into binary machine language before the program can be executed. It is the FORTRAN *compiler,* a large program itself, which performs the necessary translation. The compiler can also detect many programming errors.

Assuming the program is on cards, the compilation process can be seen as

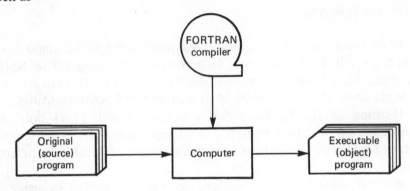

The original (source) program deck is returned in addition to a binary (object) version.[12] Another product of compilation is a *listing* of all program statements.

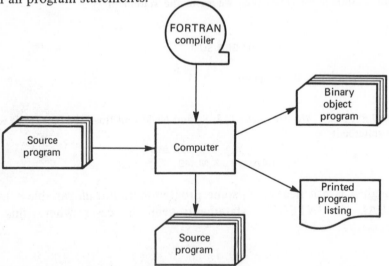

The original deck is called a *source deck,* since it is the computer's source of code. The translated version is the form which the computer uses to execute the program, and is called the *object deck.*

---

[12] One product of compilation is an object program which is loaded into main memory and executed. The programmer can request his own copy, but does not get one automatically.

EXERCISES 12.6

Flowchart and write programs for each exercise below.

1. Read e. Compute $P = 4e$, $A = e^2$, $V = e^3$. Write e, P, A, and V.

2. Do the following 50 times: read l and w, compute $P = 2l + 2w$, $A = lw$, $V = lwh$, and write l, w, P, A, and V.

*3. Form the sum of the odd integers from 1 to 99 and write their sum. Use the IF.

4. Do the N-factorial problem (see Example 12-33) by computing it as $1 \cdot 2 \cdot 3 \cdot 4 \cdots N$ rather than as $1 \cdot N \cdots 4 \cdot 3 \cdot 2$, as was done then.

5. Read n. If n is even, form the sum of the even integers from 2 to n. If n is odd, form the sum of the odd integers from 1 to n. Then write the sum.

   Hint: If fixed-point arithmetic is used

   (a) dividing an even number by 2 produces an exact result
   (b) dividing an odd number by 2 does not produce the exact quotient, since no fractional part is retained.

13

COBOL PROGRAMMING

COBOL, the *CO*mmon *B*usiness *O*riented *L*anguage, is a compiler language designed to handle commercial data processing problems. It is intended for *file processing;* that is, processing of batches of similar records which have been grouped together as a file. A good example of such processing is the determining of a company's payroll. A record (containing employee number, hours worked, and hourly wage) might be made for each employee. Then each record can be processed in nearly the same way to determine each employee's pay.

We shall investigate this payroll problem and other file processing problems that can be programmed using elementary COBOL.

LITERAL CONSTANTS

The number 2 in the formula $P = 2(l + w)$ is a constant. Its value does not change in this formula and would not change during execution if used in a program. Such numbers as 153520, -17.2, +6.2, and 0 are also constants. In COBOL they are called *numeric literals,* and they cannot have more than 18 digits. Signs and decimal points are optional; however, no numeric literal may end in a decimal point. Thus 16. should be written as 16 or as 16.0, so that the last character is not a decimal point.

Also available in COBOL are *non-numeric literals.* They are used for printing output (headings, etc.) and for character processing (rather than computing). For example, you might want as constants the literals MONDAY or 061-00-9391. Such literals are written as 'MONDAY' and '061-00-9391'. They are enclosed by quotations, cannot exceed 120 characters, and can contain any characters (even blanks) except additional quotation marks.

VARIABLES AND DATA-NAMES

Processing involves variables as well as constants. The values which variables take on can change, or vary. In algebra we use letters such as x and y as variables. In COBOL we use *data-names*. A data-name must contain 1-30 characters (letters, digits, and hyphens only), at least one of which is a letter. A data-name cannot begin or end with a hyphen.[1]

EXAMPLE 13-1   The following are acceptable data-names:

        27C
        HOURLY-RATE
        NAME-2
        X-12345
        INPUT-FILE-5
        OVERTIME

EXAMPLE 13-2.   The following are unacceptable data-names:

ABC-123-	(ends in hyphen)
HOURLY RATE	(contains illegal character, blank)
173-27	(does not contain a letter)
17.2A	(contains illegal character, period)
$12.52	(does not contain a letter and contains illegal characters . and $)

ARITHMETIC EXPRESSIONS

Arithmetic expressions are formed by combining constants and variables.[2] Such combinations are formed by using the arithmetic operators

        + addition

        – subtraction

---

[1] And the programmer must code with capital letters.
[2] The constants are numeric literals; the variables are data-names.

                           * multiplication
                             division
                          ** exponentiation.

Their use is best understood by observing some algebraic expressions
and their COBOL equivalents.

Algebra	COBOL
$x - 4$	X - 4
$\dfrac{a + b}{c + d}$	(A + B) / (C + D)
$x^2 - y^2$	X ** 2 - Y ** 2
$5x - 2.63w$	5 * X - 2.63 * W
$\dfrac{x}{-y}$	X / (- Y)

The following rules must be observed when forming arithmetic
expressions for use in COBOL programs.

1. Arithmetic operators (+ - * / **) must be preceded and followed by at least
   one blank space.[3]
2. A left parenthesis must be preceded by at least one blank space, but it must
   not be immediately followed by any blanks. A right parenthesis must not be
   preceded by any blanks, but it must be followed by at least one blank space.
3. Parentheses are used to indicate grouping as in algebra.
4. When parentheses do not completely specify the order of operations in an
   expression, then all exponentiations are performed first. Second, all
   multiplications and divisions are performed in the order they occur, from left
   to right. Last, all additions and subtractions are performed from left to right.
5. Two operation symbols cannot appear next to each other.

Some words, such as ADD, COMPUTE, EQUAL, READ, WRITE,
etc., must not be used as data-names. Each has a special meaning to the
COBOL compiler. They are called *reserved words.*[4]

---

[3]There is one exception. If a signed number is placed in parentheses, then no
   space is left between the left parenthesis and the sign. See the last COBOL
   expression (above).

[4]A complete list of reserved words is given at the end of the chapter.

EXERCISES 13.1

*1. Determine which of the following are acceptable as *numeric literals* and which are not. Indicate why in each case.

-185.632147	-4.
8.7	1000
6	3.4
150,000	5.37A
.00002	TEN
0	X
0.3	$8.35
0.0	6-3

*2. Determine which of the following are acceptable as *non-numeric literals* and which are not. Indicate why in each case.

'A + B'	'0'
'JUNE'	'-4.'
'75'	'TEN
'-27.2'	'0.00.0'
'SUM1'	'$XX.X'
LIST	'-ABC-"
'ALPHABET'	'ONE TWO'
'NAME'	'A + B - 'C' + D + E'

*3. Determine which of the following are acceptable *data-names* and which are not. Indicate why in each case.

-17B	ID-NO
25.2	1728
ABC	OUT-FILE
'X'	X1
1234-Q	X-1
PAYROLL	INTEREST-RATE
TAX-RATE	$5.23
EXIT-	X2 X3
X-Y	X,Y
P16.3	A*B/C
MASTER-IN	

4. Write COBOL expressions for each algebraic expression.

(a) $2r$

(b) x^{i+1}

(c) $\dfrac{a+b}{-c}$

(d) $m + n^3$

(e) $(m+n)^3$

(f) $(1+r)^n$

(g) $5x + 7y$ (h) $R_1 + R_2$

(i) $(2a - 3b)^2$ (j) $\dfrac{(x - 1)^2}{3x}$

STATEMENTS AND SENTENCES

The *statement* is the basic unit for indicating instructions or commands. The following are examples of statements:

ADD 5 TO X

READ MASTER-IN RECORD

COMPUTE Y = A + 10

SUBTRACT RECEIVED FROM BALANCE GIVING PURCHASE

The use and meaning of such statements will be explained later in the chapter.

A COBOL *sentence* consists of one or more statements. The last statement (only) must end in a period. Most sentences will consist of only one statement. The following are examples of sentences:

ADD 5 TO X.

IF BALANCE IS GREATER THAN 0 THEN GO TO
CHARGE OTHERWISE GO TO BALANCE-OK.

WRITE MASTER-OUT.

Several rules of punctuation must be observed when writing COBOL sentences.

1. Adjacent words (including constants and variables) must be separated by at least one blank space.
2. A period must be followed by at least one space, but must not be preceded by any spaces.

PROCEDURE DIVISION

A complete COBOL program consists of four basic parts or *divisions*. They are the Procedure Division, Data Division, Environment Division, and Identification Division. It is in the *Procedure Division* that statements are used to indicate the actual processing (input/output, computations, decisions, etc). We begin a study of the statements of the Procedure Division.

COMPUTE

In order to use arithmetic expressions in COBOL programs, you must precede each with the verb *COMPUTE.*

EXAMPLE 13-3. Indicate the computation of $x = (a + b + c)^2$.

COMPUTE X = (A + B + C) ** 2.

EXAMPLE 13-4. Indicate the COBOL for computing the WEEKLY-INCOME of a worker as the product of HOURS-WORKED and HOURLY-WAGE.

COMPUTE WEEKLY-INCOME = HOURS-WORKED * HOURLY-WAGE.

When we use the = sign with an arithmetic expression it indicates a *replacement* rather than an *equation.* In the last example HOURS-WORKED is multiplied by HOURLY-WAGE and this computed value *becomes* the value of WEEKLY-INCOME. The value of the computed product *replaces* any previous value that WEEKLY-INCOME had.

EXAMPLE 13-5. Write a COBOL statement to indicate that y shall be replaced by the value of 5x - 2.

COMPUTE Y = 5 * X - 2.

EXAMPLE 13-6. Use COBOL to indicate: increase the value of n by 2.

COMPUTE N = N + 2.

Most COBOL processing does not involve many computations, so a less symbolic form is often preferred for computations. This form uses the descriptive arithmetic verbs *ADD, SUBTRACT, MULTIPLY,* and *DIVIDE.*

EXAMPLE 13-7.   The following are acceptable forms of computation in COBOL:

ADD 5,X GIVING Y. (same as COMPUTE Y = X + 5)

ADD 1 TO I. (same as COMPUTE I = I + 1)

Computations are similar for SUBTRACT, MULTIPLY, and DIVIDE. We list all four arithmetic verbs in a table.

verb	connecting word	(optional) result indicator
ADD	TO	none
ADD	, (comma)	GIVING
SUBTRACT	FROM	GIVING
MULTIPLY	BY	GIVING
DIVIDE	INTO	GIVING

EXAMPLE 13-8

COMPUTE form	*ADD, SUBTRACT, MULTIPLY, DIVIDE form*
COMPUTE A = B - C.	SUBTRACT C FROM B GIVING A.
COMPUTE K = K - 3.	SUBTRACT 3 FROM K.
COMPUTE X = 5 * Q.	MULTIPLY Q BY 5 GIVING X.
COMPUTE M = 4 * M.	MULTIPLY M BY 4.
COMPUTE C = A/B.	DIVIDE B INTO A GIVING C.
COMPUTE R = R/2.	DIVIDE 2 INTO R.

EXERCISES 13.2

*1. Use the COMPUTE verb to indicate the following computations in COBOL.

(a) $y = 2x - 3$
(b) $x = 5(a + b)^2 - 3$
(c) $i = i + 5$
(d) $y = ax^2 + bx + c$
(e) balance = due – received

2. Write each in COBOL using the ADD, SUBTRACT, MULTIPLY, and DIVIDE verbs.

*(a) $y = 2x$ *(b) $m = m + 2$

*(c) $x = a/b$ *(d) $x = 5 - x$

(e) $n = \frac{1}{2}n$ (f) $y = mx$

(g) $t = 5t$ (h) $r = a + b$

(i) $s = x - y$ (j) $b = z - 1$

(k) $q = 3 + t$ *(l) increase i by 2

*(m) decrease n by 5   *(n) triple x

(o) $y = 2x + 3$

GO TO

The *GO TO* is used to transfer from the normal sequence of statement execution. When a GO TO is executed, transfer is made to a specified area of the program. The area is indicated by a *procedure-name* (or *label*).[5] For example, if the statement GO TO PAYROLL-OVERTIME is executed, then the next statement executed is the one which has the label PAYROLL-OVERTIME in front of it. Execution then continues at that place in the program. The label PAYROLL-OVERTIME would have a period following it to separate it from the statement which it precedes. This is true of all labels.

.
.
.

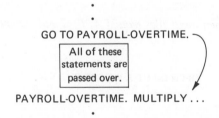

```
GO TO PAYROLL-OVERTIME.
   ┌─────────────┐
   │All of these │
   │statements are│
   │passed over. │
   └─────────────┘
PAYROLL-OVERTIME. MULTIPLY...
```

.
.
.

The transfer can be in either direction: ahead (as illustrated above) or back to a preceding statement.

The GO TO is an *unconditional branch*; that is, a transfer is always carried out when a GO TO is executed.

[5] Use the same rules for forming procedure-names (labels) as you did for forming data-names.

INPUT/OUTPUT

In COBOL we read and write *records* using input and output *files*. These files may be cards, magnetic tape, disks, or other forms of auxiliary storage. Each file which is used must be named, and each of its records must be named.

OPEN

Data is obtained from a file by reading it; that is, by using a *READ* statement. Similarly, data is placed onto a file by writing it; that is, by using a *WRITE* statement.

However, before any READ or WRITE can be executed using a particular file, the file must be initialized for reading or writing. The *OPEN* statement is used for this purpose. We illustrate its use with several examples.

EXAMPLE 13-9. Open the input file named MASTER-IN and the output file named MASTER-OUT.

OPEN INPUT MASTER-IN OUTPUT MASTER-OUT.

EXAMPLE 13-10. Open input files named A, B, C and the output files X and Y.

OPEN INPUT A B C OUTPUT X Y.

EXAMPLE 13-11. Open input file IN-FILE.

OPEN INPUT IN-FILE.

EXAMPLE 13-12. Open the output file OUT-6.

OPEN OUTPUT OUT-6.

READ

We use a *READ* statement to obtain *one record* (from an input file) for processing. The READ form is simply

| READ file-name RECORD |

which causes the reading of one record from the file named.

EXAMPLE 13-13. Indicate the READ statement for reading a record from input file MASTER-IN.

READ MASTER-IN RECORD

WRITE

The *WRITE* is used to place *one record* onto an output file. The WRITE form is simply

| WRITE record-name |

which causes a record to be written.

EXAMPLE 13-14. Write a record named OUT-REC.

WRITE OUT-REC.

CLOSE

Any file which has been opened must eventually be closed in order to complete processing. Files should be closed after all reading and writing has been completed. The form used is similar to that used with the OPEN.

EXAMPLE 13-15. Close input files A, B, C and output files X and Y.

CLOSE A B C X Y.

Note that unlike the OPEN, the CLOSE does not specify whether a file is an input file or an output file.

Not only must files be named and records on each file named, but also the individual parts of each record must be named. For example, we might read records named PAYROLL from a file named MASTER-IN. And each PAYROLL record might contain entries for EMPLOYEE-NO, HOURLY-RATE, and HOURS-WORKED (see Fig. 13-1).

Throughout this chapter we shall assume that any given file contains only one kind of record. In other words, the file of Fig. 13-1 contains PAYROLL records and therefore does not contain any records which are not PAYROLL records.

When a PAYROLL record is read it is placed in an area of storage which can be referenced as PAYROLL. We shall give an example of such a reference after introducing the MOVE statement.

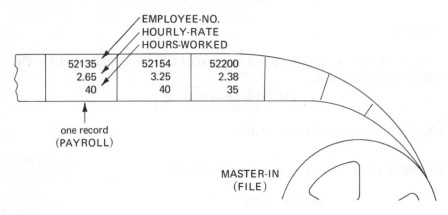

FIGURE 13-1. A File Containing Records.

MOVE

The *MOVE* is used to move a data item from one place in storage to another. The form is

> MOVE name1 TO name2

EXAMPLE 13-16. Move item EMPLOYEE-NO of record PAYROLL-IN to an area of storage from which it can be written as the EMPLOYEE-NO of a record called PAYROLL-OUT.

The statement is

MOVE EMPLOYEE-NO IN PAYROLL-IN TO EMPLOYEE-NO IN PAYROLL-OUT.

The underlined words are part of our standard form of the MOVE. They will be used regardless of the item or record names used.

You should now realize that although we intend to write the same thing that we read (that is, EMPLOYEE-NO), we must move it from the area that it was read into (namely, PAYROLL-IN) to an area from which it can be written from (namely, PAYROLL-OUT). These input and output areas are specified by the *record names*.

EXAMPLE 13-17.   Write a partial program to do the following:
a. Read records named PAYROLL-IN from file MASTER-IN. Each record contains EMPLOYEE-NO, HOURLY-RATE, and HOURS-WORKED.
b. Compute   PAY = HOURLY-RATE · HOURS-WORKED.
c. Write records named PAYROLL-OUT onto file MASTER-OUT. Each record should contain the EMPLOYEE-NO, HOURLY-RATE, HOURS-WORKED, and PAY.

In the coding below we use three *paragraphs,* named ONE, TWO, and THREE. ONE is used for opening the files, TWO for processing, and THREE for closing the files.[6]

The code:

```
ONE. OPEN INPUT MASTER-IN OUTPUT MASTER-OUT.

TWO. READ MASTER-IN RECORD AT END GO TO THREE. MOVE EMPLOYEE-NO
     IN PAYROLL-IN TO EMPLOYEE-NO IN PAYROLL-OUT. MOVE HOURLY-RATE
     IN PAYROLL-IN TO HOURLY-RATE IN PAYROLL-OUT. MOVE HOURS-WORKED
     IN PAYROLL-IN TO HOURS-WORKED IN PAYROLL-OUT. COMPUTE PAY =
     HOURLY-RATE IN PAYROLL-OUT * HOURS-WORKED IN PAYROLL-OUT.
     WRITE PAYROLL-OUT. GO TO TWO.

THREE. CLOSE MASTER-IN MASTER-OUT.
```

Two statements are underlined in this program. The combination of "AT END GO TO THREE" and "GO TO TWO" are used because there are many records on the file (one for each employee!) and each is processed the same way.[7] In other words, the process in the paragraph labeled TWO is repeated until all records have been processed. After processing (that is, "AT END") transfer is made to paragraph THREE, where the files are closed and the procedure thus completed.

The last record of any input file is followed by an *end-of-file* (EOF) mark. We are at the end of the file (that is, we have read the last record) if the EOF has been sensed. The "AT END" is simply a test for the EOF.

Since HOURLY-RATE and HOURS-WORKED are associated with both PAYROLL-IN and PAYROLL-OUT (via MOVEs), you must indicate in the computation which one you are referring to—even though they have the same value.

---

[6] A *paragraph* is one or more sentences which are combined and begin with a procedure-name. The programmer chooses each procedure-name.
[7] This is *batch processing*; that is, many records are processed similarly.

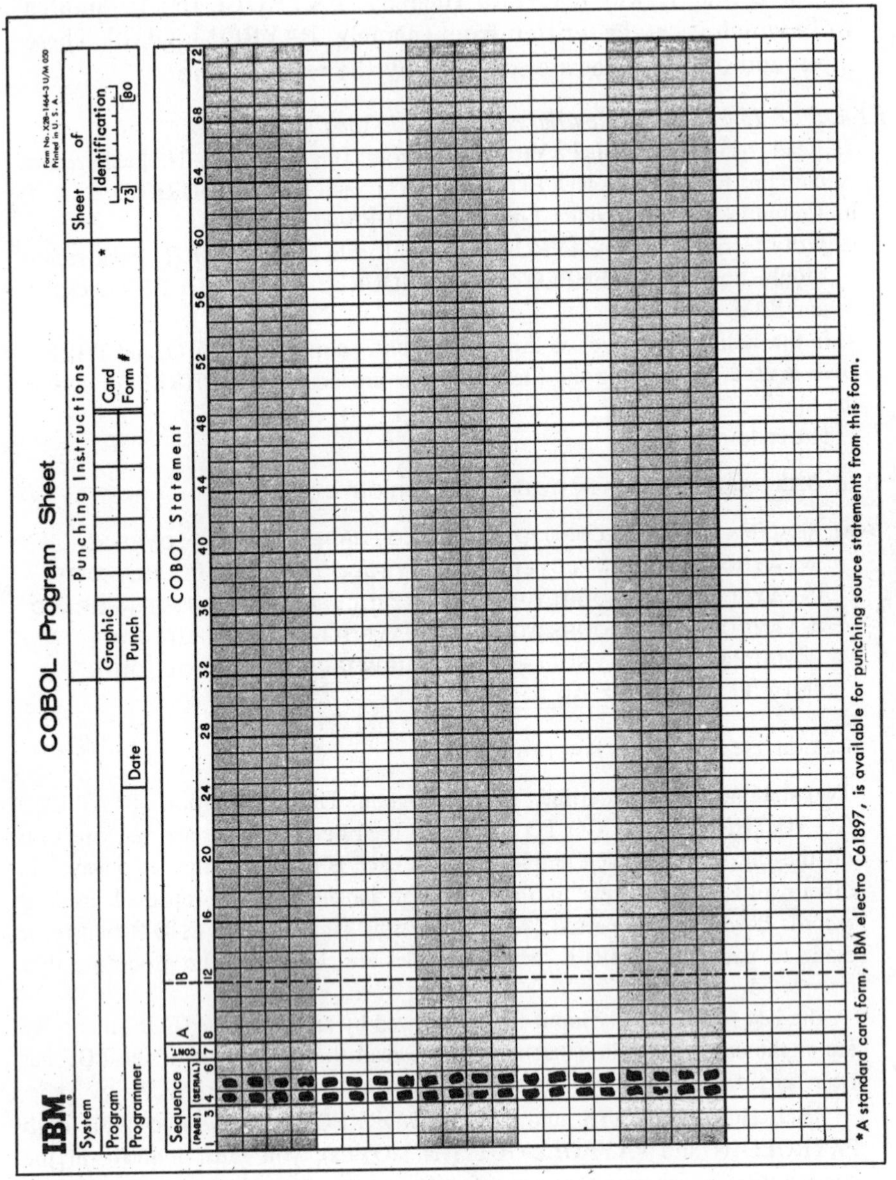

FIGURE 13-2. A COBOL Coding Form.

THE CODING FORM

We cannot present the computer with a handwritten COBOL program. Our code must be punched on cards (or entered via some other input medium), and according to a special format. We write the code on COBOL program sheets or coding forms (see Fig. 13-2).

The column numbers of the coding sheet correspond to the columns of the data processing card (see Fig. 13-3). And the code from a given line is punched into one card.

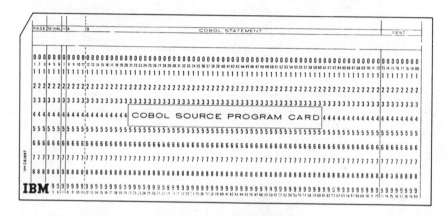

FIGURE 13-3. A COBOL Card.

Two *margins* are indicated on the coding form. The A-margin is at column 8. The B-margin is at column 12. Division names begin at the A-margin. Paragraph names also begin at the A-margin, but other lines of paragraphs begin at the B-margin (see Fig. 13-4).

Sentences are not written beyond column 72, but may be continued on the next line if necessary, and on additional lines if needed. If a *word* needs to be continued on the next line, then a hyphen must be placed in column 7 of the continuation line (see Fig. 13-4).

Figure 13-4 shows the coding of Example 13-17 as it might be written on a coding sheet. Figure 13-5 shows the cards punched accordingly. Note that the words PROCEDURE DIVISION precede the other code. The coding for any division of a COBOL program is preceded by the name of the division, followed by a period.[8]

---

[8]Each coding sheet has 25 lines. The lines of code can be numbered 001, 002, 003, 004, etc. in columns 4-6 of each line. Each page can be numbered in columns 1-3 of each line. The first page is 001, the next 002, and so on. However, we shall not number pages or lines.

COBOL Coding Form

SYSTEM				
PROGRAM EXAMPLE		PUNCHING INSTRUCTIONS		PAGE 1 OF 1
PROGRAMMER DANIEL D. BENICE	DATE 2-5-70	GRAPHIC 0 O I I	CARD FORM #	IDENTIFICATION 73 80
		PUNCH oh zero eye one		

SEQUENCE (PAGE) (SERIAL)	CONT	A	B	COBOL STATEMENT
01		PROCEDURE DIVISION.		
02		ONE. OPEN INPUT MASTER-IN OUTPUT MASTER-OUT.		
03		TWO. READ MASTER-IN RECORD AT END GO TO THREE. MOVE EMPLOYEE-NO		
04		IN PAYROLL-IN TO EMPLOYEE-NO IN PAYROLL-OUT. MOVE HOURLY-RATE		
05		IN PAYROLL-IN TO HOURLY-RATE IN PAYROLL-OUT. MOVE HOURS-WORKE		
06	-	D IN PAYROLL-IN TO HOURS-WORKED IN PAYROLL-OUT. COMPUTE		
07		PAY = HOURLY-RATE IN PAYROLL-OUT * HOURS-WORKED IN PAYROLL-		
08	-	OUT. WRITE PAYROLL-OUT. GO TO TWO.		
09		THREE. CLOSE MASTER-IN MASTER-OUT.		
10				
11				
12				
13				
14				
15				
16				
17				
18				
19				
20				

*A standard card form, IBM Electro C81887, is available for punching source statements from this form.
Instructions for using this form are given in any IBM COBOL reference manual.
Address comments concerning this form to IBM Corporation, Programming Publications, 1271 Avenue of the Americas, New York, New York 10020.

Form No. X28-1464-4 U/M 025
Printed in U.S.A.

FIGURE 13-4. A COBOL Program on a Coding Sheet.

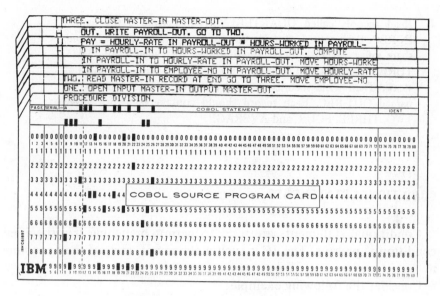

FIGURE 13-5. A COBOL Program on Cards.

EXERCISES 13.3

Write Procedure Divisions for each exercise below.

*1. Read records called DEPOSIT from a file named IN-BANK. Each record contains a value for each of ACCOUNT-NO, INVEST-MENT, and RATE. Compute INTEREST = INVESTMENT · RATE. Then write records called DIVIDEND onto a file named OUT-BANK. Each record should contain values for ACCOUNT-NO, INVESTMENT, RATE, and INTEREST.

2. Read records called QUARTERLY-SALES from a file named SALES-DATA. Each record contains an item number and four quarterly sales figures. Compute the annual sales by adding the quarterly sales. Then write the item number and its annual sales as a record named ANNUAL-SALES onto a file named SALES-RE-PORT.

*3. A file named PRE-SALE contains records named BEFORE. Each record consists of a merchandise number (MDSE-NO) and a PRICE for the item. The output file, called SALE, shall consist of records named AFTER. Each record should consist of a merchandise number and a price for the item. This sale price should reflect a 20% discount.

4. Read records called QUARTERLY-SHARE from a file named IN-REC. Each record contains the quarterly market values for one share of a certain stock. These values are called ONE, TWO, THREE, and FOUR. Compute the AVERAGE value of a share of stock. Then write records called AVERAGE-SHARE onto a file named OUT-REC. Each record should contain values for ONE, TWO, THREE, FOUR, and AVERAGE.

CONDITIONAL STATEMENTS

Conditional statements are used to permit branching if a specified condition is present. The *IF* is such a statement, and we shall examine it.

Consider the following example:

IF HOURS-WORKED IS GREATER THAN 40 THEN GO TO
OVERTIME OTHERWISE NEXT SENTENCE.

This statement has three parts to it:

1. IF HOURS-WORKED IS GREATER THAN 40
2. THEN GO TO OVERTIME
3. OTHERWISE NEXT SENTENCE

We shall discuss each of these parts separately, since this is our basic type of IF statement.

1. *A conditional expression preceded by the word IF.* A conditional expression is a phrase which is either true or false. "HOURS-WORKED IS GREATER THAN 40" is either true or else it is false. We shall have occasion to use other forms of relation; namely, *EQUAL TO* and *LESS THAN*. Comparisons of this kind can be made between two variables or a variable and a constant (in either order).

2. *A statement indicating where to continue if the preceding expression is true. The statement begins with the COBOL word THEN.* It has a built-in "GO TO." Thus, "THEN GO TO OVERTIME" indicates that transfer should be made to the statement labeled OVERTIME, if the preceding expression is true.

EXAMPLE 13-18. The sentence IF X IS LESS THAN Y THEN GO TO VALUE-2 ... indicates that transfer should be made to the statement labeled VALUE-2 *if x is less than y.*

3. *An indication of where to go if the expression is false. The statement begins with one of the words OTHERWISE or ELSE.* The "IF" example above ends with OTHERWISE NEXT SENTENCE. This indicates that if the expression is false then the next sentence in sequence is executed (that is, no transfer is made).

If you prefer to transfer if the expression is false, or if you prefer to label the next sentence (in sequence), then use a label instead of "NEXT SENTENCE." Similarly, in the "THEN" portion of the IF sentence we can indicate NEXT SENTENCE rather than a label.

EXAMPLE 13-19. Indicate a conditional statement to cause a branch from the normal sequence if GROSS is more than 7800. Branch then to a sentence labeled FICA. If GROSS is not more then 7800 take the next statement in sequence. One form might be

IF GROSS IS GREATER THAN 7800 THEN GO TO FICA OTHERWISE NEXT SENTENCE.

Another might be

IF GROSS IS LESS THAN OR EQUAL TO 7800 THEN NEXT SENTENCE OTHERWISE GO TO FICA.

EXAMPLE 13-20. Write a partial Procedure Division for the following problem. Compute INCOME as the sum of the incomes from three sources: JOB1, JOB2, and DIVIDENDS. If INCOME is greater than EXPENSES compute SAVE = INCOME - EXPENSES. If not, compute BORROW = EXPENSES - INCOME.

```
A    B    .
          .
          .
     COMPUTE INCOME = JOB1 + JOB2 + DIVIDENDS. IF
     INCOME IS GREATER THAN EXPENSES THEN GO TO WHEW
     OTHERWISE GO TO HELP.
```

HELP │. BORROW = EXPENSES – INCOME.

│   .

│   .

│   .

WHEW │. SAVE = INCOME – EXPENSES.

                        .

                        .

We could have used NEXT SENTENCE instead of GO TO HELP, in which case the label HELP would not have been needed.

EXAMPLE 13.21. Write the Procedure Division for the following problem. Read records named CREDIT-BEFORE from a file named RECORDS-IN. Each record contains an ACCOUNT-NUMBER, the amount PURCHASED, and the amount RECEIVED in payment for the purchased merchandise. Make an output file, RECORDS-OUT, containing records called CREDIT-UPDATE. Each record should contain the ACCOUNT-NUMBER and credit BALANCE (that is, PURCHASED minus RECEIVED).

A negative or zero balance will be considered favorable, since the customer owes nothing. A positive balance will be considered unfavorable, since the customer has not paid for all his purchases.

Accounts having an unfavorable balance will have a service charge of 1% added to this unpaid balance.

See Fig. 13-6 for a flowchart of the solution. The code:

```
PROCEDURE DIVISION.
OPEN-PARAGRAPH. OPEN INPUT RECORDS-IN OUTPUT RECORDS-OUT.
PROCESS-PARAGRAPH. READ RECORDS-IN RECORD AT END GO TO
    CLOSE-PARAGRAPH. MOVE ACCOUNT-NUMBER IN CREDIT-BEFORE
    TO ACCOUNT-NUMBER IN CREDIT-UPDATE. SUBTRACT RECEIVED
    FROM PURCHASED GIVING BALANCE. IF BALANCE IS GREATER
    THAN 0 THEN GO TO CHARGE OTHERWISE GO TO BALANCE-OK.
CHARGE. COMPUTE BALANCE = 1.01 * BALANCE.
BALANCE-OK. WRITE CREDIT-UPDATE. GO TO PROCESS-PARAGRAPH.
CLOSE-PARAGRAPH. CLOSE RECORDS-IN RECORDS-OUT.
```

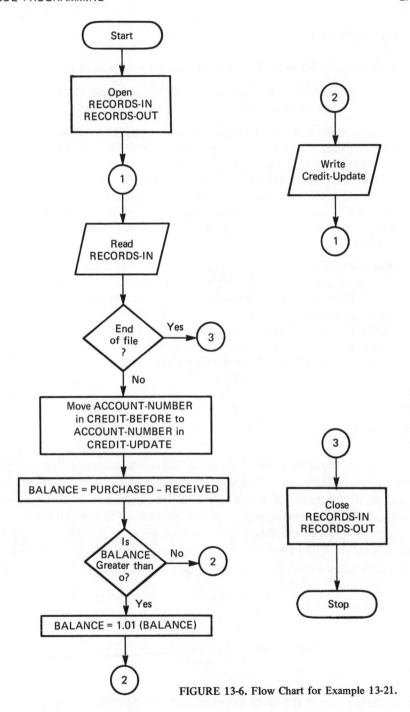

FIGURE 13-6. Flow Chart for Example 13-21.

EXERCISES 13.4

Draw flow charts and write Procedure Divisions for each exercise.

1. Redo exercise 1 of the last section with the following change: interest is given on those investments of 100 ($100) or more.

*2. Read records called TAX-IN from a file named MASTER-IN. Write records called TAX-OUT onto a file named MASTER-OUT. Each TAX-IN record contains NAME, SOC-SEC-NO, and ANNUAL-INCOME. Each TAX-OUT record consists of NAME, SOC-SEC-NO, and TAX. TAX is computed as 3 percent of ANNUAL-INCOME over $600 (that is, deduct the first $600). Incomes less than $600 are not taxed but should be reported, that is, TAX = 0 for income ≤ $600.

3. Read records called INCOME from a file called INN. Each record consists of a taxpayer's social security number (SOC-SEC-NO) and his ANNUAL-INCOME. Compute the social security PAYMENT for each taxpayer; that is, 5.2% of the first $7800 of ANNUAL-INCOME (or less if ANNUAL-INCOME is less). Then write records called SOCIAL-SECURITY onto a file called OUT. Each record should contain SOC-SEC-NO and PAYMENT.

DATA DIVISION

We have seen that the Procedure Division contains the program statements which are intended to process data. The *Data Division* contains descriptions of names used in the statements of the Procedure Division. We shall discuss only the *File Section* of the Data Division.

Each file used in the Procedure Division must be described in the File Section of the Data Division. Such a description is begun by placing the file name after the abbreviation FD (for *file description*). For example,

```
A  .  B

DATA   DIVISION.
FILE   SECTION.
FD     MASTER-IN
```

is the beginning of the Data Division and File Section describing the file MASTER-IN. Note that both DATA DIVISION and FILE SECTION begin at the A-margin and end with a period. FD also begins at the A-margin, but the file name begins at the B-margin. After the file name should be the clauses

LABEL RECORDS ARE OMITTED

and (if the records on this file are named *PAYROLL*)

DATA RECORD IS *PAYROLL.*

If the record has a name other than PAYROLL, then that name would be used in the same way that PAYROLL was used above.

The revised Data Division now appears as

```
DATA DIVISION.
FILE SECTION.
FD     MASTER-IN LABEL RECORDS ARE OMITTED
       DATA RECORD IS PAYROLL.
```

Label records are placed at the beginning and end of a file to indicate such things as date of file preparation, length of the file, and other properties which identify the file. We shall not be concerned with label records. This is why we indicate that they are omitted.

Every *record* which is mentioned in the FD must be described immediately after the DATA RECORD IS . . . clause. The record description is best explained by means of an example.

EXAMPLE 13-22. Show the Data Division for reading records called STUDENT from an input file called MASTER.

Let us assume that each record consists of a student's

NAME in columns 1-20
SOC-SEC-NO in columns 21-29
CURRICULUM in columns 30-40
YEAR of intended graduation in columns 41-42.

The remaining 38 columns (43-80) are unused (that is, blank).[9]

---

[9]We shall assume that each record originally came from a punched card, which is 80 columns (or characters) in length. Although the data may be converted to magnetic tape or disk for faster processing, the record remains 80 characters in length.

The Data Division is then

```
A     B

DATA  DIVISION.
FILE  SECTION.
FD    MASTER LABEL RECORDS ARE OMITTED
      DATA RECORD IS STUDENT.
01    STUDENT.
02    NAME PICTURE IS X(20).
02    SOC-SEC-NO PICTURE IS X(9).
02    CURRICULUM PICTURE IS X(11).
02    YEAR PICTURE IS X(2).
02    FILLER PICTURE IS X(38).
```

The following observations can be made:

1. The name of the *record,* STUDENT, is repeated after the clause DATA RECORD IS STUDENT, and has a *level-number of 01.*
2. The record (level 01) consists of four parts: NAME, SOC-SEC-NO, CURRICULUM, and YEAR. All four have the same level-number, 02.
3. The size of each field is indicated by PICTURE IS X(number of card columns).
4. FILLER is used to indicate columns which will always be blank.
5. The level-number 01 must begin at the A-margin. Any other level-number (02, etc) may be indented.
6. A period must be placed after the level 01 name and after each level 02 PICTURE description for that name.

The next example introduces an additional feature.

EXAMPLE 13-23. Write the Data Division for the following problem. Read records named PERSONNEL-ID from an input file named PERSONNEL-IN-FILE, where the format of each record is

> NAME in columns 1-18
> ID-NO in columns 20-25
> SEX in column 26
> AGE in columns 27-28
> EDUCATION in column 29

Values supplied for NAME, ID-NO, and AGE can vary considerably. However, SEX can only be male or female, for which we use the one-character abbreviations M or F. Similarly, EDUCATION might be allowed to assume only one of the following code *values:*

> 0 if elementary school education
> 1 if high school education
> 2 if college education

Level *88* is used before code values for SEX and EDUCATION, as indicated in the code below[10].

```
DATA DIVISION.
FILE SECTION.
FD  PERSONNEL-INFILE LABEL RECORDS ARE OMITTED
    DATA RECORD IS PERSONNEL-ID.
01  PERSONNEL-ID.
02  NAME PICTURE IS X(18).
02  FILLER PICTURE IS X(1).
02  ID-NO PICTURE IS X(6).
02  SEX PICTURE IS X(1).
    88 MALE VALUE IS M.
    88 FEMALE VALUE IS F.
02  AGE PICTURE IS X(2).
02  EDUCATION PICTURE IS X(1).
    88 ELEMENTARY VALUE IS 0.
    88 HIGH-SCHOOL VALUE IS 1.
    88 COLLEGE VALUE IS 2.
02  FILLER PICTURE IS X(51).
```

Thus far the discussion of the Data Division has been restricted to alphanumeric data.[11] However, we frequently process numeric data, also. The next series of examples shows how numeric data can be handled in the Data Division.

EXAMPLE 13-24. Suppose that values for a level 02 variable named AVERAGE are to be read and that AVERAGE is expected to have numeric values such as 12.3, 11.6, 49.2, and others of the form nn.n. Indicate the level 02 description of the File Section.

The form is nn.n, two digits followed by a decimal point and a third digit. We indicate this in COBOL as 99V9. Each digit is represented by a "9", and a "V" represents the decimal point. The correct position of this assumed decimal point is indicated by the proper placement of the V; however, no decimal point exists.

The COBOL is

```
02 AVERAGE PICTURE IS 99V9.
```

---

[10]The special level-number, 88, is used to indicate condition names; that is, names of values which an item may take on.

[11]Alphanumeric data consists of letters and/or digits and/or special characters, and is not used for computing.

EXAMPLE 13-25.   We provide additional examples to indicate how the input data should look, a corresponding picture description, and the effective number for computation purposes.

input data	picture description	value for computing
567	99V9	56.7
567	9V99	5.67
567	V999	.567
567	999V	567.
17	9V9	1.7
8324	9V999	8.324

Leading zeros can be indicated by using a letter P for each zero.

567	VP999	.0567
567	VPP999	.00567

Input data is given without a decimal point, but one is "supplied" according to the description given.

When *output* is numeric, it is *printed with a decimal point.* The programmer indicates where the decimal point should be placed in much the same way as he handles input; however, instead of using a "V" he uses a decimal point. Thus, a picture description input form of 99V9 would be coded as 99.9 if it were a description of output.

EXAMPLE 13-26.   Show the Data Division for the following problem. Read records called ACCOUNT-IN from a file named IN-FILE. Write records called ACCOUNT-OUT onto a file named OUT-FILE.

ACCOUNT-IN has the form
   ACCOUNT-NUMBER in characters 1-5
   AMOUNT (of form nnnnn.nn) in 10-16
   INTEREST-RATE (of form .Onnn) in 20-22
ACCOUNT-OUT has the form
   ACCOUNT-NUMBER in 1-5
   COMPUTED-INTEREST (of form nnn.nn) in 10-15

Note: Assume output records are 132 characters, one width of printed page.

The code:

```
DATA DIVISION.
FILE SECTION.
FD IN-FILE LABEL RECORDS ARE OMITTED.
    DATA RECORD IS ACCOUNT-IN.
01 ACCOUNT-IN.
02 ACCOUNT-NUMBER PICTURE IS X(5).
02 FILLER PICTURE IS X(4).
02 AMOUNT PICTURE IS 99999V99.
02 FILLER PICTURE IS X(3).
02 INTEREST-RATE PICTURE IS VP999.
02 FILLER PICTURE IS X(58).
FD OUT-FILE LABEL RECORDS ARE OMITTED
    DATA RECORD IS ACCOUNT- OUT.
01 ACCOUNT- OUT.
02 ACCOUNT-NUMBER PICTURE IS X(5).
02 FILLER PICTURE IS X(4).
02 COMPUTED-INTEREST PICTURE IS 999.99.
02 FILLER PICTURE IS X(117).
```

Editing features are available to make output easier to read and more useful. They include a ZERO SUPPRESS to replace leading zeros with blank spaces and FLOAT DOLLAR SIGN to replace leading zeros (if any) with blank spaces and a dollar sign.

EXERCISES 13.5

Write the Data Division for each exercise.

*1. Read records called SURVEY from MASTER-IN. Each record is as follows:

NAME in columns 1-25
SOC-SEC-NO in 27-35
SEX in 40
AGE in 45-46
MARITAL-STATUS in 48
DEPENDENTS in 50 (1 means one dependent, etc.)

2. Read records called WORK-REPORT from a file named WORK-FILE. Each record contains

NAME in 1-25
EMPLOYEE-NUMBER in 30-35
HOURS-WORKED (form nn) in 40-41
HOURLY-WAGE (form nn.nn) in 45-48.

*3. Write records called PAY-REPORT onto a file named PAY-FILE. The output records are determined from the input records of exercise 2.

NAME in 1-25
EMPLOYEE-NUMBER in 30-35
WEEKLY-SALARY (form nnn.nn) beginning in 50.

4. Records called INCOME are read from a file named INN. Each record begins with a 9-character social security number. Five blank spaces are next, followed by an ANNUAL-INCOME of form nnnnn.nn. The amount of social security due is computed. Then output records called SOCIAL-SECURITY are written onto a file called OUT. Each record should contain a social security number and a payment (of form nnn.nn).

5. Write records called STUDENT-REC onto a file called MASTER-OUT. Each record contains

NAME: LAST-NAME in 1-13   (*hint*: this is level 03)
              FIRST-NAME in 15-24
              MIDDLE-INITIAL in 26
CLASS in column 30 (1 for freshman, 2 for sophomore, 3 for
                               junior, 4 for senior, 5 for graduate)
DATE-FIRST-ENROLLED: MONTH in 35-36
                                            DAY in 37-38
                                            YEAR in 39-40
INTENDED-GRADUATION: MONTH in 45-46
                                            YEAR in 47-48

ENVIRONMENT DIVISION

The *Environment Division* describes the computer system for which the program is written. It contains a *Configuration Section* which indicates the source-computer and the object-computer. The *source-computer* is the computer used to compile (that is, translate) the original COBOL program deck. The *object-computer* is the one used to execute the compiled program. Very often both computers are the same; and we shall use the IBM/360-30 as both source and object-computer.

EXAMPLE 13-27. Show the Configuration Section of the Environment Division for a COBOL program to be compiled and run on an IBY/360-30.[12]

```
ENVIRONMENT DIVISION.
CONFIGURATION SECTION.
SOURCE-COMPUTER. IBM-360 D30.
OBJECT-COMPUTER. IBM-360 D30.
```

The Environment Division also contains an *Input-Output Section.* Within the section is a *file-control* which names each file used and assigns them to specific input/output devices.

EXAMPLE 13-28. Show the Environment Division for a COBOL program in which we name the input unit MASTER-IN and the output unit MASTER-OUT.

```
ENVIRONMENT DIVISION.
CONFIGURATION SECTION.
SOURCE-COMPUTER. IBM-360 D30.
OBJECT-COMPUTER. IBM-360 D30.
INPUT-OUTPUT SECTION.
FILE-CONTROL.
    SELECT MASTER-IN ASSIGN TO 'SYS005'.
    SELECT MASTER-OUT ASSIGN TO 'SYS006'.
```

The word SELECT must precede the symbolic file name. The words ASSIGN TO must always follow the (I/O) unit name.

The codes 'SYS005' and 'SYS006' are the input and output devices, respectively.

IDENTIFICATION DIVISION

The *Identification Division* must contain the program name (which you choose). Such items as author, installation, date written, date compiled, security, and remarks may be included as options. In this chapter we will use the form

IDENTIFICATION DIVISION.
PROGRAM-ID. 'program name'.
AUTHOR. name.
REMARKS. any sentence or sentences.

---

[12]The "D" used with IBM-360 D 30 indicates *D-level* COBOL; that is, 16,000 bytes of main storage are used.

EXAMPLE 13-29. A possible Identification Division.

```
IDENTIFICATION DIVISION.
PROGRAM-ID. 'SAMPLE'.
AUTHOR. DANIEL D BENICE.
REMARKS. THIS IS MERELY AN EXAMPLE SHOWING A
         POSSIBLE IDENTIFICATION DIVISION. YOU MAY
         USE SEVERAL LINES AND/OR SENTENCES FOR
         PROGRAM REMARKS OR COMMENTS.
```

ORDER OF DIVISIONS

Each COBOL program must contain all four divisions, and they must be in the following order:

> Identification Division
>
> Environment Division
>
> Data Division
>
> Procedure Division

A FINAL EXAMPLE

We present a complete COBOL program to process data as indicated in the statement of the problem below.

Problem. *Read records called WORK-REC from MASTER-IN and write records called PAY-REC onto MASTER-OUT.*

```
WORK-REC:    EMPLOYEE-NUMBER in 1-9
             HOURLY-WAGE  (of form nn.nn) in 15-18
             HOURS-WORKED (of form nn) in 20-21


PAY-REC:     EMPLOYEE-NUMBER in 1-9
             HOURLY-WAGE in 15-19 (output includes decimal point)
             HOURS-WORKED in 25-27
             WEEKLY-PAY  (of form nnn.nn) in 30-35
```

WEEKLY-PAY is computed as HOURLY-WAGE times HOURS-WORK-ED. In addition, employees are paid time-and-one-half for overtime (HOURS-WORKED over 40).

The program:

```
IDENTIFICATION DIVISION.
PROGRAM-ID. 'FINAL EXAMPLE'.
AUTHOR. DANIEL D BENICE.
REMARKS. COMPUTATION OF WEEKLY PAY.

ENVIRONMENT DIVISION.
CONFIGURATION SECTION.
SOURCE-COMPUTER. IBM-360 D 30.
OBJECT-COMPUTER. IBM-360 D 30.
INPUT-OUTPUT SECTION.
FILE-CONTROL.
    SELECT MASTER-IN ASSIGN TO 'SYS005'.
    SELECT MASTER-OUT ASSIGN TO 'SYS006'.

DATA DIVISION.
FILE SECTION.
FD MASTER-IN LABEL RECORDS ARE OMITTED
    DATA RECORD IS WORK-REC.
01 WORK-REC.
02 EMPLOYEE-NUMBER PICTURE IS X(9).
02 FILLER PICTURE IS X(5).
02 HOURLY-WAGE PICTURE IS 99V99.
02 FILLER PICTURE IS X(1).
02 HOURS-WORKED PICTURE IS 99V.
02 FILLER PICTURE IS X(59).
FD MASTER-OUT LABEL RECORDS ARE OMITTED
    DATA RECORD IS PAY-REC.
01 PAY-REC.
02 EMPLOYEE-NUMBER PICTURE IS X(9).
02 FILLER PICTURE IS X(5).
02 HOURLY-WAGE PICTURE IS 99.99..
02 FILLER PICTURE IS X(5).
02 HOURS-WORKED PICTURE IS 99.
02 FILLER PICTURE IS X(2).
02 WEEKLY-PAY PICTURE IS 999.99.
02 FILLER PICTURE IS X(97).

PROCEDURE DIVISION.
PAR-1. OPEN INPUT MASTER-IN OUTPUT MASTER-OUT.
PAR-2. READ MASTER-IN RECORD AT END GO TO PAR-5.
```

```
      MOVE EMPLOYEE-NUMBER IN WORK-REC TO EMPLOYEE-NUMBER
      IN PAY-REC. MOVE HOURLY-WAGE IN WORK-REC TO
      HOURLY-WAGE IN PAY-REC. MOVE HOURS-WORKED IN
      WORK-REC TO HOURS-WORKED IN PAY-REC. MULTIPLY
      HOURLY-WAGE IN PAY-REC BY HOURS-WORKED IN
      PAY-REC GIVING WEEKLY-PAY. IF HOURS-WORKED IN
      PAY-REC IS GREATER THAN 40 THEN GO TO PAR-3
      OTHERWISE GO TO PAR-4.
PAR-3. COMPUTE WEEKLY-PAY = .5 * (HOURS-WORKED IN
      PAY-REC. – 40) + WEEKLY-PAY.
PAR-4. WRITE PAY-REC. GO TO PAR-2.
PAR-5. CLOSE MASTER-IN MASTER-OUT.
```

EXERCISES 13.6

Write complete COBOL programs for each exercise below.

1. Read records called IN-PAY from IN-FILE and write records called
   OUT-PAY onto OUT-FILE.

```
     IN-PAY:  EMPLOYEE-NUMBER in 1-5
              GROSS-PAY (form nnn.nn) in 10-14
              FEDERAL-TAX (form nnn.nn) in 20-24
              SOCIAL-SECURITY (form n.nn) in 30-32
              STATE-TAX (form nn.nn) in 35-38
              INSURANCE-PREMIUM (Form n.nn) in 40-42
              MISC-DEDUCTIONS (form n.nn) in 45-47

     OUT-PAY: EMPLOYEE-NUMBER in 1-5
              GROSS-PAY in 10-15
              FEDERAL-TAX in 20-25
              SOCIAL-SECURITY in 30-33
              STATE-TAX in 35-39
              INSURANCE-PREMIUM in 40-43
              MISC-DEDUCTIONS in 45-48
              NET-PAY in 50-55
```

   NET-PAY is GROSS-PAY minus all deductions listed above.

2. Read records called OLD-FORM from MASTER-1 and write records
   called NEW-FORM onto MASTER-2.

OLD-FORM: SOC-SEC-NO in 1-9
               BI-WEEKLY-INCOME (form nnn.nn) in 10-14

NEW-FORM: SOC-SEC-NO in 1-9
               SEMI-MONTHLY-INCOME (form nnn.nn) in 10-15

SEMI-MONTHLY-INCOME can be computed from BI-WEEKLY-INCOME by multiplying the latter by 26 and then dividing that result by 24. The multiplication produces annual income; the division then gives 24 equal (semi-monthly) payments.

THE COBOL COMPILER

COBOL is a compiler language. It is a language of statements and descriptions which are easily written and understood by programmers. But computers work with binary code, so the COBOL statements and descriptions must be translated into binary machine language before the program can be executed. It is the COBOL *compiler,* a large program itself, which performs the necessary translation. The compiler can also detect many programming errors.

Assuming the program is on cards, the compilation process can be seen as

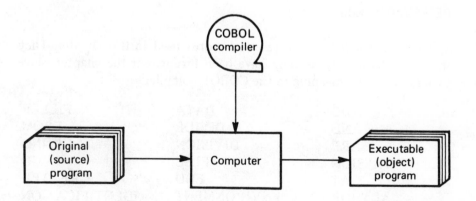

The original (source) program deck is returned in addition to a binary (object) version. An additional product of compilation is a *listing* of all program statements and descriptions.

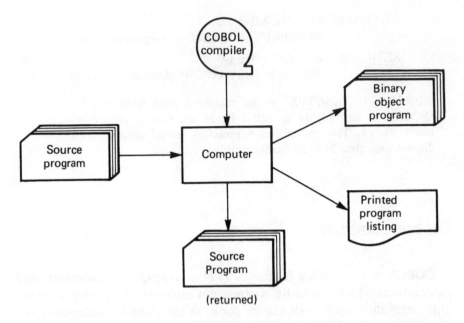

The original deck is called a *source deck* since it is the computer's source of code. The translated version is the form which the computer uses to execute the program, and is called the *object deck.*

RESERVED WORDS

We present a list of the reserved words used in this chapter. They should be used only as they have been throughout the chapter, since each has a special meaning to the COBOL compiler.

ADD	DATA	FILLER
AND	DIVIDE	FROM
ARE	DIVISION	GIVING
ASSIGN	ELSE	GO
AT	END	GREATER
AUTHOR	ENVIRONMENT	IDENTIFICATION
BY	EQUAL	IF
CLOSE	FD	IN
COMPUTE	FILE	INPUT
CONFIGURATION	FILE-CONTROL	INPUT-OUTPUT

INTO	OTHERWISE	SENTENCE
IS	OUTPUT	SOURCE-COMPUTER
LABEL	PICTURE	STANDARD
LESS	PROCEDURE	SUBTRACT
MOVE	PROGRAM-ID	THAN
MULTIPLY	READ	THEN
NEXT	RECORD	TO
OBJECT-COMPUTER	RECORDS	VALUE
OMITTED	REMARKS	WRITE
OPEN	SECTION	
OR	SELECT	

14

PL/1 PROGRAMMING

PL/1 (Programming Language One) is a compiler language which can be used equally well for scientific or commercial programming. Thus, it can serve installations as a single language replacement for FORTRAN and COBOL. This chapter introduces some of the elements of PL/1 program writing.

CONSTANTS AND VARIABLES IN PL/1

Constants are quantities whose values are explicitly stated and cannot change. We shall define two types of constants, fixed-point and floating-point.

Fixed-Point Constants

Numbers with one or more digits, with or without a decimal point, are known in PL/1 as *fixed-point constants.*

EXAMPLE 14-1. The following are fixed-point constants:

$$
\begin{array}{c}
5 \\
6.524917 \\
-72 \\
+0.7549 \\
5. \\
0
\end{array}
$$

Floating-Point Constants

Floating-point constants are those written in scientific or standard notation; the digits are followed by the letter E and the desired power of 10.

EXAMPLE 14-2   The following are floating-point constants:

> 8.36E05, which means 8.36×10^5
> 8.36E5, which means 8.36×10^5 (extra 0 is optional)
> −.62E+2, which means $-.62 \times 10^2$
> +523E−9, which means 523×10^{-9}
> 1E15, which means 1×10^{15}

(Note that the decimal point and signs are optional)

Names for Variables

In algebra we use letters such as *a, b, c* or *x, y, z* to represent variables. We can also use A, B, C or X, Y, Z in PL/1.[1] However, we do not have to restrict ourselves to single letter variables in PL/1; we can use any combination of 31 or fewer letters, digits, and break characters, as long as the first character is a letter.[2]

EXAMPLE 14-3.   The following are acceptable variable names:

> ROOT1
> SUM_SQUARED   (Use of break character)
> SUMSQUARED
> GROSS_PROFIT
> RESULT
> X
> HOURLYRATE
> HOURLY_RATE

Although a variable may take on different values throughout the executed program, all values of a particular variable must be of the same *scale;* that is, all values of that variable must be fixed-point or else all values it takes on must be floating-point.[3]

---

[1] The programmer must code with capital letters.

[2] The break character is the symbol _ .

[3] *Scale* in PL/1 means the same as *mode* in FORTRAN.

Rule. Variable names which begin with one of the letters I, J, K, L, M, or N (which we will denote in the future as [I,N]) are fixed-point. Variables which begin with any other letter are floating-point.

EXAMPLE 14-4. Acceptable variable names.

> X is a floating-point variable.
> SUM is floating-point.
> ISUM is fixed-point.
> HOURLY_RATE is floating-point.
> N7Q is fixed-point.
> A123456 is floating-point.

EXAMPLE 14-5. Unacceptable variable names.

79	does not begin with a letter
X12.5	contains a character other than a letter, digit, or break character; i.e., contains illegal character.
X + Y	contains illegal character: + .
(NAME_6)	contains illegal characters: parentheses.

EXPRESSIONS

We can combine constants and variables to form expressions, just as in algebra. We have the following operations:

> + addition
>
> − subtraction
>
> * multiplication
>
> / division
>
> ** exponentiation

Observe the use of these symbols in translating algebraic expressions into equivalent PL/1 expressions.

Algebra   PL/1

$$\frac{x}{y} \qquad X/Y$$

$$5m \qquad 5*M$$

$$4 + I \qquad 4 + I$$
$$x^2 \qquad X**2$$
$$x - z \qquad X - Z$$

Rule 1. Two operation symbols must not appear next to each other, unless the second one is + or - .[4]

EXAMPLE 14-6

> X/-Y   is valid
>
> X*/Y   is not valid

Rule 2. Parentheses are used to indicate grouping, as in algebra.

EXAMPLE 14-7. $(a + b)^2$ is written $(A + B)**2$, since $A + B**2$ represents $a + b^2$. Example 14-7 is clarified by the next rule.

Rule 3. When parentheses do not completely specify the order of operations in an expression, then all exponentiations are performed first. Second, all multiplications and divisions are performed in the order they occur (left to right). Last, all additions and subtractions are performed from left to right.

EXAMPLE 14-8

> $A + B*C$
>
> The algebraic interpretation is $a + bc$ since multiplication is performed before addition when no parentheses are used to indicate otherwise.

> $(A + B)*C$
>
> Here parentheses indicate that the addition is performed before the multiplication. The algebra is $(a + b)c$.

---

[4]The rule is a natural one, since no one would violate it in algebra. It is mentioned here because FORTRAN and COBOL will reject two adjacent symbols, even if the second is + or ⁻.

X/(Y*Z)   The result is $\frac{x}{y} \cdot z$ or $\frac{xz}{y}$ since equal level operations are performed from left to right in the order they appear. Recall that Rule 3 specifies that multiplication and division are operations of the same level, just as addition and subtraction are operations of the same level.

X/(Y*Z)   The result is $\frac{x}{yz}$ since parentheses are used.

A – B + C   The result is $(a - b) + c$.

A – (B + C)   The result is $a - (b + c)$.

Rule 4. Fixed-point quantities (constants or variables) and floating-point quantities can be mixed in the same expression. However, when a mix of such quantities appears in an expression, the fixed-point numbers are converted to floating-point by the PL/1 compiler. The arithmetic is then carried out in floating-point.

EXAMPLE 14-9. $b^2 - 4ac$ can be written any of these ways:

> B**2 – 4*A*C
> B**2 – 4.0*A*C
> B**2 – 4.0E0*A*C

And there are additional correct ways of coding the expression.

FUNCTIONS

If you had to determine the square root ($\sqrt{\ }$) of a number as part of a PL/1 program, you might wonder just how to do it. The PL/1 compiler contains a built-in *function,* called SQRT, which will determine the square root of any number (constant, variable, expression) which is enclosed in parentheses following the function name SQRT.

EXAMPLE 14-10   *Algebra*   *PL/1*

$\sqrt{x}$ SQRT(X)

$3a\sqrt{xy - 5}$ 3.0*A*SQRT(X*Y – 5.0)

Similarly, there is a function called ABS which is used to determine the absolute value of a number. There are additional functions for logarithms, trigonometric functions, etc.

EXERCISES 14.1

*1. For the list below determine which of the items are acceptable as constants, variables, or expressions, and which are unacceptable. Indicate the scale (fixed or floating) also.

(a) X   (b) 7X
(c) I*10   (d) ABC_DE7Q
(e) (X - Y)   (f) 1625E-1
(g) 1.65E02 + MU   (h) 6*A + 5.0
(i) IOTA*OMEGA   (j) A + B/C + D
(k) (A + B)(C + D)   (l) 1.5*KAPPA - 4.2E+06
(m) _TIME_OF_DAY_   (n) (XSUM*-6.3)/(A + B)
(o) DAY_OF_THE_WEEK   (p) 7.5*E-06+SQRTX

2. Write PL/1 expressions for the algebraic expressions below.

(a) $w + \dfrac{x}{y} + z$ *(b) $\dfrac{w + x}{y + z}$

(c) $a + b^2$ (d) $(a + b)^2$

*(e) $\sqrt{\dfrac{c + d}{x}}$ (f) $\left(\dfrac{a}{b}\right)^{i+1}$

(g) $17.2r + et$ (h) $27 + 5\,|3 - ax^2|$

(i) πr^2 (j) $a^x b$

*(k) $a^{i+1} x$ *(l) $\sqrt{\left(\dfrac{a}{b + c}\right)^{i+1}}$

(m) $\alpha + \beta$

STATEMENTS

PL/1 is a language of statements. A PL/1 program is a list of statements which are computer acceptable. We now begin a discussion of PL/1 statements and programs.[5]

---

[5] All PL/1 statements end with a semicolon (;). This is a signal to the compiler that the end of the statement has been reached.

Assignment Statements

The *assignment statement* handles computations involving constants, variables, and functions. The general form is

$$\boxed{\text{VARIABLE} = \text{EXPRESSION};}$$

There are four parts to the statement:

1. an equal sign
2. an *expression* to the right of the equal sign
3. a *variable* to the left of the equal sign, and
4. a semicolon at the right end (after the expression).

It should be emphasized that the assignment statement is *not* an equation. It is instead a direction to the computer to *replace* the variable which appears on the left with the computed value of the expression on the right.

EXAMPLE 14-11.   K = 5; This statement can be thought of as meaning any of the following:

1. K takes on the value 5.
2. 5 replaces the previous value of K, so that K has the value 5 for future use and reference.
3. The value of K is replaced by 5.

EXAMPLE 14-12.   IJ_DIFF = I - J; The previous value of IJ_DIFF is replaced by the difference of the current values of I and J. Suppose, for instance, that before this statement is encountered in the program we have

$$I = 19;$$
$$J = 7;$$

and *then*   IJ_ DIFF = I - J;

IJ_DIFF will be replaced by the computed value of 19 - 7. Hence IJ_DIFF becomes 12.

EXAMPLE 14-13.   N = N + 1; Execution of this statement will increase the value of N by 1. That is, 1 is added to the current value of N and this new sum (N + 1) replaces the previous value of N (note that such an equation is nonsense in algebra, although the statement is valid in PL/1).

EXAMPLE 14-14. The formula $y = ax + b$ is written in PL/1 as Y = A * X + B;.
The value of Y will be replaced by whatever results when A * X + B is computed
from supplied values of A, X, and B. Thus

$$\begin{array}{ll}
A = 3.0E0; & (a \text{ is } 3) \\
B = 4.0E0; & (b \text{ is } 4) \\
X = 1.5E0; & (x \text{ is } 1.5) \\
Y = A*X + B; &
\end{array}$$

will produce a value of 8.5E0 (or 8.5) for Y.

If the four statements of Example 14-14 are written as

$$\begin{array}{lcl}
A = 3.0; & & A = 3; \\
B = 4.0; & \text{or} & B = 4; \\
X = 1.5; & & X = 1.5; \\
Y = A*X + B; & & Y = A*X + B;
\end{array}$$

they are easier to read. However, this introduces opposite scales on the
opposite sides of the equal sign. This is permitted, and in the cases
above the constants on the right are converted from fixed-point to
floating-point before the replacements are carried out.

Rule. All expressions to the right of the equal sign are evaluated in the
scale in which they are written. If the variable on the left is of a different scale, *then* a conversion is made to that scale.

EXAMPLE 14-15. X = I + J; The sum of I and J is computed in fixed-point and
then converted to floating-point, since the variable on the left is floating-point
and must "receive" a floating-point value.

EXAMPLE 14-16. NUM = (X + Y)/A; The value of (X + Y)/A is computed in
floating-point and then converted to fixed-point, since NUM is fixed-point.

EXERCISES 14.2

*1. Write the assignment statement which corresponds to the given
formula.

(a) $v = \sqrt{2gh}$
(b) $s = \frac{1}{2}(a + b + c)$
(c) $A = \sqrt{s(s - a)(s - b)(s - c)}$
(d) $A = \pi r^2$

(e) $y = mx + b$
(f) $S = P(1 + i)^n$
(g) $F = \frac{9}{5}C + 32$

INPUT/OUTPUT

We could write a simple program to evaluate a formula for different values of its variables. But if we had to rewrite the program to supply different data each time we wanted a formula evaluation, much effort would be wasted. Instead, of course, we write the *general* formula in our program and *read* the different values for each evaluation.

To read data into storage so that it may be used by a program we use the **GET DATA** statement.

EXAMPLE 14-17. The statement GET DATA (X,Y,N); will read from a card one value of X, one value of Y, and one value of N. The values will be stored so that a reference to X, Y, or N will be a reference to the value read.

Values for X, Y, and N might be supplied on cards. For this example this could be done by punching

$$X = 1.5, \quad Y = 1.05El, \ N = 2;$$

or perhaps

$$N = 2, \quad Y = 1.05El, \ X = 1.5;$$

in any columns of a card.[6] It does not matter in what order the names and their values appear on the card, since the card contains the variables' names as well as their values (see Fig. 14-1).

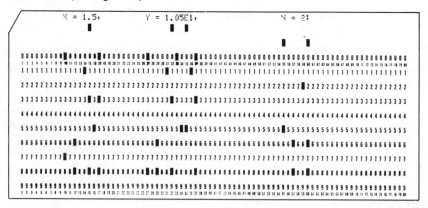

FIGURE 14-1. Data on a Card.

Once the formula has been evaluated we might want to write the result. This is done using the **PUT DATA** statement.

[6]Commas must be used to separate values, and the set of data must be terminated by a semicolon.

EXAMPLE 14-18. If the formula is RESULT $=(X + Y)^N$, then execution of

PUT DATA(X,Y,N,RESULT);

produces

X = 1.500E+00   Y = 1.050E+01   N = 2   RESULT = 1.440E+02;

as printed output.

The output is always in the order specified by the listing of the variables in the PUT DATA statement.

There might be some question in your mind about why the output form of X was changed from the original input form 1.5 to the output form 1.500E+00. Input values for floating-point variables can be of any form (with or without decimal point, with or without "E"); however, all output forms of floating-point numbers are in standard notation. The output form contains: a number between 1 and 10, the letter E, a plus or minus sign for the exponent, and a two-digit exponent.

EXAMPLE 14-19. Write PL/1 statements to do the following: read values for b_1, b_2, and h, compute $A = \frac{1}{2}(b_1 + b_2)h$, and write $b_1, b_2, h,$ and A.

```
GET DATA(B1,B2,H);
A = .5*(B1 + B2)*H;
PUT DATA(B1,B2,H,A);
```

EXERCISES 14.3

Write PL/1 statements for each problem.

*1. Read x. Compute $y = x^3 - 7x^2 - 13$. Write x and y.

2. Read HOURS, and WAGE. Compute OVERTIME = (HOURS − 40)(WAGE)1.5. Write WAGE, HOURS, and OVERTIME.

*3. Read a, b, c, d, and e. Compute their arithmetic average. Write all input and the average.

4. Calculate the simple interest on an investment of n dollars for one year at the rate of 5½% per year. Read n and write n and the interest.

5. Same as exercise 4, except *n* dollars at *m%* per year, where both *n* and m are read before computation begins.

6. Read *r,* the radius of a right circular cone. Compute the volume, *V* $=\frac{1}{3}\pi r^3$. Write *r* and *V.*

THE CODING FORM

No special coding form is used for writing PL/1 programs (unlike assembler language, FORTRAN, and COBOL). There is one restriction, however; only card columns 2 through 72 may be used. Statements may *begin* in column 2 or thereafter. You can begin different statements in different columns, place two or more statements on a single line (card), or use more than one line per statement. This *free form* of PL/1 reduces errors, since the compiler does not insist that statements begin in a certain column.[7]

PROCEDURES

Each PL/1 program is called a *procedure,* and as such requires a label and two additional statements which reference this label. The form is

label: PROCEDURE OPTIONS (MAIN);

> all other statements
> which make up the
> program

END   *label;*

The statement **PROCEDURE OPTIONS (MAIN);** will always precede all other program statements.[8] Also, the **END** statement must be the last statement of the program.

---

[7] Recall that all statements must end with a semicolon to inform the compiler when one statement ends and another begins.

[8] Our PL/1 programs will be *main* programs rather than subroutines.

Associated with the PROCEDURE and END statements is a *label*, and this label must be the same in both of these statements. We use labels in front of statements whenever they are referenced by other program statements. A colon is placed between the label and the statement in such cases.

A label consists of 31 or fewer letters, digits, and break characters. The first character of any label must be a letter.

EXAMPLE 14-20.   The following are valid labels:

> BEGIN
> LOOP
> COMPUTE_RESULT
> WRITE
> LOOP4

EXAMPLE 14-21.   Write a complete program, called ROOT, to read values for a, b, and c and compute the roots of the quadratic equation $ax^2 + bx + c = 0$ using the formula

$$x = \frac{-b \pm \sqrt{b^2 - 4ac}}{2a}$$

Then write a, b, c, x_1, and x_2, where x_1 and x_2 are the computed roots. The program:

```
ROOT: PROCEDURE OPTIONS (MAIN);
      GET DATA(A,B,C);
      X1 = (-B + SQRT(B**2 - 4*A*C))/(2*A);
      X2 = (-B - SQRT(B**2 - 4*A*C))/(2*A);
      PUT DATA(A,B,C,X1,X2);
      END ROOT;
```

Several comments can be made about the program in Example 14-21.

1. The PL/1 compiler treats any written program as one long string of statements, where each statement ends in a semicolon. Thus we *can* put more than one statement on a given line if we want to. We can indent and space however we want. The form chosen was arbitrary, but neat and easy to read.

2. The program as written is inefficient. Note that $\sqrt{b^2 - 4ac}$ is computed twice, although once would be sufficient. This is a fairly lengthy computation and should not be done twice. Waste of computer execution time should be avoided.

With the second comment in mind, we change the program and rewrite
it as

```
ROOT: PROCEDURE OPTIONS (MAIN);
        GET DATA(A,B,C);
        D = SQRT(B**2 −4*A*C);
        X1 = (−B + D)/(2*A);
        X2 = (−B − D)/(2*A);
        PUT DATA(A,B,C,X1,X2);
        END ROOT;
```

EXERCISES 14.4

Write complete PL/1 programs for each exercise below.

1-6. Rewrite exercises 1-6 of the previous section, making each a
complete program (i.e., a procedure).

7. Read x and y. Compute $z = x^3y^2 - 7(x + y)$. Write x, y, and z.

*8. Read a, b, and c, which are lengths of the sides of a triangle.
Compute the area (A) of the triangle by computing the semi-
perimeter (s) as $s = \frac{1}{2}(a + b + c)$ and $A = \sqrt{s(s - a)(s - b)(s - c)}$.
Write a, b, c, s, and A.

9. Read r, the radius of a sphere, and compute the volume of the
sphere as $V = \frac{4}{3}\pi r^3$. Write r and V.

GO TO

We introduce the unconditional transfer statement, the **GO TO**.

EXAMPLE 14-22

GO TO LOOP;

When executed, the statement causes control to be transferred so that the next
statement executed is the one labeled LOOP.

EXAMPLE 14-23

GO TO SUM_OF_THE_VARIABLES;

Execute next the statement labeled SUM_OF_THE_VARIABLES.

IF

The **IF** is used for conditional transfer of control. The statement includes a test for a condition. If the condition is true, a transfer is made to another part of the program. If the condition is false, the next statement in normal sequence is taken.

In addition to the usual arithmetic operations (+ - */**) we use the logical operators:

>	greater than
<	less than
=	equal to
>=	greater than or equal to
<=	less than or equal to

EXAMPLE 14-24.

.
.
.

```
If X > 3 THEN GO TO COMPUTE;
PUT DATA(X);
```

.
.

If $x > 3$, than a transfer is made so that the statement labeled COMPUTE is executed next (the statement is not actually written in the example, but it could be either before or after the IF statement). If x is not greater than 3, then the PUT DATA is executed next. In other words, a transfer is made if $x > 3$; otherwise no transfer is made.

There is always a built-in GO TO following the word THEN in our IF statement. Thus, the IF is a conditional transfer.

EXAMPLE 14-25

.
.
.

```
IF X**2 + 1 > = Y**2 THEN GO TO ERROR;
Z = (X + Y)**3 - SQRT(X/Y);
```

.
.

```
ERROR:Z = X**2 + Y**2;
```

Transfer is made to the statement labeled ERROR if $x^2 + 1 \geqslant y^2$; otherwise the statement immediately below the IF is executed.

The examples suggested the general form

$$\text{IF \_\_\_\_ THEN GO TO \_\_\_\_ ;}$$

EXAMPLE 14-26. Flowchart and code a complete program (name it FUNCTION) which reads values for k, r, x, and y and then computes a result called F_RESULT. However, F_RESULT is computed differently according to the size of the k which is read.

> If $k \geqslant 0$, then F_RESULT = $(x + y)r$.
> If $k < 0$, then F_RESULT = $x(y + r)$.

After F_RESULT is computed, write *k, r, x, y,* and F_RESULT.
    The flow chart:

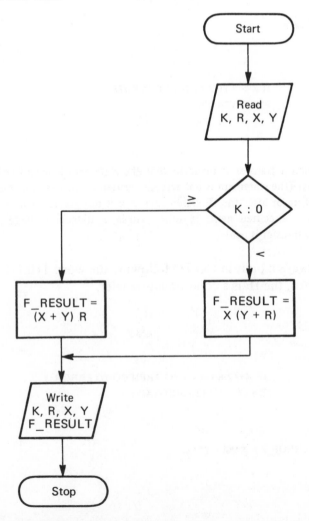

Note that we use the same "write" and "stop" instructions after either computation of F_RESULT. This, of course, is arranged by using the GO TO statement.

The flow chart in this instance has been made to agree with the coding. In other words, coding directly from the chart above will place the END statement very naturally at the end of the code, which is where it must be.

```
FUNCTION:PROCEDURE OPTIONS (MAIN);
        GET DATA (K,R,X,Y);
        IF K >= 0  THEN GO TO KPOSITIVE;
        F_RESULT = X*(Y + R);
        GO TO WRITE;
KPOSITIVE:F_RESULT = (X + Y)*R;
    WRITE:PUT DATA(K,R,X,Y,F_RESULT);
        END FUNCTION;
```

EXERCISES 14.5

Flowchart and write complete PL/1 programs for each exercise.

1. Read INCOME. If INCOME is less than 600, TAX = 0. If INCOME is greater than 600, TAX = .03(INCOME - 600). Compute and write TAX.

*2. Read x and y. Determine which is larger and write it.

3. Read x and y. If they have the same sign, compute $ABSXY = xy$. If their signs are different, compute $ABSXY = -xy$. Write $ABSXY$. *Hint:* Two numbers have opposite signs if their product is negative.

*4. A stock purchase plan is set up so that an employee receives a share of stock as soon as his contributions equal (or exceed) the price of one share. And every time he receives a share the cost of one share is subtracted from his contributions. Read CONTRIBUTE (the amount an employee currently has in the stock purchase fund), SHARES (the number of shares of stock he currently owns), and PRICE (the current price of one share). Determine whether or not the employee has enough in the fund to buy a share. If not, write the values of CONTRIBUTE and SHARES that were read. If a share can be purchased, increase SHARES by 1, subtract PRICE from CONTRIBUTE, and write the new CONTRIBUTE and SHARES. Assume that the employee's contributions are small compared to the price of a share of stock, so that he cannot purchase more than one share at a time.

5. Read x. Determine which of $x^2 - 4x + 7$ or $x^2 + 5x - 1$ is larger.
    Write x and the larger of the two computed values.

6. Read a_1, a_2, and a_3. Determine which is largest, call it BIG, and
    write it.

LOOPS

Let us rewrite the program of Example 14-26 so that the procedure
will be carried out 200 times.

A very general flow chart:

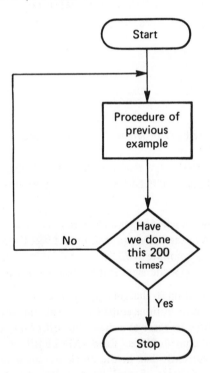

We shall use a variable, say I, to keep count of how many times we
have performed the procedure. I will be set to zero before the
procedure has been performed, and increased by one after each
performance. After the increment, we will use an IF to test whether we
have done the procedure 200 times.

The flow chart (showing loop construction):

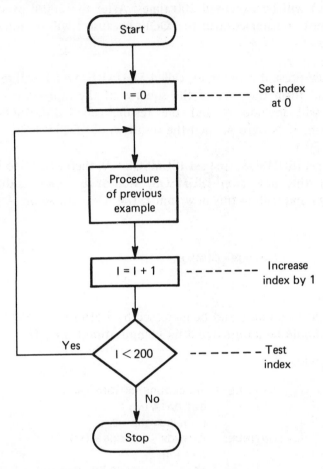

The program:

```
TWO_HUNDRED:    PROCEDURE OPTIONS (MAIN);
                I = 0;
LOOP:           GET DATA(K,R,X,Y);
                IF K > = 0  THEN GO TO KPOSITIVE;
                F_RESULT = X*(Y + R);
                GO TO WRITE;
KPOSITIVE:      F_RESULT = (X + Y)*R;
WRITE:          PUT DATA (K,R,X,Y,F_RESULT);
                I = I + 1;
                IF I < 200 THEN GO TO LOOP;
                END TWO_HUNDRED;
```

The reader should note that all statements from the GET to the IF (inclusive) will be executed 200 times. After the 200th execution the IF will not transfer control to LOOP, because I will no longer be less than 200.

We now present a program, called SQUARE, which will read a value for N and form the sum of the squares of the integers from 1 to N. Output will include N and the result, called ISUMSQS. (As an illustration, if N were 4, then the result would be $1^2 + 2^2 + 3^2 + 4^2$, which is 30.)

To form ISUMSQS, first set ISUMSQS = 0, then add 1^2 to ISUMSQS and call this new sum ISUMSQS. Repeat by then adding 2^2 to ISUMSQS and calling this new sum ISUMSQS, and so on. A statement such as

```
ISUMSQS = ISUMSQS + I**2;
```

is needed.

I should begin at 1 and be increased by 1 after each calculation. The process should be terminated after computation for I = N.

The code:

```
SQUARE:     PROCEDURE OPTIONS (MAIN);
            GET DATA (N);
            I = 1; ISUMSQS = 0;
CONTINUE:   ISUMSQS = ISUMSQS + I**2;
            I = I + 1;
            IF I <= N THEN GO TO CONTINUE;
            PUT DATA(N,ISUMSQS);
            END SQUARE;
```

The flow chart is on page 309.

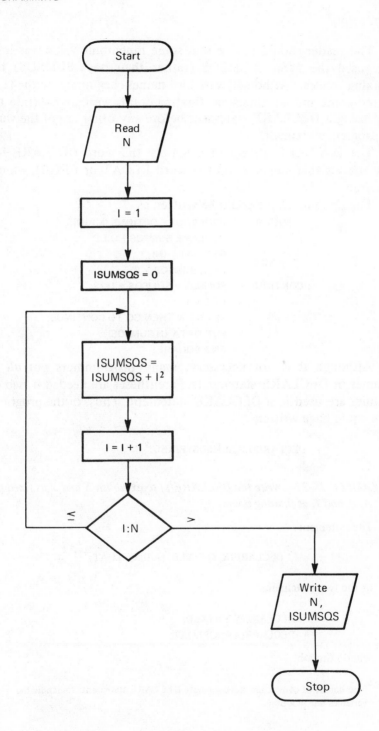

DECLARE

The reader should realize that some mnemonic value was lost when we used the name ISUMSQS (rather than, say, SUMSQS) to avoid mixing scales. Although variable names beginning with [I,N] are fixed-point and all others are floating-point, we may override this rule by using a **DECLARE** statement before any other use of the variable in a program statement.

The DECLARE statement is simply the word DECLARE followed by the variable name(s) and the word FLOAT or FIXED, whichever is desired.

The program above could be written as

```
SQUARE:     PROCEDURE OPTIONS (MAIN);
            DECLARE SUMSQS FIXED;
            GET DATA (N);
            I = 1; SUMSQS = 0;
CONTINUE:   SUMSQS = SUMSQS + I**2;
            I = I + 1;
            IF I <= N THEN GO TO CONTINUE;
            PUT DATA (N,SUMSQS);
            END SQUARE;
```

Although it is not necessary, many programmers put *all* variable names in DECLARE statements. Parentheses are needed if two or more names are used in a DECLARE statement. Thus, in the program above we could have written

DECLARE(I,N,SUMSQS) FIXED;[9]

EXAMPLE 14-27. Write the DECLARE(s) to extablish X and Y as fixed-point and A, B, and K as floating-point.

The statement

DECLARE(X,Y) FIXED, (A,B,K)FLOAT;

or the two statements

DECLARE(X,Y)FIXED;
DECLARE(A,B,K)FLOAT;

will do the job.

---

[9] You could, of course, use three separate DECLARE statements to handle the variables one at a time.

COMMENTS

The programmer can put remarks or comments anywhere in his program by enclosing his comments within /* and */ symbols. The following are examples of acceptable comments:

```
/* USE COMMENTS WISELY */
/*   (A+B)(C+D)  IS OK AS A COMMENT   */
/*              */
```

It is not necessary to have comments in programs, but they are generally helpful to both the programmer writing the program and to anyone who might later read or use the program.

The comment is *not* translated by the compiler. It is not executed, unlike all other PL/1 statements. The comment is merely printed as part of the listing of the program instructions.

EXAMPLE 14-28. Rewrite the last program with suitable comments.

```
SQUARE:    PROCEDURE OPTIONS (MAIN);
           DECLARE SUMSQS FIXED;
           GET DATA (N);
  /*    INITIALIZE BY SETTING COUNT = 1 AND SUM OF SQUARES = 0     */
           I = 1; SUMSQS = 0;
  /*    ADD I**2 TO SUM TO FORM NEW SUM   */
CONTINUE:  SUMSQS = SUMSQS + I**2;
  /*    ADD 1 TO COUNT    */
           I = I + 1;
  /*    TEST FOR TERMINATION OF LOOPING   */
           IF I <= N THEN GO TO CONTINUE;
           PUT DATA (N,SUMSQS);
           END SQUARE;
```

The purpose of Example 14-28 was to emphasize the use of comments within a program. In practice you might use comments less freely, although the choice is yours.

ADDITIONAL PL/1 CAPABILITIES

It is beyond the scope of this book to discuss all PL/1 capabilities. However, it should be noted that among them are DO-loops similar to those of FORTRAN, I/0 formats resembling those of FORTRAN, and descriptions similar to those in the COBOL Data Division.

THE PL/1 COMPILER

PL/1 is a compiler language. It is a language of statements which are easily written and understood by programmers. But computers work with binary code, so the statements must be translated into binary machine language before the program can be executed. It is the PL/1 *compiler,* a large program itself, which performs the necessary translation. The compiler can also detect many programming errors.

Assuming the program is on cards, the compilation process can be seen as

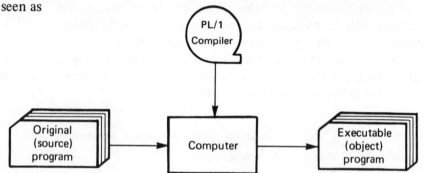

The original (source) program deck is returned in addition to a binary (object) version.[10] An additional product of compilation is a *listing* of all program statements.

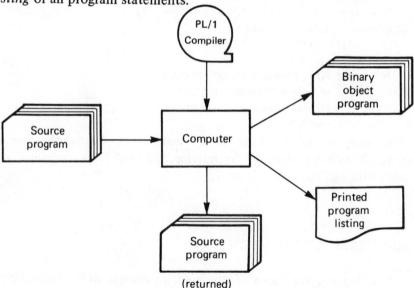

---

[10]One product of compilation is an object program which is loaded into main memory and executed. The programmer can request his own copy, but does not get one automatically.

The original deck is called a *source deck* since it is the computer's source of code. The translated version is the form which the computer uses to execute the program, and is called the *object deck*.

EXERCISES 14.6

Flowchart and write separate and complete PL/1 programs to do each of the following. Include at least one comment in each program.

1. Read values for a^2 and a, determine which is larger, store the larger value in **LARGER**, and write it.

2. Place in location **IJBIG** whichever of I or J is larger in absolute value.

*3. Do the following 350 times: read values for a, b, c, d and e, compute $x = a^2 \ \sqrt{(b^2 \ c - d)/(e + 1)^2}$, and write a, b, c, d, e, and x.

4. Read a value for a variable named **LAST** and compute and write the sum of the integers from 1 up to **LAST**.

5. Compute and write N_FACTORIAL (N!), for an N which is read in. As illustrations, $5! = 5 \cdot 4 \cdot 3 \cdot 2 \cdot 1$ (or $1 \cdot 2 \cdot 3 \cdot 4 \cdot 5$, if you prefer) and $8! = 8 \cdot 7 \cdot 6 \cdot 5 \cdot 4 \cdot 3 \cdot 2 \cdot 1$.

*6. Read a value for **NUMBER** and form the square of the sum of the integers from 1 to **NUMBER**. Write **NUMBER** and the result. For example, if **NUMBER** is 5, then compute $(1 + 2 + 3 + 4 + 5)^2$.

7. Read values for a, b, and c. Compute DISCRMNT $= b^2 - 4ac$. If DISCRMNT is positive, store +1 in **TYPE**; if it is zero, store 0 in **TYPE**; or if it is negative, put –1 in **TYPE**. Then write a, b, c, and **TYPE**.

15

REPORT PROGRAM
GENERATOR—RPG

INTRODUCTION

Report Program Generator (RPG) is a compiler language used to accept specified input data from cards and perform unit-record (EAM) type processing of the data. The results are produced as a report, a printed document.

The programmer must code

1. Input specifications
2. Calculation specifications
3. Output-format specifications.

Computer manufacturers supply specific forms for use in coding RPG programs (see Fig. 15-1).

We shall examine the following RPG data processing functions:

1. Describing a record and its fields (input)
2. Adding and subtracting (calculation)
3. Detail printing (output)
4. Control fields (input, calculation, output)
5. Total calculations (calculation)
6. Detail and total printing (output).

314

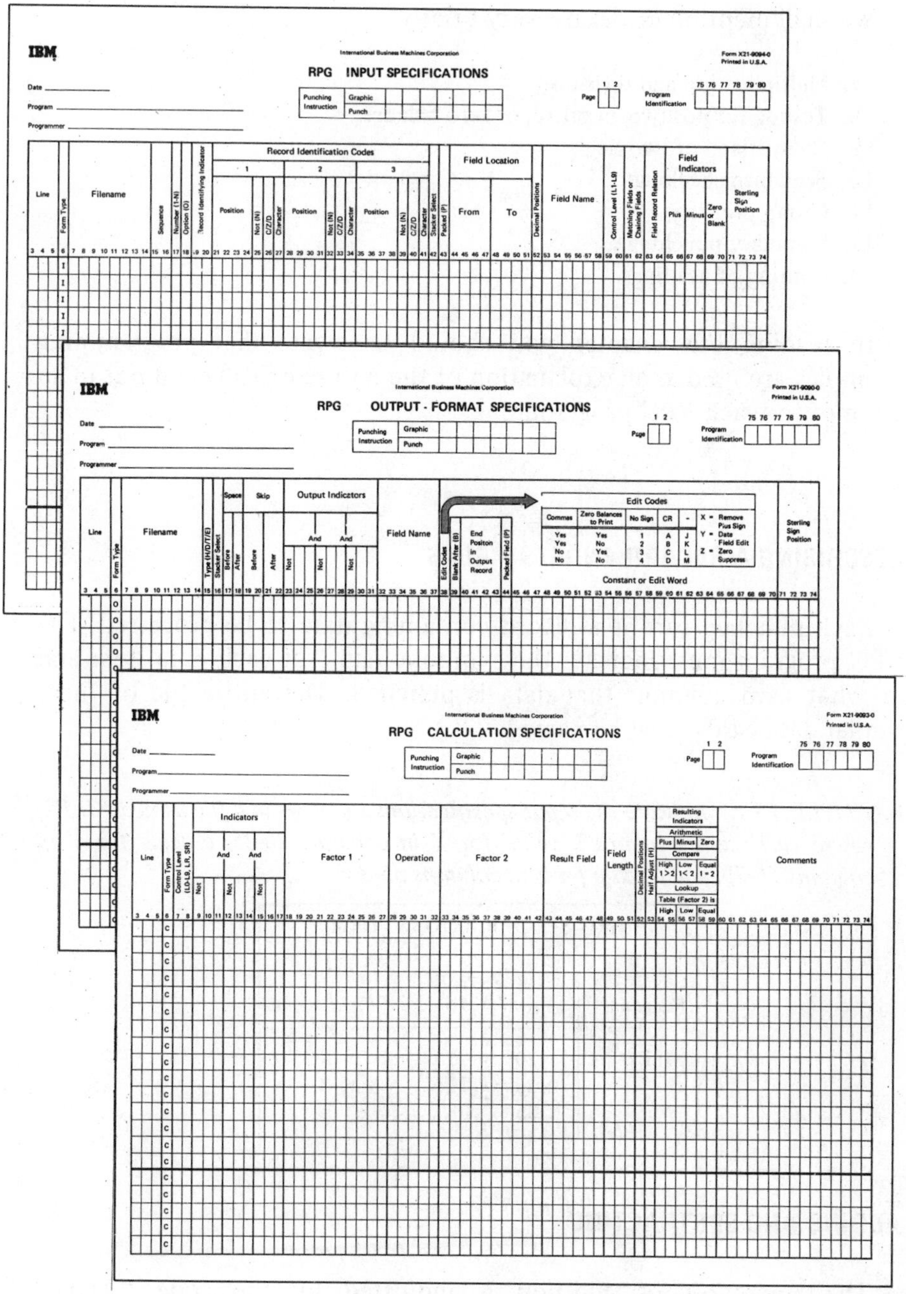

FIGURE 15-1. RPG Coding Forms.

We shall mention or discuss very briefly

7. Multiplication and division
8. Testing for positive, negative, or zero balance
9. Comparison of two fields
10. Sequence checking
11. Group printing
12. Summary punching
13. Printing of headings.

In reading this chapter you should be aware that programming examples are used as an explanation of the nature of RPG and not in an attempt to teach RPG programming.

DESCRIBING A RECORD AND ITS FIELDS

Each punched card is a record containing data to be processed. The RPG program must indicate the symbolic name of each data item and in what card columns that data is punched. The entire file of these similar data cards must be named.

EXAMPLE 15-1. Indicate the input specifications for cards in a file named FILE1, where each card contains a value for X in columns 20-25, a value for Y in columns 26-29, and a value for Z in columns 35-38.

INPUT SPECIFICATIONS FORM			
	Field Location		
Filename	From	To	Field Name
FILE1	20	25	X
	26	29	Y
	35	38	Z

ADDING AND SUBTRACTING

The *operation* of addition is indicated by the code "ADD." Subtraction is indicated by "SUB." The programmer must specify the two *factors* in an addition or subtraction, the name of the field where the *result* should be placed, and its *field length* (or number of columns the result might occupy).

EXAMPLE 15-2. *Show the calculation specifications for adding the previously specified X and Y and putting the result in a field named RESULT.*

CALCULATION SPECIFICATIONS FORM				
Factor 1	*Operation*	*Factor 2*	*Result Field*	*Field Length*
X	ADD ·	Y	RESULT	6

Later we will need to specify just where X, Y, and the 6-column RESULT will be placed on the output report.

If we had placed the sum (X + Y) in either X or Y (instead of in some new location, RESULT), we would have lost the original X or Y and could not output it later.

EXAMPLE 15-3. *Show the calculation specifications for RESULT = X + Y − Z.*

CALCULATION SPECIFICATIONS FORM				
Factor 1	*Operation*	*Factor 2*	*Result Field*	*Field Length*
X	ADD	Y	RESULT	6
RESULT	SUB	Z	RESULT	6

Note that RESULT is used to hold the temporary result (X + Y) first and then the final result (X + Y − Z). Each data name (X, Y, Z, RESULT) is actually a symbolic name for a storage location.

You must be careful of order in an operation like subtraction. As coded above, Z will be subtracted from RESULT. Factor 2 is always subtracted from factor 1.

EXERCISES 15.1

1. Show the input specifications for processing cards which contain values for SOCSEC in the first 9 columns, WAGE1 in columns 20-27, WAGE2 in columns 30-37, WAGE3 in columns 40-47, and WAGE4 in columns 50-57. Be sure to name the input file.

2. Indicate the calculation specifications for computing

WAGET = WAGE1 + WAGE2 + WAGE3 + WAGE4,

where WAGE1, WAGE2, WAGE3, WAGE4 are those of exercise 1.

3. When we perform the calculations in exercise 2, we introduce a new variable, WAGET. Is it necessary to change the input specifications to take care of this new variable? Why or why not?

4. Show the input specifications for RPG processing of cards containing values for variables A, B, C, D, E, F, G, H. Each value should be allowed five card columns and should be separated from adjacent values by five card columns. Assume A begins in column 6.

5. Indicate the calculation specifications for computation of

SUM1 = A + B + C
SUM2 = D + E + F
SUM3 = G + H
DIFF = SUM1 – SUM2 – SUM3,

where A, B, C, D, E, F, G, H are those of exercise 4.

DETAIL PRINTING

Since the purpose of RPG is to generate printed reports, let us consider one form of printing. *Detail printing* is the printing of data that has just been read from cards and of results of computations with that data. Detail printing is specified by the letter "D" in the proper column of the output-format specifications sheet.[1]

Just as an input file (of cards) must be named so must an output file (printed report) be named.

Just as the position (say columns 21-25) of data on the input card must be specified, so must the position of data for output (on the printed report) be specified. You merely indicate the column in which the *last digit* of the data item should be printed. The number is then positioned accordingly, since the input specifications indicate the size of input items and the calculation specifications tell the size of computed results.

---

[1] The printing of headings is specified by "H"; total printing is indicated by "T." Heading and total printing will be discussed later.

No one would go to all the trouble of writing an RPG program if there was only one input card of a given specification. You should realize then, that there are perhaps several hundred cards that will be read and processed. Consequently, there may be several hundred lines of output printed according to your output-format specifications. If you want each line to appear immediately under the one before it (single-spaced) you specify "1" in the *space* column. A "2" causes double-spacing, etc.

EXAMPLE 15-4. In a previous example we read X, Y, Z and then computed RESULT. Show the corresponding output-format specifications for single-spaced output, with X values ending in column 10, Y in column 20, Z in column 30, and RESULT in column 50. Call the file OUT1.

OUTPUT-FORMAT SPECIFICATIONS FORM				
Filename	*H/D/T*	*Space*	*Field Name*	*End Column*
OUT1	D	1		
			X	10
			Y	20
			Z	30
			RESULT	50

CONTROL FIELDS

Let us write an RPG program to generate a sales report. The report will list the number of each ITEM along with separate SALES figures for that item. In addition, the TOTAL of the separate sales for each item will be placed immediately after the list of all sales for that item. For example, we might have

ITEM numbers		separate SALES
5203	6	
5203	10	
5203	12	
5203	7	
5203	5	

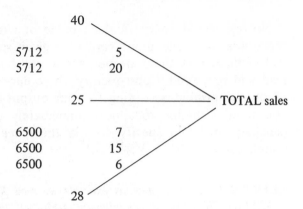

We have shown above the generated report for a sample of three items—numbers 5203, 5712, and 6500. Item 5203 has a sales total of 40, item 5712 a total of 25, and item 6500 a total of 28.

Assuming that each line containing an item number and a sales figure came from one data processing card, then a total of ten cards was used as input.

One consideration in handling a situation such as the one above is determining when the item number has changed; that is, determining when a total should be computed and a new sum begun. A *control field* is established by the programmer to instruct the computer to compare the contents of a specified (control) field for each card. When a change in the contents of a control field (such as the ITEM field above) occurs this is called a *control break*. When a control break occurs special calculations are made. One example of such calculations is the calculation of totals.

In this section we have used only one control field (the ITEM field). In other words, only one *control level* has been used. This is referred to as "L1" on the RPG input specifications sheet.

TOTAL CALCULATIONS

Let us continue the example of the last section, and indicate how totals can be computed at a control break.

We assume that each input card contains an ITEM number and four sales figures called ONE, TWO, THREE, FOUR (quarterly sales figures). The RPG program will compute the sum for each card and print this as the SALES figure opposite the ITEM number for that card.

In addition to printing the ITEM number and SALES total for each card, we want the TOTAL sales (from all cards) for each item and the total sales (called GTOTAL) of all items (see Fig. 15-2, page 324).

The input specifications might be

	INPUT SPECIFICATIONS FORM			
	Field Location			
Filename	*From*	*To*	*Field Name*	*Control Level*
SALESIN	1	4	ITEM	L1
	10	15	ONE	
	20	25	TWO	
	30	35	THREE	
	40	45	FOUR	

since each card contains an ITEM number and numbers for the quarterly sales (ONE, TWO, THREE, FOUR).

The calculation specifications are

	CALCULATION SPECIFICATIONS FORM				
Control Level	*Factor 1*	*Operation*	*Factor 2*	*Result Field*	*Field Length*
	ONE	ADD	TWO	SALES	6
	THREE	ADD	SALES	SALES	6
	FOUR	ADD	SALES	SALES	6
	TOTAL	ADD	SALES	TOTAL	7
L1	GTOTAL	ADD	TOTAL	GTOTAL	7

where

1. The first three lines merely indicate computation of the yearly SALES total for a given ITEM, *from one card.* This is done for each card.
2. The fourth line indicates computation of the TOTAL of all sales of a given ITEM (from all cards having that ITEM number).
3. The first four lines of computations occur for all detail cards which are read, the TOTAL being gradually accumulated.
4. Only the first four lines of computations will occur as long as there is no change in the ITEM number.
5. A change in ITEM number represents a control break, since ITEM was previously (in the input specifications) established as a control level, L1.
6. Such a control break causes execution of the fifth ADD. The TOTAL of all sales for this first ITEM number becomes the first part of GTOTAL (the grand total of all sales).

7. The TOTAL is then set to zero and the SALES for the next ITEM are totaled.[2] In other words, the first four lines are repeated for each card with the second ITEM number (5712 in our example). This process is continued until another change in ITEM number causes another control break.
8. The control break causes this second TOTAL to be added to GTOTAL. TOTAL is then set to zero and the process continues with a third ITEM's sales considered. And so on, for as many ITEMs as there are.

DETAIL AND TOTAL PRINTING

Let us continue with the example discussed above under TOTAL CALCULATIONS. Our concern now is the output-format specifications.

We shall call the output filename SALESRPT. ITEM and SALES shall be single-spaced. This information is detail printed (D) since it comes directly from each input (detail) card.

Thus, we have the output-format specifications

OUTPUT-FORMAT SPECIFICATIONS FORM				
Filename	*H/D/T*	*Space*	*Field Name*	*End Column*
SALESRPT	D	1		
			ITEM	10
			SALES	20

where columns 10 and 20 are arbitrary choices.

Note additionally that we have computed some totals: TOTAL and GTOTAL. When these are printed the operation is called *total printing,* and must be specified by the letter "T" in the H/D/T type column.

TOTAL is the SALES total for a particular ITEM and should be printed each time a control break occurs. This must be indicated on the coding sheet by placing the code L1 in the control level field.

GTOTAL is the total of all SALES for *all* ITEMs and should be printed only after all cards have been processed. This must be indicated on the coding sheet by "LR," to indicate that GTOTAL is the final total to be printed.

---

[2]The TOTAL for the first ITEM's SALES is available (briefly) for output, and we shall see how this is handled in the next section.

The revised output-format specifications:

OUTPUT-FORMAT SPECIFICATIONS FORM					
Filename	*H/D/T*	*Space*	*Control Level*	*Field Name*	*End Column*
SALESRPT	D	1			
				ITEM	10
				SALES	20
	T	2	L1		
				TOTAL	16
	T	3	LR		
				GTOTAL	16

We are allowing double-spacing for the TOTALs and triple-spacing for GTOTAL. Also, these totals are not lined up with the SALES values. This makes them easier to spot. Figure 15-2 shows sample output.

Our example uses only one control level, L1. For more complex problems additional levels (L2, L3, . . . ,L9) are available. Had our ITEMs come from different divisions of the company we might have been concerned with sales totals for each division, as well as for each ITEM. We would then have used L1 and L2.

EXERCISE 15.2

1. Show the input specifications, calculation specifications, and output-format specifications for the sales report example, if
   (a) the quarterly sales figures are in card columns 20-27, 30-37, 40-47, and 50-57.
   (b) the quarterly sales figures are renamed FIRST, SECOND, THIRD, and FOURTH.
   (c) ITEM numbers are printed (on the report) in columns 25-30. Be sure to make appropriate changes for other output figures.
   (d) spacing separating all lines is doubled when compared with the original example. Thus, single-spacing becomes double-spacing, etc.

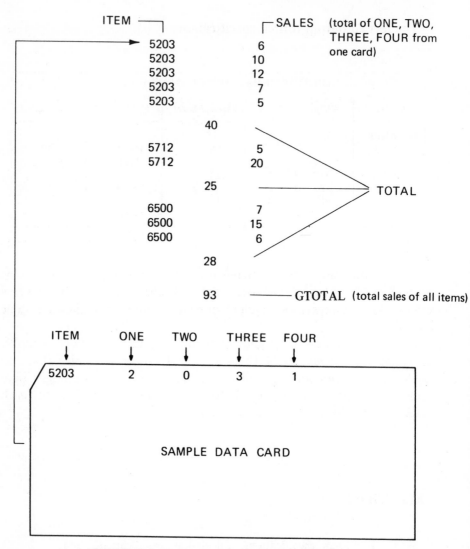

FIGURE 15-2. Printing for Total Calculations Example.

AN EXAMPLE

The amount of tax collected by the federal government from any taxpayer (call it TAX) is either

1. the amount originally deducted from earnings (DEDUCT) minus the amount to be returned (RETURN), when too much was deducted, or

2. the amount originally deducted (DEDUCT) plus the amount still due (DUE), when not enough was deducted.

We combine these two computations as

$$TAX = DEDUCT - RETURN + DUE,$$

since any particular taxpayer either must pay additionally (DUE) or else he has money returned (RETURN).[3] Thus one of the two (DUE or RETURN) is zero for any given taxpayer.

Taxpayers are identified by social security numbers. Their states of residence are indicated by numbers from 01 to 50.

The Detail Card

Each input card contains

1. the state of residence of the taxpayer in columns 1-2
2. the social security number of the taxpayer in columns 5-13
3. the amount deducted by the federal government in columns 20-29
4. the amount to be returned to the taxpayer in columns 40-49
5. the amount still due the federal government in columns 60-69

The Problem

Write an RPG program to list

1. *for each detail card* one line containing state, taxpayer, deducted tax, amount returned, amount due, and total tax collected.
2. *for each state* the total tax collected by the federal government from residents of that state.[4]
3. the total tax collected from all U.S. citizens.

Notation

STATE   the state of residence of the taxpayer
TAXPAY   the social security number of the taxpayer

---

[3] Unless, of course, the amount deducted was exactly correct, in which case he owes nothing and will have nothing returned.

[4] We assume the cards for all taxpayers from a given state are grouped together.

DEDUCT   the amount already deducted for the federal government
RETURN   the amount to be returned to the taxpayer
DUE   the amount still due the federal government by the taxpayer
TAX   the total tax collected from the taxpayer
STTOT   the total taxes paid by all residents of a given state
USATOT   the total taxes paid by all U.S. taxpayers

The Program

INPUT SPECIFICATIONS FORM				
Filename	Field Location From To		Field Name	Control Level
TAXIN	1	2	STATE	L1
	5	13	TAXPAY	
	20	29	DEDUCT	
	40	49	RETURN	
	60	69	DUE	

CALCULATION SPECIFICATIONS FORM					
Control Level	Factor 1	Operation	Factor 2	Result Field	Field Length
	DEDUCT	SUB	RETURN	TAX	10
	TAX	ADD	DUE	TAX	10
	STTOT	ADD	TAX	STTOT	10
L1	USATOT	ADD	STTOT	USATOT	10

OUTPUT-FORMAT SPECIFICATIONS FORM					
Filename	H/D/T	Space	Control Level	Field Name	End Column
TAXOUT	D	2			
				STATE	2
				TAXPAY	13
				DEDUCT	29
				RETURN	49
				DUE	69
				TAX	80
	T	3	L1		
				STTOT	50
	T	3	LR		
				USATOT	45

Since choices for output columns are arbitrary, we conveniently used the same columns for output as we used for input.

OTHER FEATURES

We have already seen some of the processing functions which can be used in RPG. The reader should have some feeling about the place of RPG as a programming language. RPG is used for the rapid generation of reports and documents; it computerizes many of the functions of the unit record (EAM) equipment. Although RPG is a programming language, it is unlike any other (FORTRAN, COBOL, PL/1, Assembler) studied in this text. These other languages are designed for handling more complex logic and processing than is RPG, but RPG is better designed for report generation.

Multiplication and Division

RPG can handle multiplication and division. The codes used are "MULT" and "DIV."

Testing for Positive, Negative, or Zero Balance

Specifications are executed in the sequential order in which they are written, unless a transfer is made from the normal sequence.

You can test the number in an input field of a card and transfer if the value is zero (or positive, or negative).

Similarly, you can test the result of some calculations and transfer if that value is zero (or positive, or negative).

Comparison of Two Fields

You can compare the numbers in two different fields and transfer according to their relative size (greater than, less than, or equal).

Sequence Checking

Several types of sequence checking (see Chapter 2) can be handled using RPG.

Group Printing

Group printing resembles detail and total printing; however, only one line (the total) is printed for each group of detail cards.

Summary Punching

Summary punching provides a more condensed report of transactions than does detail and total printing. Each total requested is *punched* on a separate card, along with enough information to indicate just what it is a total of. Detail information is omitted.

Printing of Headings

To print a heading you must place an "H" in the type column of the output-format specifications form. You must also indicate the actual message by placing it in a special section of the coding form, and including it in quotations.

SPECIFICATIONS

Filenames must contain 1-8 letters and/or digits. The first must be a letter. If you are using the standard coding forms (see Fig. 15-1), then the name should always begin in column 1; that is, it should be left justified. Also, the RPG compiler only recognizes the first 7 characters of any name. Thus, two names such as OBJECT10 and OBJECT15 would be considered identical for processing purposes. This could be disastrous, since different files must have different names (within the same program).

Field names must contain 1-6 characters (letters and/or digits). The first must be a letter.

ORDER OF ENTRIES ON CODING FORMS

Entries on the calculation specifications form should be in the order in which they are to be executed.

The field names used on the input specifications sheet and the output-format sheet need not be placed in order according to the columns allowed for them. However, it is usually easier to write or follow a program if this natural order is preserved.

INDICATORS

We have used L1 as a control-level indicator, and we have neglected to use any other indicators. Some of their uses are listed below.

1. Indicators are used to determine the record type for which a specified set of calculations is to be carried out, also preventing such calculations for records of different type.
2. Control-level indicators are used to allow some calculations only at control break occurrences.
3. Codes can be used to control calculations according to conditions that resulted from previous calculations.
4. Halt indicators are used to end execution of the program if an error caused by calculations has occurred.

RPG VERSUS EAM

RPG is used for efficient computerization of processing which had previously been handled almost exclusively by EAM equipment. RPG uses the computer to process data and generate reports. Such processing is faster than the electro-mechanical and manual operation of EAM. Fewer errors are likely with RPG, since human intervention is minimized. And RPG programs are easy to write!

We have seen that RPG can be used to handle the calculation, summarizing, and reporting otherwise carried out by the calculator and accounting machine. All collator functions (matching, merging, match-merging, sequence checking, and selecting) can also be programmed in RPG.

COBOL ACKNOWLEDGEMENT

The following extract from Government Printing Office Form Number 1962-0668996 is presented for the information and guidance of the user:

"This publication is based on the COBOL System developed in 1959 by a committee composed of government users and computer manufacturers. The organizations participating in the original development were:

Air Material Command, United States Air Force
Bureau of Standards, United States Department of Commerce
Burroughs Corporation
David Taylor Model Basin, Bureau of Ships, United States Navy
Electronic Data Processing Division, Minneapolis-Honeywell Regulator Company
International Business Machines Corporation
Radio Corporation of America
Sylvania Electric Products, Inc.
UNIVAC Division of Sperry Rand Corporation

"In addition to the organizations listed above, the following other organizations participated in the work of the Maintenance Group:

Allstate Insurance Company
The Bendix Corporation, Computer Division
Control Data Corporation
E. I. du Pont de Nemours and Company
General Electric Company
General Motors Corporation
Lockheed Aircraft Corporation
The National Cash Register Company
Philco Corporation
Royal McBee Corporation
Standard Oil Company (New Jersey)
United States Steel Corporation

"This COBOL-61 manual is the result of contributions made by all of the above-mentioned organizations. No warranty, expressed or implied, is made by any contributor or by the committee as to the accuracy and functioning of the programming system and language. Moreover, no responsibility is assumed by any contributor, or by the committee, in connection therewith.

"It is reasonable to assume that a number of improvements and additions will be made to COBOL. Every effort will be made to insure that the improvements and corrections will be made in an orderly fashion, with due recognition of existing users' investments in programming. However, this protection can be positively assured only by individual implementors.

"Procedures have been established for the maintenance of COBOL. Inquiries concerning the procedures and the methods for proposing changes should be directed to the Executive Committee of the Conference on Data Systems Languages.

"The authors and copyright holders of the copyrighted material used herin: FLOW-MATIC,* Programming for the UNIVAC* I and II, Data Automation Systems 1958, 1959, Sperry Rand Corporation; IBM Commercial Translator, Form No. F28-8013, copyrighted 1959 by IBM; FACT, DSI 27A5260-2760, copyrighted 1960 by Minneapolis-Honeywell, have specifically authorized the use of this material, in whole or in part, in the COBOL specifications. Such authorization extends to the reproduction and use of COBOL specifications in programming manuals or similar publications.

"Any organization interested in reproducing the COBOL report and initial specifications, in whole or in part, using ideas taken from this report or utilizing this report as the basis for an instruction manual or any other purpose is free to do so. However, all such organizations are requested to reproduce this section as part of the introduction to the document. Those using a short passage, as in a book review, are requested to mention 'COBOL' in acknowledgement of the source, but need not quote this entire section."

*Trademark of Sperry Rand Corporation.

ANNOTATED
BIBLIOGRAPHY

Chapter 1. A Brief History of Computing and Computers

Newman, James R., *The World of Mathematics*. New York: Simon and Schuster, Inc., 1956. A wealth of material covering computing devices and methods from ancient times to ENIAC. Selections by George Boole, John Von Neumann, A. M. Turing, Claude Shannon, and others.

Rosen, Saul, *Programming Systems and Languages*. New York: McGraw-Hill, Inc., 1967. Begins with a historical survey of computers and languages from 1947 to present. Many manufacturers and their computers are mentioned. Comments on software (programming) development.

Chapter 2. The Punched Cards and EAM Equipment

Claffey, William J., *Principles of Data Processing*. Belmont, California: Dickenson Publishing Company, Inc., 1967. A good explanation of EAM, but not as thorough as the Micallef text (see below).

Langenbach, Robert G., *Introduction to Automated Data Processing*. Englewood Cliffs, N.J.: Prentice-Hall, Inc., 1968. Describes many areas of data processing: including pegboards, keysorting, metal plates, microfilming, aperture cards, punched tags, edge-punched cards, and others which are not covered in my text.

Micallef, Benjamin A., *Electric Accounting Machine Fundamentals*. Reading, Mass.: Addison-Wesley Publishing Company, Inc., 1968. In-depth explanations of functions and operations of the keypunch, sorter, interpreter, reproducer, collator, and accounting machine. Many photos and illustrations.

Chapter 3. Number Systems

Bartee, Thomas C., *Digital Computer Fundamentals* (Second Edition). New York: McGraw-Hill, Inc., 1966. The author devotes an entire chapter to number systems; Topics including decimal, binary, octal, and hexadecimal systems, addition, subtraction, multiplication, division, pulses, transmission, complements, excess three code, and binary-coded decimal.

Chapter 4. Computer Logic and Boolean Algebra

Litton Industries, *Digital Computer Fundamentals*. Englewood Cliffs, N.J.: Prentice-Hall, Inc., 1965. Treats computer logic and gates in detail.

Whitesitt, J. Eldon, *Boolean Algebra and Its Applications*. Reading, Mass.: Addison-Wesley Publishing Company, Inc., 1961. Detail on Boolean algebra and switching circuits.

Chapter 5. The Electronic Computer

Desmonde, William H., *Real-Time Data Processing Systems: Introductory Concepts*. Englewood Cliffs, N.J.: Prentice-Hall, Inc., 1964. A general introduction to real-time systems. Includes chapters on environment, multiprogramming, storage allocation, on-line computer centers, transmission control, simulation, and planning a system. Applications include SABRE system and Project Mercury.

Ziegler, James R., *Time-Sharing Data Processing Systems*. Englewood Cliffs, N.J.: Prentice-Hall, Inc., 1967. Detail on time-sharing systems. Includes what they are and their economics. Many applications. A wealth of information on software and hardware (CPU, storage, and terminals).

Chapter 6. Storage and Input/Output

IBM, *Introduction to IBM System/360 Direct Access Storage Devices and Organization Methods*. White Plains, New York: International Business Machines Corporation, 1969. (C20-1649). Detailed explanations of the functions, physical features, and addressing of IBM addressable storage devices.

Chapter 8. The Central Processing Unit

Gear, C. William, *Computer Organization and Programming*. New York: McGraw-Hill, Inc., 1969. Contains information on the CPU and control.

Hassitt, Anthony, *Computer Programming and Computer Systems*. New York: Academic Press, Inc., 1967. Includes comparison of the central processing units of the CDC 1604, 3600, and 6600, the IBM 1620, 1401, 7090, 360, and several others.

Chapter 9. Languages and Applications

Bobrow, Davis B., and Judah L. Schwartz, *Computers and the Policy-Making Community*. Englewood Cliffs, N.J.: Prentice-Hall, Inc., 1968. A collection of papers on various applications of computers, including simulations, CRT, computer logic, information retrieval, cost analysis, artificial intelligence, etc.

Boutell, Wayne S., *Computer-Oriented Business Systems*. Englewood Cliffs, N.J.: Prentice-Hall, Inc., 1968. An introduction to business information systems: hardware, software, batch-processing, design. Emphasis on IBM 1401 and IBM 360.

Deardon, John, and F. Warren McFarlan, *Management Information Systems*. Homewood, Illinois: Richard D. Irwin, Inc., 1966. Text material on information systems, management problems of data processing, PERT, simulation, and information retrieval. Additionally, over 20 case studies are given.

Hare, Van Court, Jr., *Systems Analysis: A Diagnostic Approach*. New York: Harcourt, Brace, and World, Inc., 1967. Describes systems in general and system patterns. Intended for "problem solvers." Includes system definition, variety and control, simplification methods, systems analysis, search problems, systems simulation, logic, and probability. Matrices are used.

Sammett, Jean E., *Programming Languages: History and Fundamentals*. Englewood Cliffs, N.J.: Prentice-Hall, Inc., 1969. Explanation and comparison of programming languages—including all the ordinary ones and many others.

Chapter 10. Program Flowcharting

Moursund, David G., *How Computers Do It*. Belmont, California: Wadsworth Publishing Company, Inc., 1969. Many flow charts, examples, and problems involving flowcharting. Additional material on algorithms.

Steinbach, Robert C., *Programming Exercises for Problem-Oriented Languages.* Beverly Hills, California: Glencoe Press, 1969. Many examples and exercises in flowcharting.

Chapter 11. System/360 Assembler Language Programming

Germain, Clarence B., *Programming the IBM 360.* Englewood Cliffs, N.J.: Prentice-Hall, Inc., 1967. A complete guide to programming the IBM 360. Many short examples.

Golden, James T., and Richard M. Leichus, *IBM 360 Programming and Computing.* Englewood Cliffs, N.J.: Prentice-Hall, Inc., 1967. A good text for additional information and reading on System/360 assembler language. Many programming examples.

IBM, *A Programmer's Introduction to the IBM System/360 Architecture, Instructions, and Assembler Language.* White Plains, N.Y. International Business Machines Corporation, 1969. (C20-1646). An IBM Student Text. Contains good introductory examples, explanations, and programs.

Chapter 12. FORTRAN Programming

Computer Usage Company, Inc., and Eric A. Weiss, *Computer Usage 360 FORTRAN Programming.* New York: McGraw-Hill, Inc., 1969. An introduction to FORTRAN programming for the IBM 360.

Malcom, Robert E., and Malcolm H. Gotterer, *Computers in Business: A FORTRAN Introduction.* Scranton, Pa.: International Textbook Company, 1968. A good introduction to FORTRAN for business applications. Many complete programs. Foldouts with flow charts and programs.

Organick, Elliott I., *A FORTRAN IV Primer.* Reading, Mass.: Addison-Wesley Publishing Company, 1966. A clear and comprehensive treatment of FORTRAN IV. Many helpful flow charts and illustrations.

Stuart, Fredric, *FORTRAN Programming.* New York: John Wiley & Sons, Inc., 1969. A clear introduction to FORTRAN IV programming. Examples, etc. do not assume a lot of mathematics. Specifications are given for 152 computers.

Chapter 13. COBOL Programming

Jones, Robert Lloyd, *Fundamental COBOL or IBM System/360.* Englewood Cliffs, N.J.: Prentice-Hall, Inc., 1969. Explains COBOL statements and divisions with a minimum of words. Several case studies with complete programs and explanations.

McCracken, Daniel D., *A Guide to COBOL Programming*. New York: John Wiley & Sons, Inc., 1963. Complete explanation of COBOL. Very clearly written. Many examples. Orientation is second generation.

Spitzbarth, Laurel M., *Basic COBOL Programming*. Reading, Mass.: Addison-Wesley Publishing Co., Inc., 1970. A self-instructional approach. Many examples, including flow charts, code, cards, and listings.

Chapter 14. PL/1 Programming

Sprowls, R. Clay, *Introduction to PL/1 Programming*. New York: Harper and Row, Publishers, Inc., 1969. A good introduction to PL/1. Contains actual program listings. Many examples. Excellent, readable format.

Weinberg, Gerald M., *PL/1 Programming Primer*. New York: McGraw-Hill, Inc., 1966. A fine introduction to PL/1 programming. Many examples.

Chapter 15. Report Program Generator—RPG

Gildersleeve, Thomas R., *Computer Data Processing and Programming*. Englewood Cliffs, N.J.: Prentice-Hall, Inc., 1970. A self-teaching introduction to RPG programming.

IBM, *IBM System/360 Disk and Tape Operating Systems Report Program Generator Specifications*. White Plains, N.Y.: International Business Machines Corporation, 1968. (C26-3570-4). A reference manual for RPG. Many examples.

Saxon, James A., *System 360/20 RPG Programming*. Belmont, California: Dickenson Publishing Company, Inc., 1968. A self-instructional manual.

ANSWERS TO
SELECTED EXERCISES

CHAPTER 1

6. (b)   9
19   10   4
33   14

7. (a)   2,000,000

(b) $\frac{1}{2}$

(c)   3,000,000

(d)   5 milliseconds

(e)   .2 microsecond

CHAPTER 3

Section 3.1

2.   19
3.   26
5.   100001
6.   1010111
9.   63
11.   62
14.   249
15.   316
18.   DO
19.   10001011
22.   231
23.   1502

Section 3.2

1. (a) 1100
    (b) 10111
    (c) 10010
    (d) 110000
    (e) 1111
    (f) 11010
2. (a) 101
    (b) 1017
    (c) 133
    (d) 1450
    (e) 135
3. (a) AE
    (b) 178
    (c) 1AAB
    (d) 1663
    (e) CB3

Section 3.3

1. (a)   17
    (b)   6
    (c)   53
    (d) 231
2. (a) 4E
    (b) 24
    (c) 3D
    (d) E
3. (a) 10
    (b) 11
    (c) 1010
    (d) 1101

Section 3.4

1. (a) 11001
    (b) 1111110
    (c) 10010110
    (d) 1011000

2.   (a)   430
      (b)   3445
      (c)   12351
      (d)   130003
3.   (a)   8E5
      (b)   8CE8
      (c)   312A
      (d)   A4A06

Section 3.5

1.   70
3.   27
6.   10001111
8.   8D
9.   55
12.   110101100
13.   1FF
14.   37C
15.   5274
16.   6757
17.   1.125 or $1\frac{1}{8}$
18.   1.75 or $1\frac{3}{4}$
19.   6.5 or $6\frac{1}{2}$
20.   1001.011
21.   7.5 or $7\frac{1}{2}$
22.   12.25 or $12\frac{1}{4}$
23.   114.5
24.   1D.C

CHAPTER 4

Section 4.1

4. $A \cdot B \cdot C \cdot (D + E \cdot F)$
6. $A + B \cdot C + D \cdot E \cdot F$
7. $A \cdot (B + C + D \cdot E)$
11. $A \cdot (E + F) + B \cdot (C + D)$
13. $A \cdot (B \cdot C \cdot D + E + F) \cdot G$

14.   (a)   1
          (b)   1
          (c)   1
          (d)   0
          (e)   0

Section 4.2

9. $A \cdot B + C$
11. $A \cdot (B + C)$
13. $\overline{A \cdot B + \overline{C}}$

CHAPTER 7

1.   binary: 1111011
         EBCDIC: F1 F2 F3
         ASCII: 51 52 53

2.   (a)   C3 E2 F1 F0 F1
                  11000011 11100010 11110001 11110000 11110001
          (b)   D4 D1 C3
                  11010100 11010001 11000011
          (c)   F7 F5
                  11110111 11110101

3.   (a)   A3 B3 51 50 51
                  10100011 10110011 01010001 01010000 01010001
          (b)   AD AA A3
                  10101101 10101010 10100011
          (c)   57 55
                  01010111 01010101

CHAPTER 11

Section 11.1

2.   16,000 halfwords, 8000 fullwords
3.   40,150
4.   40, 160, 400, 656, 1000
7.   − 12:   11111111 11110100
         − 73:   11111111 10110111
         −205:   11111111 00110011

Section 11.2

3.

200	L	3,624
204	M	2,628
208	A	3,620
212	A	3,632
216	M	2,636
220	ST	3,640
224	EOJ	

5. 6

Section 11.3

3.

	START	200
	BALR	13,0
	USING	*,13
	L	5,B
	M	4,C
	A	5,A
	ST	5,R
	S	5,D
	M	4,E
	ST	5,S
	EOJ	
A	DS	F
B	DS	F
C	DS	F
D	DS	F
E	DS	F
R	DS	F
S	DS	F
	END	

4.

	START	200
	BALR	13,0
	USING	*,13
	L	9,X
	M	8,FIVE
	L	11,Y
	M	10,TEN
	AR	9,11
	ST	9,Z

(continued)

```
            EOJ
    X       DS      F
    Y       DS      F
    Z       DS      F
    FIVE    DC      F'5'
    TEN     DC      F'10'
            END
```

10. 15A, 19,B17.3, EXERCISE2
12. 00000000 00000000 00000000 00100111
13. 11111111 11111111 11111111 11101100

Section 11.4

```
2.          START   200
    IN      DTFCD   BLKSIZE = 80
                    DEVICE = 2501
    OUT     DTFPR   BLKSIZE = 132
                    DEVICE = 1403
            BALR    13,0
            USING   *,13
            OPEN    IN,OUT
            GET     IN    I,R
            L       5,I
            M       4,R
            ST      5,E
            M       4,I
            ST      5,P
            PUT     OUT   I,R,E,P
            CLOSE   IN,OUT
            EOJ
    I       DS      F
    R       DS      F
    E       DS      F
    P       DS      F
            END


5.          START   200
    IN      DTFCD   BLKSIZE = 80
                    DEVICE = 2501
    OUT     DTFPR   BLKSIZE = 132
                    DEVICE = 1403
            BALR    13,0
            USING   *,13
```
                                        (continued)

```
        OPEN    IN,OUT
        GET     IN  A,B,C
        L       5,B
        M       4,B
        L       7,A
        M       6,C
        M       6,FOUR
        SR      5,7
        ST      5,D
        GET     IN  X
        L       3,X
        M       2,X
        M       2,A
        L       5,X
        M       4,B
        AR      5,3
        A       5,C
        ST      5,Y
        PUT     OUT  A,B,C,D,X,Y
        CLOSE   IN,OUT
        EOJ
A       DS      F
B       DS      F
C       DS      F
D       DS      F
X       DS      F
Y       DS      F
FOUR    DC      F'4'
        END
```

Section 11.5

```
2.          START   200
    READ    DTFCD   BLKSIZE = 80
                    DEVICE = 2501
    WRITE   DTFPR   BLKSIZE = 132
                    DEVICE = 1403
            BALR    13,0
            USING   *,13
            OPEN    READ,WRITE
            LA      9,75
    LOOP    GET     READ  V0,T,G
            L       5,G
```
(continued)

```
          M        4,T
          L        7,V0
          SR       7,5
          ST       7,V
          PUT      WRITE  V0,G,T,V
          BCT      9,LOOP
          CLOSE    READ,WRITE
          EOJ
   G      DS       F
   T      DS       F
   V0     DS       F
   V      DS       F
          END
```

5.
```
          START    200
   READ   DTFCD    BLKSIZE = 80
                   DEVICE = 2501
   WRITE  DTFPR    BLKSIZE = 132
                   DEVICE = 1403
          BALR     13,0
          USING    *,13
          OPEN     READ,WRITE
          GET      READ  NUMBER
          L        9,NUMBER
   LOOP   GET      READ  WAGE,HOURS
          L        5,HOURS
          M        4,WAGE
          ST       5,PAY
          PUT      WRITE  WAGE,HOURS,PAY
          BCT      9,LOOP
          CLOSE    READ,WRITE
          EOJ
   WAGE   DS       F
   HOURS  DS       F
   PAY    DS       F
   NUMBER DS       F
          END
```

6.
```
          START    200
   READ   DTFCD    BLKSIZE = 80
                   DEVICE = 2501
   WRITE  DTFPR    BLKSIZE = 132
                   DEVICE = 1403    (continued)
```

```
                    BALR      13,0
                    USING     *,13
                    OPEN      READ,WRITE
                    GET       READ  X
                    LA        9,6
                    L         5,X
          LOOP      M         4,X
                    BCT       9,LOOP
                    ST        5,Y
                    PUT       WRITE  X,Y
                    CLOSE     READ,WRITE
                    EOJ
          X         DS        F
          Y         DS        F
                    END
```

11.

```
                    START     200
          READ      DTFCD     BLKSIZE = 80
                              DEVICE = 2501
          WRITE     DTFPR     BLKSIZE = 132
                              DEVICE = 1403
                    BALR      13,0
                    USING     *,13
                    OPEN      READ,WRITE
                    GET       READ  M,B
                    PUT       WRITE  M,B
                    LA        9,10
          LOOP      L         5,X
                    M         4,M
                    A         5,B
                    ST        5,Y
                    PUT       WRITE  X,Y
                    L         8,X
                    A         8,ONE
                    BCT       9,LOOP
                    CLOSE     READ,WRITE
                    EOJ
          M         DS        F
          B         DS        F
          X         DC        F'1'
          ONE       DC        F'1'
          Y         DS        F
                    END
```

Section 11.6

1.
```
           START    200
  READ     DTFCD    BLKSIZE = 80
                    DEVICE = 2501
  WRITE    DTFPR    BLKSIZE = 132
                    DEVICE = 1403
           BALR     13,0
           USING    *,13
           OPEN     READ,WRITE
           GET      READ  M,V
           L        5,M
           M        4,V
           M        4,V
           SRL      5,1
           ST       5,E
           PUT      WRITE  M,V,E
           CLOSE    READ,WRITE
           EOJ
  M        DS       F
  V        DS       F
  E        DS       F
           END
```

4.
```
           START    200
  READ     DTFCD    BLKSIZE = 80
                    DEVICE = 2501
  WRITE    DTFPR    BLKSIZE = 132
                    DEVICE = 1403
           BALR     13,0
           USING    *,13
           OPEN     READ,WRITE
           GET      READ  A,B,C
           L        5,A
           SLL      5,1
           L        8,B
           SLL      8,2
           AR       5,8
           L        10,C
           SLL      10,3
           SR       5,10
           ST       5,X
           PUT      WRITE  A,B,C,X
           CLOSE    READ,WRITE            (continued)
```

```
              EOJ
    A         DS         F
    B         DS         F
    C         DS         F
    X         DS         F
              END
```

9.   8

Section 11.7

```
1.              START      200
    READ        DTFCD      BLKSIZE = 80
                           DEVICE = 2501
    WRITE       DTFPR      BLKSIZE = 132
                           DEVICE = 1403
                BALR       13,0
                USING      *,13
                OPEN       READ,WRITE
                GET        READ  Q
                BC         4,SQUARE
                L          5,Q
                A          5,FIVE
                ST         5,P
                BC         15,OUTPUT
    SQUARE      L          5,Q
                M          4,Q
                ST         5,P
    OUTPUT      PUT        WRITE  Q,P
                CLOSE      READ WRITE
                EOJ
    Q           DS         F
    P           DS         F
    FIVE        DC         F'5'
                END
```

```
3.              START      200
    READ        DTFCD      BLKSIZE = 80
                           DEVICE = 2501
    WRITE       DTFPR      BLKSIZE = 132
                           DEVICE = 1403
                BALR       13,0
                USING      *,13            (continued)
```

```
            OPEN     READ,WRITE
            GET      READ   X
            L        5,X
            S        5,TEN
            BC       2,BIGGER
            L        5,X
            M        4,NINE
            ST       5,Y
            BC       15,OUT
BIGGER      L        5,X
            M        4,X
            ST       5,Y
OUT         PUT      WRITE   X,Y
            CLOSE    READ,WRITE
            EOJ
X           DS       F
Y           DS       F
NINE        DC       F'9'
TEN         DC       F'10'
            END
```

CHAPTER 12

Section 12.1

1. (a)   Floating-point variable or expression
    (b)   Unacceptable
    (c)   Unacceptable
    (d)   Floating-point expression
    (e)   Floating-point expression
    (f)   Mixed expression
    (g)   Mixed expression
    (h)   Unacceptable
    (i)   Floating-point expression
    (j)   Mixed expression
    (k)   Floating-point expression
    (l)   Fixed-point expression
    (m)   Floating-point expression
    (n)   Mixed expression
    (o)   Mixed expression
    (p)   Floating-point expression
2. (a) $(A + B)/(C - D)$
    (h) $A**(M + 1)*G$

(i)   (X/(P + Q))**(I + 1)
(o)   7*(ALPHA + BETA)

Section 12.2

1.   (h)   S = .5*G*T**2 + V0*T
      (i)   DR = SQRT(B**2 – 4.0*A*C)
      (j)   AO = ABS(X1 ÷ X2)
      (n)   AR = SQRT(S*(S – A)*(S – B)*(S – C))
2.   (a)   N = N + 1
      (b)   I = I – 2
      (c)   Y = X
      (d)   J = 0
      (e)   Y = 2*X
3.   (a)   6
      (b)   6.
      (c)   7
      (d)   25.
      (e)   0.
      (f)   0
      (g)   1.
      (h)   0
      (i)   5
      (j)   5.6
      (k)   .9999999
      (l)   0
      (m)   0.
      (n)   11

Section 12.3

1.   (a)   READ(5,100)J,K,L
                  100 FORMAT (3I2)

      (c)   READ(5,100)A1,A2,I
                  100 FORMAT(2F 4.1,I2)

      (e)   READ(5,100)P,R
                  100 FORMAT(2F6.1)

2.   (a)   WRITE(6,200)I,K,JSUM,N,M1
                  200 FORMAT(3I3,2I1)

(d)   WRITE(6,200)H,O,QVAL
                200 FORMAT(2F3.1,F6.5)

(e)   WRITE(6,200)Z,I,Q
                200 FORMAT(F4.1,I4,F4.1)

Section 12.4

2.   READ(5,100)X
                   100 FORMAT(F10.4)
                      IF(X)3,4,4
                    3 Y = X**2
                      GO TO 50
                    4 Y = X**3
                   50 WRITE(6,200)X,Y
                   200 FORMAT(2F10.4)
                      STOP
                      END

3.   READ(5,100)A,B
                   100 FORMAT(2F10.2)
                      IF(A – B)70,90,90
                   70 BIG = B
                      SMALL = A
                      GO TO 40
                   90 BIG = A
                      SMALL = B
                   40 WRITE(6,200)BIG,SMALL
                   200 FORMAT(2F10.2)
                      STOP
                      END

7.   READ(5,100)X
                   100 FORMAT(F10.2)
                      IF(X)1,2,2
                    1 AB = –X
                      GO TO 500
                    2 AB = X
                   500 WRITE(6,200)AB
                   200 FORMAT(F10.2)
                      STOP
                      END

Section 12.5

1.
```
            I = 0
        12 READ(5,100)X
       100 FORMAT(F10.1)
            Y = X**2 + 1.0
            WRITE(6,200)X,Y
       200 FORMAT(F10.1,F15.2)
            I = I + 1
            IF(I - 100)12,13,13
        13 STOP
            END
```

4.
```
            READ(5,100)M
       100 FORMAT (I4)
            J = 0
         8 READ(5,200)EYE,N,P
       200 FORMAT(F4.0,I3,F8.2)
            S = P*(1.0 + EYE)**N
            WRITE(6,300)EYE,N,P,S
       300 FORMAT(F4.0,I3,F8.2,F12.2)
            J = J + 1
            IF(I - M)8,9,9
         9 STOP
            END
```

8.
```
            READ(5,100)A,B,N
       100 FORMAT(2F10.3,I3)
            W = (A + B)**N + SQRT(A*B)
            WRITE(6,200)A,B,N,W
       200 FORMAT(2F10.3,I3,F12.4)
            STOP
            END
```

10.
```
            READ(5,100)K
       100 FORMAT(I3)
            KPROD = 1
            J = K
         7 KPROD = KPROD*J
            J = J - 1
            IF(J.GT.1) GO TO 7
            WRITE(6,200)K,KPROD
       200 FORMAT(I3,I10)
            STOP
            END
```

Section 12.6

3.
```
                ISUM = 0
                I = 1
              5 ISUM = ISUM + I
                I = I + 2
                IF(I – 99)5,5,7
              7 WRITE(6,100)ISUM
            100 FORMAT(I10)
                STOP
                END
```

CHAPTER 13

Section 13.1

1. Unacceptable:
    150,000   (commas not allowed)
    –4.   (ends with decimal point)
    5.37A   (letters not allowed)
    TEN   (letters not allowed in *numeric* literals)
    X   (letters not allowed in *numeric* literals)
    $8.35   ($ not allowed)
    6-3   (– not allowed)

2. Unacceptable:
    LIST   (not enclosed by quotes)
    'TEN   (right quote missing)
    'A + B –'C' + D + E'   (has additional quotes)

3. Unacceptable:
    –17B   (begins with a hyphen)
    25.2   (contains decimal point)
    'X'   (contains quotes)
    EXIT-   (ends with a hyphen)
    P16.3   (contains decimal point)
    1728   (does not contain a letter)
    $5.23   (contains illegal characters $.)
    X2 X3   (contains blank)
    X,Y   (contains comma)
    A*B/C   (contains illegal characters * /)

Section 13.2

1. (a)   COMPUTE Y = 2 * X – 3.
    (b)   COMPUTE X = 5 * (A + B) ** 2 – 3.

   (c)   COMPUTE I = I + 5.
   (d)   COMPUTE Y = A * X ** 2 + B * X + C.
   (e)   COMPUTE BALANCE = DUE – RECEIVED.
2. (a)   MULTIPLY X BY 2 GIVING Y.
   (b)   ADD 2 TO M.
   (c)   DIVIDE B INTO A GIVING X.
   (d)   SUBTRACT X FROM 5 GIVING X.
   (l)   ADD 2 TO I.
   (m)   SUBTRACT 5 FROM N.
   (n)   MULTIPLY X BY 3.

Section 13.3

1.   PROCEDURE DIVISION.
            FIRST. OPEN INPUT IN-BANK OUTPUT OUT-BANK.
            SECOND. READ IN-BANK RECORD AT END GO TO
                 THIRD. MOVE ACCOUNT-NO IN DEPOSIT TO
                 ACCOUNT-NO IN DIVIDEND. MOVE INVESTMENT
                 IN DEPOSIT TO INVESTMENT IN DIVIDEND.
                 MOVE RATE IN DEPOSIT TO RATE IN DIVIDEND.
                 COMPUTE INTEREST = INVESTMENT IN DEPOSIT
                 * RATE IN DEPOSIT. WRITE DIVIDEND. GO
                 TO SECOND.
            THIRD. CLOSE IN-BANK OUT-BANK.
3.   PROCEDURE DIVISION.
            ONE. OPEN INPUT PRE-SALE OUTPUT SALE.
            TWO. READ PRE-SALE RECORD AT END GO
                 TO THREE. MOVE MDSE-NO IN BEFORE
                 TO MDSE-NO IN AFTER. COMPUTE
                 SALE-PRICE = PRICE IN BEFORE * .80.
                 WRITE AFTER. GO TO TWO.
            THREE. CLOSE PRE-SALE SALE.

Section 13.4

2.   PROCEDURE DIVISION.
            ONE. OPEN INPUT MASTER-IN OUTPUT MASTER-OUT.
            TWO. READ MASTER-IN RECORD AT END GO TO FIVE.
                 MOVE NAME IN MASTER-IN TO NAME IN
                 MASTER-OUT. MOVE SOC-SEC-NO IN

MASTER-IN TO SOC-SEC-NO IN MASTER-OUT.
IF ANNUAL-INCOME IS GREATER THAN
600 THEN GO TO THREE OTHERWISE
NEXT SENTENCE. COMPUTE TAX = 0. GO TO FOUR.
THREE. COMPUTE TAX = (ANNUAL-INCOME – 600) * .03.
FOUR. WRITE TAX-OUT. GO TO TWO.
FIVE. CLOSE MASTER-IN MASTER-OUT.

Section 13.5

1.   DATA DIVISION.
                FILE SECTION.
                FD MASTER-IN LABEL RECORDS ARE OMITTED
                    DATA RECORD IS SURVEY.
                01 SURVEY.
                02 NAME PICTURE IS X(25).
                02 FILLER PICTURE IS X(1).
                02 SOC-SEC-NO PICTURE IS X(9).
                02 FILLER PICTURE IS X(4).
                02 SEX PICTURE IS X(1).
                    88 MALE VALUE IS M.
                    88 FEMALE VALUE IS F.
                02 FILLER PICTURE IS X(4).
                02 AGE PICTURE IS X(2).
                02 FILLER PICTURE IS X(1).
                02 MARITAL-STATUS PICTURE IS X(1).
                    88 SINGLE VALUE IS S.
                    88 MARRIED VALUE IS M.
                    88 DIVORCED VALUE IS D.
                02 FILLER PICTURE IS X(1).
                02 DEPENDENTS PICTURE IS X(1).
                    88 ONE VALUE IS 1.
                    88 TWO VALUE IS 2.
                    88 THREE VALUE IS 3.
                    88 FOUR VALUE IS 4.
                    88 FIVE VALUE IS 5.
                    88 MORE-THAN-5-VALUE IS 6.
                02 FILLER PICTURE IS X(30).

3.   DATA DIVISION.
                FILE SECTION.
                FD PAY-FILE LABEL RECORDS ARE OMITTED
                    DATA RECORD IS PAY-REPORT.

```
01  PAY-REPORT.
02  NAME PICTURE IS X(25).
02  FILLER PICTURE IS X(4).
02  EMPLOYEE-NUMBER PICTURE IS X(6).
02  FILLER PICTURE IS X(14).
02  WEEKLY-SALARY PICTURE IS 999.99.
02  FILLER PICTURE IS X(78).
```

CHAPTER 14

Section 14.1

1.   (a)   Floating-point variable or expression
    (b)   Unacceptable
    (c)   Fixed-point expression
    (d)   Floating-point variable or expression
    (e)   Floating-point expression
    (f)   Floating-point constant or expression
    (g)   Mixed expression
    (h)   Mixed expression
    (i)   Mixed expression
    (j)   Floating-point expression
    (k)   Unacceptable
    (l)   Mixed expression
    (m)   Unacceptable
    (n)   Mixed expression
    (o)   Floating-point variable or expression
    (p)   Unacceptable

2.   (b) $(W + X)/(Y + Z)$
    (e) $SQRT((C + D)/X)$
    (k) $A**(I + 1)*X$
    (l) $SQRT((A/(B + C))**(I + 1))$

Section 14.2

1.   (a) $V = SQRT(2*G*H);$
    (b) $S = .5*(A + B + C);$
    (c) $AR = SQRT(S*(S - A)*(S - B)*(S - C));$
    (d) $A = 3.1416*R**2;$
    (e) $Y = M*X + B;$
    (f) $S = P*(1 + I)**N;$
    (g) $F = 1.8*C + 32;$

Section 14.3

1.
```
GET DATA(X);
Y = X**3 – 7*X**2 – 13;
PUT DATA(X,Y);
```

3.
```
GET DATA(A,B,C,D,E);
AVERAGE = (A + B + C + D + E)/5;
PUT DATA(A,B,C,D,E,AVERAGE);
```

Section 14.4

8.
```
AREA: PROCEDURE OPTIONS(MAIN);
     GET DATA(A,B,C,);
     S = .5*(A + B + C);
     AR = SQRT(S*(S – A)*(S – B)*(S – C));
     PUT DATA(A,B,C,S,AR);
     END AREA;
```

Section 14.5

2.
```
LARGER: PROCEDURE OPTIONS(MAIN);
         GET DATA(X,Y);
         IF X < Y THEN GO TO YBIG;
         BIG = X;
         GO TO OUT;
   YBIG: BIG = Y;
    OUT: PUT DATA(BIG);
         END LARGER;
```

4.
```
STOCK_PLAN: PROCEDURE OPTIONS(MAIN);
            GET DATA(CONTRIBUTE,SHARES,PRICE);
            IF CONTRIBUTE < PRICE THEN GO TO NO_BUY;
            SHARES = SHARES + 1;
            CONTRIBUTE = CONTRIBUTE – PRICE;
    NO_BUY: PUT DATA(CONTRIBUTE,SHARES);
            END STOCK_PLAN;
```

Section 14.6

3.
```
EX: PROCEDURE OPTIONS(MAIN);
    I = 0;
```

```
LOOP: GET DATA(A,B,C,D,E);
      X = A**2*SQRT((B**2*C - D)/(E + 1)**2);
      PUT DATA(A,B,C,D,E,X);
      I = I + 1;
      IF I < 350 THEN GO TO LOOP;
      END EX;
```

6.
```
SQUARE: PROCEDURE OF OPTIONS(MAIN);
        GET DATA(NUMBER);
        I = 1;
        ISUM = 0;
LOOP: ISUM = ISUM + I
      I = I + 1;
      IF I < = NUMBER THEN GO TO LOOP;
      ISUM = ISUM**2;
      PUT DATA(NUMBER,ISUM);
      END SQUARE;
```

INDEX

A

A, 185
Abacus, 1–2
Access time, 100
Accounting machine, 38–39
Addition in number systems, 49–53
Address, 104, 141, 176, 184
Addressable storage, 104
AH, 189
Aiken, Howard, 6
ALGOL, 149
Alphabetic sorting, 32
Alphanumeric, 130
American Standard Code, 131–133
Analog computer, 2
Analysis, 84
Analytical engine, 4
AND, 69
AND gate, 75
AR, 182
Arithmetic unit, 140
ASCII, 131–133
Assembler, 216–218
Assembler language:
  A, 185

Assembler language (*cont.*):
  AH, 189
  AR, 182
  BALR, 191–192
  BC, 212–215
  BCT, 206
  BLKSIZE, 198–200
  branching, 212–215
  characters, 190
  CLOSE, 201
  comments, 194
  DC, 193–194
  DEVICE, 198–201
  DS, 192–193
  DTFCD, 198–200
  DTFPR, 200–201
  END, 193
  EOJ, 183–184
  fixed-point numbers, 177–178
  floating-point numbers, 189
  GET, 198–200
  halfword processes, 189
  input/output, 198–202
  instructions, 180–215
  L, 185
  LA, 206